Television Women from Lucy to *Friends*

TELEVISION WOMEN FROM LUCY TO *FRIENDS*

Fifty Years of Sitcoms and Feminism

Lynn C. Spangler

Westport, Connecticut
London

Library of Congress Cataloging-in-Publication Data

Spangler, Lynn C.
    Television women from Lucy to "Friends" : fifty years of sitcoms and feminism / by
Lynn C. Spangler.
      p. cm.
   Includes bibliographical references and index.
   ISBN 0-313-28781-3 (acid-free paper)
   1. Women on television. 2. Television comedies—United States. I. Title
PN1995.9.W6 S69 2003
791.45′652042—dc21   2002192498

British Library Cataloguing in Publication Data is available.

Library of Congress Catalog Card Number: 2002192498
ISBN: 0–313–28781–3

First published in 2003

Praeger Publishers, 88 Post Road West, Westport, CT 06881
An imprint of Greenwood Publishing Group, Inc.
www.praeger.com

Printed in the United States of America

The paper used in this book complies with the
Permanent Paper Standard issued by the National
Information Standards Organization (Z39.48–1984).

10 9 8 7 6 5 4 3 2 1

This book is dedicated to my best friend, my mom, who taught me by example to cherish female friends.

CONTENTS

Photo essay follows chapter 4.

ILLUSTRATIONS

PREFACE

One month and four days before the fiftieth anniversary of the debut of *I Love Lucy,* the unthinkable happened. Terrorists hijacked four commercial flights, crashing into and destroying the twin towers of the World Trade Center and a segment of the Pentagon. The brave, heroic souls on the fourth hijacked plane learned of their hijackers' plans and fought, crashing their jet into a field in Pennsylvania before it could reach Washington, D.C., and do further damage. More than 3,000 innocent people were killed, people who had just gone to work or were flying to vacation destinations to celebrate friendships and birthdays. People said what happened was surreal, like a movie, yet the reality made us numb, angry, scared. Nothing else seemed to matter as we repeatedly watched the planes crashing into the towers and people fleeing for their lives as each came down. We hungrily watched television for answers to who did such evil and why, and what we could do to prevent it from ever happening again. We saw dozens of people on the news holding up pictures of their loved ones, hoping they were truly just "missing." As the days passed, however, it became clear that among the tons of rubble that were once two 110-story office buildings full of people and hopes and dreams, there would be no more survivors. And nothing else seemed to matter.

In the face of such horror and fear that it could happen again, I was working on the final chapters of this book on situation comedy. The research and ideas that I had been passionate about throughout many years seemed trivial now. Why couldn't I have spent these years doing something more worthwhile, like learning how to save lives and prevent disasters? Other questions arose too, like how could people hate us so much and was there really something wrong with our way of life? As it became known who was behind the attacks, news reports and documentaries told of the ways of the terrorists and how they brutalized women.[1] Other reports made it evident that millions of women around the world lacked basic human rights, much less equal rights. Perhaps it *was* a good time to reflect on women's rights in this country too. Despite the fact that we knew life would never be the same again, we struggled to return to some sense of normalcy, and that included watching entertainment television. Situation comedies in particular became a great escape, in both syndication and their original network run. *Friends,* more popular than ever, offered us a glimpse of lower Manhattan untouched by terrorism, where our biggest concern was whether the pregnant Rachel would marry the adoring Joey or the baby's father, Ross.

This book is indeed a reflection about the roles of women in the United States, and it uses the situation comedy as a kind of mirror. Whether that mirror is reflective, instructive, or more like the "mirror, mirror on the wall" that tells us what we wish to hear, a look at the most consistently popular genre on the small screen seems timely after all as we celebrate fifty years of loving Lucy, the grand dame of sitcoms, and contemplate on where we are heading in the twenty-first century.

While sitcoms must attract a diverse audience to achieve the impressive Nielsen ratings they have gotten over the past half century, they have been particularly attractive to women and children, perhaps because it is the genre where most women and child characters can be found. Soap operas also have been particularly important to female audiences where their stories include many female characters. Interestingly and perchance not coincidentally, these two genres historically have been much maligned by media critics and the general public, yet they have been extensively researched and discussed by feminists. Scholars such as Bonnie Dow and Andrea Press have written about how important particular programs and genres are to them, both as significant childhood memories as well as current pleasures.[2] In the preface to her excellent book exploring prime-time feminism in five series (four of them sitcoms), Dow wrote that watching reruns of *The Mary Tyler Moore Show* was "a reassuring anchor in a strange place" during her early college years.[3] In the introduction to her important research on women's responses to television, Press writes that she was much influenced by the images on television and that it "more than any other medium, has always been a pervasive presence" in her life.[4] Susan Douglas, in *Where the Girls Are: Growing up Female with the Mass Media,* has, like many women and girls, a love/hate relationship with the media, including television. Like her, I grew up "internalizing an endless film loop of fairy-tale princesses, beach bunnies, witches, flying nuns, bionic women, and beauty queens."[5] Also like her, I am a white, middle-class and middle-aged female college professor who recognizes that my gender, race, social class, education, and age affect my interpretations of what I have seen on television. While television texts are polysemic (that is, open to multiple interpretations) and how we "read" television depends on a number of variables, both of a demographic and a personal nature (including how we feel at the moment), we have been exposed to the same images over the years. This book is an exploration of what those images are and have been in the cultural context of their times, particularly in relationship to women's rights.

Born in 1951, I too celebrated my fiftieth year about the same time *I Love Lucy* did. While I laughed heartily at the episodes I viewed throughout the 1950s and 1960s, my feminist consciousness was raised in the 1970s, and I became appalled as I reinterpreted some of the scenes and the general tone of the series. Lucy was clearly afraid of Ricky at times. Whenever she "misbehaved" and he found out, she would keep out of his way for fear that he would hit her. And he did hit her—in at least two episodes it is evident he spanked her, once in front of the approving Ethel and Fred Mertz. Years later, however, as I read a female student's media autobiography for an introductory mass media class, I learned with surprise that she enjoyed *I Love Lucy* because Lucy was such a feminist! Indeed, Lucy was always fighting against Ricky's domineering ways. This student saw Lucy as a woman who fought for her personal autonomy, including her right to work outside the home. My consciousness was raised again! In discussing series in this book, I often refer to the interpretations and studies of others as well as my own in recognition of the multiplicity of meanings that people make.

Regardless of the various ways in which people interpret sitcoms, the important point is that these images can affect us—how we feel about ourselves, what we think we can achieve in life, and even how we treat other people. While millions of dollars have been spent over the past few decades to research the effects of television (usually focusing on the negative, particularly violence), our most compelling evidence is within ourselves. This book is an invitation to think about your life in relationship to television sitcoms, cultural history, and gender.

My approach in discussing fifty years of television sitcoms is from a cultural and feminist perspective, both terms that mean a lot of different things to different people and which will be discussed in more detail in chapter 1. Each decade of television situation comedy is put into its historical and cultural context with the recognition that television and other media are important parts of our culture, both reflecting and influencing our personal and public lives. The business of television is also addressed in each chapter; as the industry undergoes major changes over the decades in its quest for high ratings, program content is inevitably affected. Six situation comedies are highlighted for each decade, although both television programming and women's roles in sitcoms in general are also discussed.

Every author must make tough choices in deciding what to include and exclude in a book. It is, of course, impossible to cover all of television situation comedy history in one publication, much less the cultural history of the United States over the past fifty years. The focus on women, with men discussed primarily only in relationship to women, is from my own personal concerns as a woman. It still astounds me when I think of the fact that my grandmothers were both married with children when women finally got the vote. Although in some ways we "have come a long way, baby," particularly in comparison to women in other parts of the world, our struggle for equal rights and opportunities is not over.[6]

The first chapter of this book presents a context for understanding and analyzing television sitcoms. It starts with a discussion of the nature of humor in general and situation comedy in particular. Several studies based on content analyses are summarized to give a quantitative picture of how women have been depicted on television, and theories about how television affects audiences are addressed. Cultural and critical studies are discussed as ways of examining the interpretation of television programs, and various definitions of feminism and concepts in feminist criticism are considered. The remaining chapters approach our cultural history and television sitcoms by decade, ending with a summarizing chapter. This division of television programming is a matter of convenience and part of how we tend to organize history and our memories, although the end of a decade can be very different from its beginning. The choice of which programs to highlight was based on a combination of their popularity and the presence of significant female roles. In discussing each series, I emphasize the major female characters and focus on the following areas: relationships with men, female friendships, work, sexuality and reproduction, and other social issues.[7] In determining the areas on which to focus, I used general concerns of feminists as well as more traditional areas discussed in television character analyses.

While situation comedies and our relatively privileged lives in watching them may seem trivial in light of 9/11 and the distress around the world, they are a part of who and what we are, and we need not apologize.

Reflecting on who and what we are and how we got here is important and what this book, in its own way, is about.

NOTES

1. See, for example, Richard Lacayo, "About Face: An Inside Look at How Women Fared under Taliban Oppression and What the Future Holds for Them Now," *Time,* 3 December 2001: 34–49; and Lisa Beyer, "The Women of Islam," *Time,* 3 December 2001: 50–59.

2. In particular, see Bonnie J. Dow, *Prime-Time Feminism: Television, Media Culture, and the Women's Movement Since 1970* (Philadelphia: University of Pennsylvania Press, 1996); and Andrea Press, *Women Watching Television: Gender, Class, and Generation in the American Television Experience* (Philadelphia: University of Pennsylvania Press, 1991).

3. Dow, xii.

4. Press, 9.

5. Susan J. Douglas, *Where the Girls Are: Growing up Female with the Mass Media* (New York: Times Books, 1994, 1995), 18.

6. This was the slogan in television commercials for "women's" cigarettes, Virginia Slims, which were aired in the late 1960s and 1970. The Federal Communications Commission banned the broadcasting of cigarette advertisements, starting in January 1971, primarily based on the Surgeon General's report that connected smoking to cancer. Many feminists thought the commercial connection of women's liberation to cigarette smoking was another good reason to ban it!

7. For the importance of female friendships, see Lynn C. Spangler, "A Historical Overview of Female Friendships on Prime-Time Television," *Journal of Popular Culture* 22.4 (1989): 13–23. To compare to male friendships, see Lynn C. Spangler, "Buddies and Pals: A History of Male Friendships on Prime-Time Television," *Men, Masculinity, and the Media,* ed. Steve Craig (Newbury Park, CA: Sage, 1992), 93–110.

ACKNOWLEDGMENTS

I'd like to thank Joel Persky for getting me started on this manuscript and my wonderful friend, Carole Levin, for her great encouragement in keeping me working on it. I also thank Georgia Spangler for spending hours with me talking about television sitcom women. My husband, Richard Wollmann, also has been very supportive and patient as I converged with my computer, books, articles, and videotapes. Several other friends throughout the past few decades also have taught me the meaning of friendship that is such an important part of TV sitcom women, especially Denise, Laura, Didi, and Pat.

Besides the many feminist writers who have written insightful critiques of television, other resources were very useful. Many websites were immeasurably helpful with sitcom episode synopses and sometimes even transcripts of episodes, such as epguides.com and www.durfee.net, filling in gaps of memory and viewing. Scott Sobel of archivehollywood.com was terrific at getting me hard-to-find VHS copies of *Private Secretary* and *The Goldbergs*. Photofest in New York City was great at helping me to find wonderful pictures for this book. I also thank Eric Levy at Greenwood Press for his enthusiasm and support. Last, but not least, I'd like to thank the many people in television over the past fifty-five years who have brought us the several inspiring, uplifting, and funny women and girls in sitcoms.

Chapter 1

LIFE WITH TELEVISION

For more than fifty years now, prime-time network television's most consistently popular genre, the situation comedy, has been inspiring laughter and tears. Between the domestic screwball life of the New York newlyweds on *Mary Kay and Johnny* in the late 1940s and the angst of the many single friends in New York City in the early twenty-first century are a wealth of characters that have provided us entertainment, role models, and even public controversy. Their history is part of our history. In the early 1950s, Lucy Ricardo *(I Love Lucy)* made motherhood a national event during the postwar baby boom. Laura and Rob Petrie *(The Dick Van Dyke Show)* were a middle-class version of the Kennedys in the early 1960s. Mary Richards *(The Mary Tyler Moore Show)* was a thirtyish single woman trying to "make it on her own" during the second wave of feminism in the 1970s, while Archie, Edith, Mike, and Gloria debated the Vietnam War and racism in *All in the Family*. The 1980s brought us divorced women pooling their resources to raise their children *(Kate & Allie)* as well as the traditional nuclear family in both upper-middle-class *(The Cosby Show)* and lower-middle-class *(Roseanne)* versions. A single, career woman in her forties caused a national debate about "family values" when she decided in the early 1990s to have a child on her own *(Murphy Brown)*. Single friends and their relationships *(Friends, Seinfeld, Living Single)* became prevalent in the last decade before the twenty-first century, but the struggles of a formerly abused, divorced single mother who was a recovering alcoholic *(Grace Under Fire)* reminded us of more bleak economic and social realities. As our lives have changed over the past half century, so too has television.

Although a few network programs were offered the first two years following World War II, 1948 marks the first fairly complete broadcast network prime-time schedule.[1] By 1960, 87 percent of U.S. homes had television, a figure that has grown to about 98 percent since 1981.[2] Once regularly scheduled programming was available, the way Americans spent their leisure time changed significantly, with the images on the small screen occupying a large part of our waking hours. Commercial networks ABC, CBS, and NBC dominated the television industry until the 1980s when cable networks in particular and three new commercial broadcast networks started to seriously erode their audience. Sitcoms, both new and old, continued to be popular, even on cable, and the role of women in creating these programs began to increase.[3] Our need to laugh seems deep and enduring.

HUMOR AND SITCOMS

There are dozens of theories about what makes people laugh. A researcher of humor for many years, Charles Gruner claims that seventeenth-century philosopher Thomas Hobbes's superiority theory can explain every instance of humor.[4] Hobbes believed that laughing at the misfortune, stupidity, clumsiness, or similar actions of someone else makes us feel superior. In *Jokes and Their Relation to the Unconscious,* Sigmund Freud divided jokes into the categories of "innocent" and "tendentious."[5] When it is not innocent, Freud wrote that "it is either a *hostile* joke (serving the purpose of aggressiveness, satire, or defence [sic]) or an *obscene* joke (serving the purpose of exposure)."[6] Others believe much humor is based on incongruity, involving a difference between what one expects and experiences.

Over the past fifty years, what we generically refer to as situation comedy has been divided into a number of categories, often based on the type of humor to be found. In his ground-breaking work that approached television as an art, Horace Newcomb made a distinction between situation comedy and domestic comedy. In the former, "the situation is simply the broad outline of events, the special funny 'thing' that is happening this week to a special set of characters."[7] Complications (usually involving some sort of human error or mistake) and confusion are also part of the formula for sitcoms, according to Newcomb, as seen in *I Love Lucy.* In domestic comedy, there is more emphasis on characters and setting (the home) than there is on situation. Newcomb wrote that "the wisdom of the father, with assists from the mother, is the prime value asserted by the structures of domestic comedy."[8] *Father Knows Best* is an obvious example.

In David Marc's analysis of comedy, he compared sitcoms to standup comedy and concluded that "whereas sitcoms depend on familiarity, identification, and redemption of popular beliefs, standup comedy often depends on the shocking violation of normative taboos.... The sitcom, despite several attempts to push it in deviant directions, insists on a portrayal of reality that can best be defended with statistics."[9] He claimed that, even after television sitcoms began to confront "post-adolescent issues," their narrative structure remained directly traceable to radio, with episodes beginning with the familiar status quo followed by a ritual error made, a ritual lesson learned, and then a return to the familiar status quo.[10]

In Barry Putterman's analysis of television comedy, he discussed both physical comedy, such as that in *I Love Lucy,* and verbal comedy, exemplified by Eve Arden in *Our Miss Brooks.*[11] He wrote of Jack Benny's tremendous influence "in the traditionalist sense of creating a more complex character by blending styles, and in the modernist sense of creating a surreal normality by blending spaces and repeating ideas in unexpected ways."[12] Putterman claimed that much of current television comedy can be traced to the early days of television, including Jackie Gleason's working-class comedy and Ernie Kovac's free-associative conceptual modernist comedy.[13] According to Putterman, "the 1970s saw the last major aesthetic innovations within the traditional sitcom form. *The Mary Tyler Moore Show* redirected the female-dominated sitcom towards low-key naturalism, and *All in the Family* redirected the family sitcom towards a highly charged theatricality."[14]

Television sitcoms have been classified in a number of other ways, including by setting (workplace, military, family), main characters (single woman, black), and tone (warmedy, dramedy, character, put-down, surreal). Many scholarly television critics discuss sitcoms in relationship to ideology, acknowledging television as "an extremely powerful vehicle for storytelling, a medium whose intimate presence in our lives...lends its stories a sense of truthfulness that tends to obscure their status as fiction."[15] Cultural critic Hal Himmelstein defined ideology as "a constructed belief system that explains economic, political, and social reality to people and establishes collective goals of a class, group, or, in the case of a dominant ideology, the entire society."[16] Himmelstein labeled many sitcoms of the 1950s and 1960s as "suburban-middle-landscape," comedies primarily of reassurance where principles of fair play prevailed.[17] Using *Leave It to Beaver* as a prime example, he concluded that the woman in this society, while not lazy, as are the children, is represented instead as vacuous.... The woman does not think in this milieu, and is not a part of the events that frame the world outside the house; in other words, in a world in which the woman's place is in the kitchen or at the beauty parlor, the woman is not a socially relevant being.[18]

In "rural-middle-landscape" comedies, such as *The Beverly Hillbillies,* he found class tension that was expressed "through the often bizarre acts of some very odd central characters...thus concealed, rendered both comedic and sterile."[19] Urban comedy was a genre that developed "most naturally from the life experience of the creative television workers who represent the New York-Hollywood connection."[20] In series such as *Make Room for Daddy* and *The Mary Tyler Moore Show,* "urban comedy offers us transient togetherness disguised as humanity in a highly competitive white-collar work context best described as professional-entrepreneurial."[21] In social or self-reflexive comedies, such as *All in the Family* and *M*A*S*H,* Himmelstein claimed that we recognize "television's peculiar ability to present us ostensibly significant social commentary that, in its deeper layers, reinforces traditional values, and thereby makes the threatening unthreatening and incorporates potentially emergent oppositional social strategies into the social fabric as demanded by the dominant values of the culture."[22]

Other critics have explored situation comedies based simply on the class of the primary characters and have found significant gender differences. For example, in his study of four decades of sitcoms, Richard Butsch concluded that, in the few working-class comedies there have been, "the stock image of the ineffectual, even buffoonish working-class man has persisted as the dominant image" in contrast to the "consistently competent working-class wives and children and middle class fathers."[23] Cultural critic Darrell Hamamoto found that "more than the simple reflection of hegemonic class interests, reduced to the 'dominant ideology' of the corporate capitalist order, the situation comedy has embodied emancipatory beliefs proven to have had deep resonance with its diverse audience."[24] He referred to the discourse found in television sitcoms as being "liberal democratic ideology," validating and renewing three "generic values": freedom, equality, and democracy.[25]

It could be argued that these values are what some critics consider in comedies labeled as feminist. In her essay on feminist sitcoms, Lauren Rabinovitz wrote that

feminism's capacity to disrupt and upset cultural categories has always been so ambiguously presented on television that it lends itself to a range of political interpretations. Although television consistently articulates feminism as reformist, liberal, and progressive, it simultaneously disavows any racial or class determinants. Television allows for the expression of a feminist critique but represses feminism's potential for radical social change.[26]

Rabinovitz said that feminine excess is central to some feminist sitcoms as a binary opposition and is used as a focus of humor on such shows as *Designing Women* and *The Golden Girls*:

> The notion that femininity and feminism are in a mutual relationship in the feminist sitcom depends on two important assumptions about femininity. First, femininity is not an essential property of women; it is an image that is usually correlated with women's appearances. Second, the function of femininity, as elaborated by numerous feminist critics, is to provide cover for the female's Otherness and to distance the female spectator from finding fullness in self-identification.[27]

Feminist Andrea Press divided television programming into prefeminist, feminist, and postfeminist categories.[28] In the years before second-wave feminism, which started in the late 1960s, Press said that in prefeminist television women were rarely shown to be mature, independent individuals, yet some characters, such as Lucy Ricardo on *I Love Lucy,* offered a subtext of resistance.[29] The relatively brief era of feminist television, Press concluded, depicted strong women in nontraditional roles, but the focus was on individualism, not any collective women's movement.[30] Finally, postfeminist television gives women a work identity, but the emphasis is on their family role. Significantly, Press wrote that there is almost no conflict between the sexes now, unlike in prefeminist television where women "were often shown in warlike alliance with their female friends against their husbands."[31]

In black situation comedies, the central characters are predominantly African American. Researcher Robin Coleman saw the roots of black sitcoms in both minstrel shows, where "blackface" was worn and the humor was quite racist, and in broadcast radio shows, such as *Amos 'n' Andy,* which also dealt with stereotyped, unflattering images.[32] Black sitcoms are divided into six eras, starting with TV minstrelsy in the early 1950s and ending with neo-minstrelsy from 1990 to the present.[33] Coleman said the latter is "defined by its Sambo, coon, Nat/bad buck, prized criminals character types. It ridicules Black culture and promotes racial separation and inequality."[34] In contrast, the Cosby era, specifically through *The Cosby Show,* presented an ideal supportive family of African Americans.

In his foreword to Coleman's book, psychiatrist and former consultant to *The Cosby Show* Alvin Poussaint wrote that

> Bill Cosby's talent at finding humor in everyday life allowed universal identification with the ups and downs of the Huxtables' daily lives. The show deliberately avoided put-down humor while seeking to model a family unpretentiously steeped in Black culture.[35]

In addition to the potential benefits of positive role models in sitcoms, research has found many other benefits to humor. For example, researchers Howard Pollio and John Edgerly wrote that "the comedian, and all of his or her kind...provide a situation which allows each of us a bit of transcendence; a bit of transcendence designed to make sport of those situations, events and taboos that lie heaviest upon us if seen only from an earnest and serious perspective."[36] Darrell Hamamoto found a special function for situation comedy over the years in that "it has remained consistently true to its twin, often conflicting, origins in liberal democratic ideology and corporate capitalism. Through narratives that assimilate social contradictions into everyday personal experience, the situation comedy has stood as an enduring sociodramatic model that has helped 'explain' American society to itself."[37] With their built-in conflict through contrasting characters, sitcoms, particularly since the 1970s, have been the site of contested discourses. According to British researcher Paul Wells, in America "it is clear that both implicitly and explicitly the sitcom has done much to challenge and dissolve old boundaries by laughing at their very existence."[38]

THE EFFECTS OF TELEVISION

Since the beginning of broadcast network television in the late 1940s, people have been concerned about its effects, including what viewing in general can potentially do, such as ruin eyesight, decrease attention spans, lessen learning potential, take away from time with family and friends, and even make viewers fat as they become "couch potatoes." Most research, however, has concerned itself with specific types of content, particularly violence. Role portrayals have been another major concern, and hundreds of studies have been conducted in various disciplines.

In a very ambitious study that combined both quantitative and interpretive research in addition to interviews with television writers, Diana Meehan analyzed the roles of women in television programming between 1950 and 1980.[39] Using several examples, she concluded that female characters in prime-time television could be put into ten categories: imp (Lucy Ricardo in *I Love Lucy*), goodwife (Laura Petrie in *The Dick Van Dyke Show*), harpy (Margaret Houlihan in *M*A*S*H*), bitch (title character in *Maude*), victim (in many action shows), decoy (as in *Charlie's Angels*), siren (seductress who leads to destruction of male partner, often in action shows), courtesan (Flo on *Alice*), witch (Samantha on *Bewitched*), and matriarch (Victoria Barkley on *Big Valley*). Several years later, Meehan added an eleventh female character type—the androgyne, who was both strong and soft, such as Claire Huxtable on *The Cosby Show*.[40]

Over the years, dozens of content analyses have been conducted to see how various categories of people and issues are being portrayed on television. As one might suspect, both women and minorities have usually been found to be underrepresented and stereotyped. Many years ago, Cedric Clark discussed four stages of minority portrayals: nonrecognition, ridicule, regulation (protectors of the existing order, such as police officers), and respect (having the same full range of roles as the majority).[41] These four areas can be reduced to two, recognition and respect, to discuss whether and to what extent any group appears on television and how they are portrayed when they do. In Signorielli and Bacue's analysis of characters on prime-time television between 1967 and 1998, the authors operationalized respect in terms of three key elements: program genre, age, and occupation.[42] They found that of the 8,293 characters in their sample, only 34.5 percent were women, moving from 28 percent in the 1960s and 1970s to 39 percent in the 1990s. More than 40 percent of these female characters were found in situation comedies in the 1960s–1970s and 1990s and close to that number in the 1980s. Women were always judged to be about four years younger than men. They also found that more women were seen employed outside the home and in jobs with a little more prestige in more recent years. In their analysis of network series featuring working women in the 1980s, Atkin, Moorman, and Lin found that the highest expansion of such series corresponded roughly to the period of competition accompanying the growth of cable and the Fox network in the late 1980s, suggesting that competitive pressures, not feminism, facilitated series devoted to working women.[43] The authors also credited female producers such as Diane English *(Murphy Brown)* and Linda Bloodworth-Thomason *(Designing Women)* for the more assertive or competent feminine roles.

David Atkin analyzed television series with minority lead characters (black, Hispanic, or Asian) that were broadcast between 1948 and 1991, predicting changes in representation in relationship to television network economics.[44] Of the fifty-four series he found, 80 percent addressed blacks. The most common occupational format for minority female leads involved maid or domestic roles, and situation comedy was the genre in which all roles were "broken in."[45] Atkins noted that

> minority-lead series continue to underrepresent women in both number and occupational status. Such characters represent something of a "double minority" to producers and audiences, remaining outside the realm of co-optation. This is especially true of Asian and Hispanic females, who have yet to garner as many series as have, for example, animals (e.g., *Mister Ed, Flipper*). Given their perceived cultural unfamiliarity, they are unlikely to increase in visibility until advertisers recognize them as a distinctive revenue source.[46]

Greenberg and Collette looked at the demographics of new series from 1966 to 1992 and found a steady increase in black characters over the years (from 6 percent in the late 1960s to 14 percent in the early 1990s).[47] Asians, Hispanics, and American Indians constituted less than 1 percent each, however. The researchers cautioned that "though television is a fictionalized drama, it remains an important cultural forum where its characters and stories may be representational of those things valued within our society."[48] Many years ago, Gaye Tuchman wrote of the symbolic annihilation of women on television and in other media.[49] While content analyses indicate that women and blacks are getting at least some recognition and respect now, other groups have neither.

The concept of what constitutes a family and how families are portrayed in general has been a concern of many researchers. In his study of prime-time television families from 1947 through 1990, Marvin L. Moore found a trend toward more equal presentation of conventional (with married couples) and nonconventional families, but few divorced or female single parents and few minority families.[50] He concluded that "in contrast to men, the changing roles of women and the consequences of these changes have been largely ignored in the programming. For example, the predominance of female single parents, the number of women working outside the home, and the feminization of poverty have rarely been dealt with in these programs."[51] In their study of television families between 1950 and 1989, Skill and Robinson found that families were most frequently presented in the situation comedy context, although this trend has steadily decreased since the 1950s.[52] Overall they found that "the television family has lagged real life families in presenting controversial or complex situations such as divorce, separation, and single motherhood."[53] Looking specifically at family conflict and jealousy on prime-time television, Comstock and

Strzyzewski found that, in general, "female characters in all program types engaged in more conflict than male characters. On situation comedies, females were involved in more conflictual situations and those conflicts lasted longer than conflicts involving males. Additionally, conflicts initiated by wives were most often portrayed as antisocial."[54]

While many studies cross genres, some have focused specifically on comedies. Using more than 300 undergraduate students to evaluate four "generations" of domestic comedy, Douglas and Olson concluded that their "study yielded no support for the claim that family life and family relations have deteriorated across time in the television family although there was evidence that working-class families are seen to be less functional than higher socio-economic status families."[55] In another study of college students' evaluation of situation comedies in terms of gender roles, Olson and Douglas concluded that "equality, similarity, and dominance do not change in a linear pattern over time, as gender roles have transformed."[56] They found, for example, that subjects saw *The Cosby Show* as portraying the most equality between spouses and *Home Improvement* the least. Reep and Dambrot asked college students to name the first television mother and father that came to mind (the most frequently named were all from sitcoms) and then rate them for gender traits and parental effectiveness.[57] They found that the subjects "saw the mothers in current programs as more independent and more decisive than the mothers on noncurrent programs. However, viewers did not perceive much loss of expressive and nurturing traits at the same time that instrumental [e.g., active, independent] traits increased."[58] Basing her research on the theory that humorous exchanges are often expressions of power between the joke teller and the target of the joke, Erica Scharrer found that, in family-oriented sitcoms, "modern television fathers and working class television fathers are more likely to be portrayed foolishly than fathers of the past or fathers of higher socioeconomic classes."[59] Such a finding indicates a power shift among male and female characters over the years, with women becoming more powerful in the 1980s and 1990s.

Body image and sexuality in comedies have also been studied, often with the concern about their potential to influence the self-esteem and health of young women and girls. Fouts and Burggraf did a content analysis of eighteen prime-time television situation comedies in 1997 and found that 76 percent of the female characters were below average in weight.[60] They also found that many negative comments were expressed on the shows for being average or heavier in weight and that there was laughing at derogatory comments toward heavier women, reinforced by audience reactions.[61] In studying sexuality themes in the most popular prime-time television shows with children and teens from 1992 to 1993, L. Monique Ward found that even though ten out of the twelve programs were sitcoms, more than one in four interactions related to sex.[62] Accounting for almost one-third of the messages, the male sexual role included suggestions that men typically see women as sexual objects and value them based on their physical appearance. Ward theorized that the nature of the situation comedy may even contribute to the prevalence of comments about sexuality because "they rely on a number of standard devices to convey humor, including sexual innuendo, double entendres, irony, and visual exaggeration of characters' body parts and flirtations."[63] In their summary of sex in prime-time television, Greenberg and Hofschire said the single largest study, looking at five months of programming in 1998, found that 77 percent of sitcom episodes had sexual content, the most of all genres.[64] Only 3 percent of those sitcoms, however, had messages dealing with the risk and responsibility of sexual behavior. Greenberg and Hofschire also concluded in their review of studies that girls are more likely to use the media to educate themselves about sex and relationships, and messages have the most impact when teens perceive them as realistic.[65] Focusing specifically on sexual harassment, Grauerholz and King found that 84 percent of the shows aired on prime-time television between September and November 1991 had at least one incident of an unwelcome sexually related encounter, with an average of 3.4 incidents in such programs.[66] They concluded that

> these acts of sexual harassment remain largely invisible in that none of the behaviors was labeled as sexual harassment. They are presented in humorous ways, and victims are generally unharmed and very effective at ending the harassment.... [T]hey perpetuate several myths about sexual harassment, such as that sexual harassment is not serious and that victims should be able to handle the situations themselves.[67]

Content analyses and similar research do important groundwork by telling us what is on television, and they raise important concerns about how such content can affect audiences. However, they can only theorize or guess at television's impact on the lives of real people. A variety of methodologies have been used to measure media effects, based on a number of theories. Socialization theory, for example, recognizes television as one of many influences, including family, friends, school, and church; the challenge to researchers, of course, is isolating television's role. Cognitive theory asserts that "information processing is constructive; that is, people do not literally encode and retrieve information that they read or hear in the media. Rather, as they comprehend, they interpret in accordance with their prior knowledge and beliefs and the context in which the message is received."[68] People develop schemas that are used to interpret new data. Psychologist Richard Harris has said "one consequence of this for information processing is that the individual is likely to go beyond the information actually presented to draw inferences about people or events that are congruent with previously formed schemas."[69] Scripts are schemas about an activity that we can learn from both television and real life, such as dating. Television can be the only or primary source of information for some people about certain things, including what different people are like.[70] As psychologist John Condry has pointed out, "regardless of whether the information is presented as fiction or nonfiction, true or not, it is still information to which television viewers are exposed that they may incorporate into their knowledge structures."[71] *Framing* is a term that "refers to the way events and issues are organized and made sense of, especially by the media, media professionals, and their audiences."[72] Beyond the schemas of individuals, then, "frames are organizing principles that are socially shared and persistent over time, that work symbolically to meaningfully structure the social world."[73] A related concept is the agenda-setting function of the media that hypothesizes that they can determine even *what* we think about, let alone how we think about it. This applies to not only news events, but also such fictional events as the birth of the title character's baby in *Murphy Brown* and the use of ethnic and racial putdowns in *All in the Family.*

A theory that looks at the cumulative effects of television content is cultivation analysis, which

> attempts to determine the extent to which people who watch greater amounts of television (generally referred to as *heavy viewers*) hold different conceptions of social reality from those who watch less, other factors held constant. The basic hypothesis is that heavy viewers will be more likely to perceive the real world in ways that reflect the most stable and recurrent patterns of portrayals in the television world.[74]

In conjunction with content analyses that show television content to both stereotype and under-represent women, cultivation research has shown, for example, that heavy viewers of television score higher on a test that supposedly measures sexism.[75] In contrast to a cumulative effect of television portrayals, communication researcher Bradley Greenberg offered his "drench" hypothesis, which posits that some characterizations may have a significantly larger impact on individuals.[76] Researchers Cynthia Hoffner and Joanne Cantor have discussed how audience members engage in impression formation of characters and concluded that "they have implications for various components of attraction, such as liking, perceived similarity, and the desire to be like characters. These reactions, in turn, have been shown to influence viewers' tendencies to identify with or take the perspective of characters, and to attend to and imitate their behaviors."[77]

Uses and gratifications theory, according to communication researcher Alan Rubin, "sees communication influence as being socially and psychologically constrained and affected by individual differences and choice."[78] People watch television for a variety of reasons, including for information, relaxation, escape, companionship, excitement, and mood management, as well as to conform with what others are doing and to pass time. One study, for example, illustrated how women use particular television genres for mood management during their menstrual cycle (it was found that female undergraduate students preferred comedy programs just before and during their periods).[79] Uses of television have been categorized as either ritualized (watching out of habit and for diversion or to consume time) or instrumental (seeking specific content for information). According to Rubin, "instrumental orientations may produce stronger attitudinal and behavioral effects than ritualized orientations because instrumental orientations incorporate greater motivation to use and involvement with messages."[80] If a teenage girl is watching *Friends* to learn about dating and living on one's own, for example, the series could theoretically have more impact on her than it would on someone who is casually watching to pass the time.

A variety of methods have been used in effects research, including laboratory research where variables are tightly controlled, and in natural environments, such as people's homes where subjects may be observed and interviewed.[81] No method is without criticism, so similar results from a variety of methodologies tend to be more convincing. Many researchers, including several who are feminists, have turned their focus onto the audience and its role in making their own meaning of television, including its effects on their lives. Using the technique of extensive interviews, Andrea Press found that, despite their disclaimers of the lack of realism on television, middle-class women are even more likely than working-class women to absorb television's subtle dictates about how to be a person, in particular how to be a woman."[82] She also found that working-class women related first as members of the working class, then as women. Robin Coleman used extensive interviews with African Americans of varying ages to discuss black situation comedies. One of the findings revealed was "clear acknowledgment that some viewers are relying, in part, upon television for knowledge and guidance. This was seen as being especially useful to young viewers who must confront all sorts of growing pains."[83] Coleman also found that "the female participants exhibited a pattern of seeing themselves in only those female characters who are powerful, strong, and independent in the face of dominating structures (e.g., patriarchy, racism, workplace inequities)."[84]

CULTURAL AND CRITICAL STUDIES

Cultural and critical studies have been summarized by George Comstock as "an examination of the process of production, the content of messages, and the way in which those messages are received and interpreted, with emphasis on the complexity and cultural context of these processes and outcomes, to uncover the modes by which a predominant ideology is disseminated and sometimes resisted."[85] Feminist Ien Ang further explicated that "it is the contradictory, continuous and open-ended *social process* of the production, circulation and consumption of meaning that cultural studies is about, not 'culture' defined as a more or less static, bounded and objectified set of ideas, beliefs, and behaviours."[86] Cultural studies is associated with a variety of approaches and theories also used by scholarly television critics, including those related to Marxism, political economy, semiotics, structuralism, postmodernism, psychoanalysis, mythology, literary criticism, reception theory, rhetoric, sociology, and feminism.[87] A number of key concepts are integral to cultural studies, including hegemony, which can be defined as "the process of making, maintaining and reproducing the governing sets of meanings [dominant ideology] of a given culture."[88] Audience members (often referred to as "readers") are considered active and television content (the "text") is polysemic—that is, open to a number of interpretations.[89] How audiences read television texts has been divided in terms of their relationship to the dominant ideology with the assumption that it is the beliefs and ways of the ruling class that are reproduced in television programming. A "preferred" reading is one that accepts the dominant ideology and status quo, while an "oppositional" reading does not. Meanings in texts are often "negotiated" between the existing "subject" position (the reader/viewer) and "the one proposed by the text itself, and in this negotiation the balance of power lies with the reader."[90] The dominant and preferred reading of *I Love Lucy,* for example, is that women should stay home and care for the household and men should earn the money. Despite the fact that Lucy's schemes to get into show business or earn her own money always end up with her happily returning home, some viewers have interpreted her as a feminist, rebelling against her sex-typed role as housewife and the power structure (represented by her husband) that limits her. Discussed earlier, Coleman's finding that African American women saw themselves only in strong characters can be seen as evidence that the "female participants negotiate dominant messages by resisting characters and portrayals that lack empowerment."[91]

To be popular, a series must appeal to a variety of people, so the potential for multiple readings is desirable in the television industry. However, as the developers of cultivation theory explain, "to say that audiences' interactions with media texts can produce enormous diversity and complexity does not negate that there can be important commonalities and consistencies as well across large bodies of media output."[92] As a matter of fact, many would argue that this is how hegemony works and the ruling class stays in power, by tolerating other ideas and lulling people into a false sense of things getting better for all people or by indicating they are better off as they are. In an interesting study of social mobility in television sitcoms, for example, Lewis Freeman found that characters who strive to improve their circumstances often find it is not worth the price they paid to achieve it or, if they fail to achieve a mobility goal, they benefit personally somehow.[93] Freeman concluded that "television comedies reinforce the myth that the United States is a land of economic opportunity where anyone can become anything through industry and persistence. Paradoxically, the same comedy programs would seem to deter individuals' aspirations for significant mobility and discourage challenges to the current social and economic order."[94]

FEMINISM, FEMININE GENRES, AND FEMINIST CRITICISM

There are many types of feminism and feminists. Liberal feminism, which has dominated the feminist movement in the United States, is marked by a belief that equality can be achieved through the existing social and political structure by rational arguments and changing laws.[95] According to Josephine Donovan, cultural feminism is based on a matriarchal vision, "the idea of a society of strong women guided by essentially female concerns and values. These include, most importantly, pacifism, cooperation, nonviolent settlement of differences, and a harmonious regulation of public life."[96] Radical feminism was developed during the second wave of feminism in the late 1960s and 1970s when women in the "New Left" political movement became disgusted with the contemptuous treatment they received by male radicals.[97] Their central beliefs include

> the idea that the personal is political; that patriarchy, or male-domination—not capitalism—is at the root of women's oppression; that women should identify themselves as a subjugated class or caste and put their primary energies in a movement with other women to combat their oppressors—men; that men and women are fundamentally different, have different styles and different cultures, and that the women's mode must be the basis of any future society.[98]

Marxist and socialist feminists believe "that class oppression under capitalism is a fundamental factor in women's oppression."[99] According to Donovan, ecofeminists, with their emphasis on ecology, have their roots in cultural and radical feminism.

Other ideologies and theories have influenced feminist thought as it has developed over the years, including psychoanalysis and existentialism. More recently, theories of postmodernism and poststructuralism have made a large impact. Postmodernism, according to feminist Myra Macdonald, is a cultural response to cataclysmic global changes, particularly since the 1970s, in "information provision, the economy, work patterns and technology. This response has been characterized by a loss of faith in meaningfulness and originality, and a celebration of fragmentation, surface texture and the breaking down of old boundaries."[100] Macdonald has described poststructuralism as "an analytical movement that challenges the notion of a unified subject.... Influenced by psychoanalysis, it prefers to think of the individual as riven by fragmented subjectivities."[101] Ien Ang wrote that, according to poststructuralism, "a female person cannot be presumed to have a pregiven and fixed gender identity as a woman. Rather, an individual's gendered subjectivity is constantly in process of reproduction and transformation. Being a woman can mean many different things, at different times and in different circumstances."[102] Charlotte Brunsdon referred to Michele Barrett and Anne Phillips' distinction between " 'modernist' 1970s feminism, with its optimism about discovering the cause of women's oppression, and postmodern 1990s feminism, with its sense of the fragmentation of the category 'woman,' and its stress on the significance of difference."[103] The concept of postmodernism is intricately connected to "third-wave" feminists who, according to Shugart, Waggoner, and Hallstein, "define themselves first in terms of what they are not; namely, they reject the feminism of the second wave, claiming that it reflects almost exclusively the perspectives and values of white, middle-class, heterosexual women who define themselves primarily as oppressed victims of patriarchy."[104] Third-wave feminism "features a celebration of difference in terms of identity construction, in which signifiers such as race and binary gender are rejected in favor of ambiguity and multiple positionalities."[105] Shugart, Waggoner, and Hallstein wrote that "the politics of difference that drive third-wave feminism... are manifest in an embracing of contradiction so that apparently inconsistent political viewpoints coexist in the name of third-wave feminism."[106] Certainly most would agree that women's realities vary, and that there are differences based on race, ethnicity, and age, among other things. But, as Macdonald has pointed out, "within feminist thinking, postmodernism is viewed either as an unprecedented opportunity for women to forge their own identities and explore their own subjectivities, or as a cultural movement that stifles the possibility of meaningful action just as feminism is beginning to make a political and social impact."[107] Foss, Foss, and Griffin, however, feel the variety of definitions and perspectives on feminism that have developed over the years "opens up choices and possibilities and speaks to the very nature of feminism. It is rooted in choice and self-determination and does not prescribe one 'official' position that feminists must hold. Feminism also is an evolving process that necessarily changes as conditions in the world change and as feminists develop new understandings."[108]

Some early feminist research and criticism rejected what many have referred to as "women's genres" in media, particularly soap operas and romance novels, finding them filled with stereotypical images of gender roles.[109] Many feminists have embraced so-called women's genres, however, and find them liberating. Mary Ellen Brown, a feminist who has conducted much research on television soap operas and their audiences, claims that the insistence of women

> on their right to their own pleasure is not only an act of cultural resistance within the politics of the family in that it defies masculine power within the patriarchal family, but such insistence is also a recognition that the differences between masculine and feminine tastes can be understood in terms of a power relationship of domination and resistance. The term "trash" is so rich because it contains within it the social struggle for power articulated in terms of cultural taste and preference.[110]

In her research, Brown has found that "much of the pleasure in soap opera fanship lies in the discursive network among women that builds around the viewing of a program that is designed for them."[111] Brown also wrote of the power of laughter among the groups of soap opera fans she has interviewed. Basing her analysis on the concept of "carnival which involved role reversal in which the established hierarchies of life were ignored as people dressed and acted in unconventional ways,"[112] Brown found that the

> carnivalesque laughter with its droll view of the world produces a position of defiance for women within discursive networks, and it is such discursive networks that ultimately define reality. When women talk and joke in recognition of their subordination, they break boundaries and assert their power. This inversion of power can be a threat to dominant institutions and transgress the barriers of polite society.[113]

Dorothy Hobson has found in her research on women's talk at work that "women use television programs as part of their general discourse on their own lives, the lives of their families and friends and to add interest to their working lives."[114] Brown has connected such talk about television to the notion of consciousness raising used by the feminist movement in the 1970s, a political tool that

> might be thought of as a form of gossip although more formal and purposeful. Women gathered in small groups and took turns talking about their personal issues. In this way they discovered the power of the idea that the personal is political. Their personal stories, when taken collectively, outlined the parameters of their oppression. In other words, these are not personal problems but structural limitations built into a system that oppresses them.[115]

Whether women are laughing in groups as they recount plots and characters in soap operas or are laughing individually as they watch a situation comedy, humor can be liberating, as can the contemplation of gender portrayals. Should we hate *I Love Lucy* because it prescribes the role of housewife for women, or should we love it because Lucy continuously resists that narrow definition of who she should be? The answer could be both or neither. What is important is that we explore these characters and their stories, and reflect on their impact in our lives. We can also laugh and enjoy the carnival of images.

The following chapters are not meant as a definitive interpretation of women in situation comedy over the past half century, but as an invitation to reminisce, to think about your own interpretations and how such characters have influenced your life, to talk about them with others, and, perhaps most important, to reflect on where we should go from here.

NOTES

1. Tim Brooks and Earle Marsh, *The Complete Directory to Prime Time Network and Cable TV Shows 1946–Present,* 7th ed. (New York: Ballantine, 1999), 1167–1169.

2. Margaret S. Andreasen, "Patterns of Family Life and Television Consumption from 1945 to the 1990s," in *Media, Children, and the Family: Social Scientific, Psychodynamic, and Clinical Perspectives,* ed. Dolf Zillmann, Jennings Bryant, and Aletha C. Huston (Hillsdale, NJ: Erlbaum, 1994), 23.

3. Research indicates that it makes at least some difference in the portrayal of female characters when women are behind the scenes. For example, a study by Martha M. Lauzen and David M. Dozier of the 1995–1996 television season found that programs with female executive producers had more female characters and that they "speak more often, have the last word, and interrupt others more often than female characters on shows with no female executive producer" ("Making a Difference in Prime Time: Women On Screen and Behind the Scenes in the 1995–1996 Television Season," *Journal of Broadcasting & Electronic Media* 43 (1999): 13).

4. Charles R. Gruner, *The Game of Humor: A Comprehensive Theory of Why We Laugh* (New Brunswick, NJ: Transaction, 1997).

5. Sigmund Freud, *Jokes and Their Relation to the Unconscious,* trans. and ed. James Strachey with a biographical introduction by Peter Gay (New York: Norton, 1960), 106–107.

6. Freud, 115.

7. Horace Newcomb, *TV: the Most Popular Art* (Garden City, NY: Anchor, 1974), 31.

8. Newcomb, 56.

9. David Marc, *Comic Visions: Television Comedy & American Culture,* 2nd ed. (Oxford: Blackwell, 1997), 20.

10. Marc, 190.

11. Barry Putterman, *On Television and Comedy: Essays on Style, Theme, Performer and Writer* (Jefferson, NC: McFarland, 1995), 16–18.

12. Putternam, 30.

13. Putterman, 33.

14. Putternam, 21.

15. Hal Himmelstein, *Television Myth and the American Mind* (New York: Praeger, 1984), 84.

16. Himmelstein, 3.

17. Himmelstein, 88.

18. Himmelstein, 96.

19. Himmelstein, 97.

20. Himmelstein, 112.

21. Himmelstein, 116.

22. Himmelstein, 121.

23. Richard Butsch, "Class and Gender in Four Decades of Television Situation Comedy: Plus ca Change...," *Critical Studies in Mass Communication* 9 (1992): 397.

24. Darrell Y. Hamamoto, *Nervous Laughter: Television Situation Comedy and Liberal Democratic Ideology* (New York: Praeger, 1989), 2.

25. Hamamoto, 3–4.

26. Lauren Rabinovitz, "Ms.-Representation: The Politics of Feminist Sitcoms," *Television, History, and American Culture,* ed. Mary Beth Haralovich and Lauren Rabinovitz (Durham, NC: Duke University Press, 1999), 145.

27. Rabinovitz, 149.

28. Andrea L. Press, *Women Watching Television: Gender, Class, and Generation in the American Television Experience* (Philadelphia: University of Pennsylvania Press, 1991); and Andrea Press and Terry Strathman, "Work, Family, and Social Class in Television Images of Women: Prime-Time Television and the Construction of Postfeminism," *Women and Language* 16.2 (1993): 7–15.

29. Press, 29.

30. Press, 37.

31. Press, 48.

32. According to Coleman, the other eras are nonrecognition (1954–1967) where there are no blacks in major roles, assimilationist (1968–1971) where black characters appear but there is no reference to black culture, the Lear era (1972–1983) where black subjectivity and social relevancy are ridiculed, and The Cosby era (1984–1989) where there is a celebration of black culture and equal status.

33. Coleman, 104.

34. Alvin F. Poussaint, M.D., foreword, *African American Viewers and the Black Situation Comedy,* by Robin R. Means Coleman (New York: Garland, 2000), xiii.

35. Howard R. Pollio and John W. Edgerly, "Comedians and Comic Style" in *Humor and Laughter: Theory, Research, and Applications,* ed. Antony J. Chapman and Hugh C. Foot (New Brunswick, NJ: Transaction, 1996), 240.

36. Hamamoto, 133.

37. Paul Wells, " 'Where Everybody Knows Your Name': Open Convictions and Closed Contexts in the American Situation Comedy," *Because I Tell a Joke or Two: Comedy, Politics and Social Difference,* ed. Stephen Wagg (London: Routledge, 1998), 199.

38. Diana Meehan, *Ladies of the Evening: Women Characters of Prime-Time Television* (Metuchen, NJ: Scarecrow, 1983).

39. Diana M. Meehan, "The Strong-Soft Woman: Manifestations of the Androgyne in Popular Media," *Television as a Social Issue,* ed. Stuart Oskamp (Newberry Park, CA: Sage, 1988), 103–112.

40. Cedric Clark, "Television and Social Control: Some Observations on the Portrayals of Ethnic Minorities," *Television Quarterly* 8 (1969): 18–22.

41. Nancy Signorielli and Aaron Bacue, "Recognition and Respect: A Content Analysis of Prime-Time Television Characters across Three Decades," *Sex Roles* 40 (1999): 527–44.

42. David J. Atkin, Jay Moorman, and Carolyn A. Lin, "Ready for Prime Time: Network Series Devoted to Working Women in the 1980s," *Sex Roles* 25 (1991): 683.

43. David Atkin, "An Analysis of Television Series with Minority-Lead Characters," *Critical Studies in Mass Communication* 9 (1992): 337–49.

44. Atkin, 345.

45. Atkin, 347.

46. Bradley S. Greenberg and Larry Collette, "The Changing Faces on TV: A Demographic Analysis of Network Television's New Seasons, 1966–1992," *Journal of Broadcasting & Electronic Media* 41 (1997): 8.

47. Greenberg and Collette, 11.

48. Gaye Tuchman, "Introduction: The Symbolic Annihilation of Women by the Mass Media," *Hearth and Home: Images of Women in the Mass Media,* ed. Gaye Tuchman, Arlene Kaplan Daniels, and James Benet (New York: Oxford University Press, 1978), 3–38.

49. Marvin L. Moore, "The Family as Portrayed on Prime-Time Television, 1947–1990: Structure and Characteristics," *Sex Roles* 26 (1992): 41–61.

50. Moore, 58.

51. Thomas Skill and James D. Robinson, "Four Decades of Families on Television: A Demographic Profile, 1950–1989," *Journal of Broadcasting and Electronic Media* 38 (Fall 1994): 449–64.

52. Skill and Robinson, 463.

53. Jamie Comstock and Krystyna Strzyzewski, "Interpersonal Interaction on Television: Family Conflict and Jealousy on Primetime," *Journal of Broadcasting & Electronic Media* 34 (Summer 1990): 277.

54. William Douglas and Beth M. Olson, "Beyond Family Structure: The Family in Domestic Comedy," *Journal of Broadcasting & Electronic Media* 39 (1995): 236–61.

55. Beth Olson and William Douglas, "The Family on Television: Evaluation of Gender Roles in Situation Comedy," *Sex Roles* 36 (1997): 422.

56. Diana C. Reep and Faye H. Dambrot, "TV Parents: Fathers (and Now Mothers) Know Best," *Journal of Popular Culture* 28 (1994): 13–24.

57. Reep and Dambrot, 16.

58. Erica Scharrer, "From Wise to Foolish: The Portrayal of the Sitcom Father, 1950s–1990s," *Journal of Broadcasting & Electronic Media* 45 (2001): 23.

59. Gregory Fouts and Kimberley Burggraf, "Television Situation Comedies: Female Weight, Male Negative Comments, and Audience Reactions," *Sex Roles* 42 (2000): 929.

60. Fouts and Burggraf, 931.

61. L. Monique Ward, "Talking about Sex: Common Themes about Sexuality in the Prime-Time Television Programs Children and Adolescents View Most," *Journal of Youth and Adolescence* 24 (1995): 595–615.

62. Ward, 612.

63. Bradley S. Greenberg and Linda Hofschire, "Sex on Entertainment Television," *Media Entertainment: The Psychology of Its Appeal,* ed. Dolf Zillmann and Peter Vorderer (Mahwah, NJ: Erlbaum, 2000), 93–111. The large study to which they refer is D. Kunkel, K.M. Cope, W.J. Maynard Farinola, E. Biely, E. Rollin, and E. Donnerstein, *Sex on TV: A Biennial Report to the Kaiser Family Foundation* (Menlo Park, CA: Kaiser Family Foundation, 1999).

64. Greenberg and Hofschire, 104. For more on the portrayal of sexuality in the media and its effects, see Jane D. Brown, Jeanne R. Steele, and Kim Walsh-Childers, eds., *Sexual Teens, Sexual Media: Investigating Media's Influence on Adolescent Sexuality* (Mahwah, NJ: Erlbaum, 2002); and L. Monique Ward and Rocio Rivadenya, "Contributions of Entertainment Television to Adolescents' Sexual Attitudes and Expectations: The Role of Viewing Amount versus Viewer Involvement," *Journal of Sex Research* 36 (1999): 237–49.

65. Elizabeth Grauerholz and Amy King, "Prime Time Sexual Harassment," *Violence Against Women* 3 (April 1997): 129–49.

66. Grauerholz and King, 129.

67. Richard Jackson Harris, *A Cognitive Psychology of Mass Communication,* 3rd ed. (Mahwah, NJ: Erlbaum, 1999), 26.

68. Harris, 26.

69. For example, in a survey questionnaire given to both Japanese international and white students in the United States about African Americans, Yuki Fujioka found that the effects of the mass media are more significant when direct information is limited. Furthermore, it was found that the greater the number of perceived positive television portrayals of African Americans, the more positive the stereotypes of African Americans. With the white students, negative stereotypes increased as the perceived negative stereotypes increased. See Yuki Fujioka, "Television Portrayals and African-American Stereotypes: Examination of Television Effects When Direct Contact Is Lacking," *Journalism & Mass Communication Quarterly* 76 (1999): 52–75.

70. John Condry, *The Psychology of Television* (Hillsdale, NJ: Erlbaum, 1989), 5.

71. Stephen D. Reese, "Prologue–Framing Public Life: A Bridging Model for Media Research," in *Framing Public Life: Perspectives on Media and Our Understanding of the Social World,* ed. Stephen D. Reese, Oscar H. Gandy, and August E. Grant (Mahwah, NJ: Erlbaum, 2001), 7.

72. Reese, 11.

73. Michael Morgan and Nancy Signorielli, "Cultivation Analysis: Conceptualization and Methodology," in *Cultivation Analysis: New Directions in Media*

Effects Research, ed. Nancy Signorielli and Michael Morgan (Newbury Park, CA: Sage, 1990), 9–10.

74. See, for example, Nancy Signorielli, "Television and Conceptions about Sex Roles: Maintaining Conventionality and the Status Quo," *Sex Roles* 21 (1989): 337–56; and "Children, Television, and Conceptions about Chores: Attitudes and Behaviors," Sex Roles 27 (1992): 157–70. For a good summary of cultivation analysis research, see George Gerbner, Larry Gross, Michael Morgan, Nancy Signorielli, and James Shanahan, "Growing up with Television: Cultivation Processes," *Media Effects: Advances in Theory and Research,* ed. Jennings Bryant and Dolf Zillmann, 2nd ed. (Mahwah, NJ: Erlbaum, 2002), 43–67.

75. Bradley S. Greenberg, "Some Uncommon Television Images and the Drench Hypothesis," *Television as a Social Issue,* ed. Stuart Oskamp (Newbery Park, CA: Sage, 1988), 88–102.

76. Cynthia Hoffner and Joanne Cantor, "Perceiving and Responding to Mass Media Characters," *Responding to the Screen: Reception and Reaction Processes,* ed. Jennings Bryant and Dolf Zillmann (Hillsdale, NJ: Erlbaum, 1991), 64.

77. Alan M. Rubin, "The Uses-and-Gratifications Perspective of Media Effects," *Media Effects: Advances in Theory and Research,* ed. Jennings Bryant and Dolf Zillmann, 2nd ed. (Mahwah, NJ: Erlbaum, 2002), 538.

78. James B. Weaver III and Elizabeth A. Laird, "Mood Management during the Menstrual Cycle through Selective Exposure to Television," *Journalism and Mass Communication Quarterly* 72 (1995): 139–46.

79. Rubin, 536.

80. For a good introduction to research methodologies, see Roger D. Wimmer and Joseph R. Dominick, *Mass Media Research: An Introduction* (Belmont, CA: Wadsworth, 2000). They discuss three distinct approaches to social science research: positivism (objective, quantitative, more traditional), interpretive (qualitative, including field observations, focus groups, intensive interviews, and case studies), and critical (analysis, ideology). Most of the book focuses on quantitative research, although there is a good introduction to qualitative methods.

81. Press, 86.

82. Coleman, 186–87.

83. Coleman, 246.

84. George Comstock, "Television Research: Past Problems and Present Issues," *Research Paradigms, Television, and Social Behavior,* ed. Joy Keiko Asamen and Gordon L. Berry (Thousand Oaks, CA: Sage, 1998), 27.

85. Ien Ang, *Living Room Wars: Rethinking Media Audiences for a Postmodern World* (London: Routledge, 1996), 133.

86. For more on these approaches, see Chris Barker, *Cultural Studies: Theory and Practice* (London: Sage 2000); as well as Arthur Asa Berger, *Cultural Criticism: A Primary of Key Concepts* (Thousand Oaks, CA: Sage, 1995); and Leah R. Vande Berg, Lawrence A. Wenner, and Bruce E. Gronbeck, *Critical Approaches to Television* (Boston: Houghton Mifflin, 1998).

87. Barker, 385.

88. Some would argue, though, that what others have called polysemy is actually "polyvalence"—rather than creating different meanings from a text, viewers are receiving the same messages but evaluating them differently. See Celeste Condit, "The Rhetorical Limits of Polysemy," *Critical Studies in Mass Communication* 6 (1989): 103–22.

89. John Fiske, *Television Culture* (London: Methuen, 1987), 66.

90. Coleman, 246.

91. George Gerbner et al., 48.

92. Lewis Freeman, "Social Mobility in Television Comedies," *Critical Studies in Mass Communication* 9 (1992): 400–406.

93. Freeman, 405.

94. For a discussion of various feminist theories in relationship to media studies, see H. Leslie Steeves, "Feminist Theories and Media Studies," *Critical Studies in Mass Communication* 4 (1987): 95–135.

95. Josephine Donovan, *Feminist Theory: The Intellectual Traditions of American Feminism,* New Expanded Edition (New York: Frederick Ungar, 1985), 32.

96. Donovan, 141.

97. Donovan, 142.

98. Steeves, 106.

99. Myra Macdonald, *Representing Women: Myths of Femininity in the Popular Media* (London: Edward Arnold, 1995), 226.

100. Macdonald, 227. A subjectivity, according to Macdonald, is "the persona that we are invited to adopt as a result of the way that we are addressed, either face to face or via cultural and media discourses. Each individual on this reckoning will experience a number of different, and competing, subjectivities" (228).

101. Ang, 119.

102. Charlotte Brunsdon, "The Role of Soap Opera in the Development of Feminist Television Scholarship," *To Be Continued... Soaps Operas Around the World,* ed. Robert C. Allen (London: Routledge, 1995), 51. Brunsdon's reference is to Michele Barrett and Anne Phillips, "Introduction," in *Destabilizing Theory,* ed. Michele Barrett and Anne Phillips (Cambridge: Polity, 1992).

103. Helene A. Shugart, Catherine Egley Waggoner, and D. Lynn O'Brien Hallstein, "Mediating Third-Wave Feminism: Appropriation as Postmodern Media Practice," *Critical Studies in Media Communication* 18 (2001): 194–195.

104. Shugart, Waggoner, and Hallstein, 195.

105. Shugart, Waggoner, and Hallstein, 195. In another article, Helene Shugart argues that third-wave feminism is more appropriately understood as a "Gen X" subculture than as an evolutionary phase of feminism. See Helene A. Shugart, "Isn't It Ironic? The Intersection of Third-Wave Feminism and Generation X," *Women's Studies in Communication* 24 (2001): 131–68.

106. Macdonald, 34.

107. Karen A. Foss, Sonja K. Foss, and Cindy L. Griffin, *Feminist Rhetorical Theories* (Thousand Oaks, CA: Sage, 1999), 3.

108. For example, John Fiske, in *Television Culture* (London: Methuen, 1987), explores what he calls "gendered" television, distinguishing between masculine genres (typified by action adventure) and feminine (in particular, soap operas).

109. Mary Ellen Brown, *Soap Opera and Women's Talk: The Pleasure of Resistance* (Thousand Oaks, CA: Sage, 1994), 116.

110. Brown, 1.

111. Brown, 134.

112. Brown, 149.

113. Dorothy Hobson, "Women Audiences and the Workplace," *Television and Women's Culture: The Politics of the Popular,* ed. Mary Ellen Brown (London: Sage, 1990), 62.

114. Brown, 179.

Chapter 2

1940s AND 1950s: HOUSEWIVES AND SECRETARIES

Television broadcasting officially began in 1941, but its growth was interrupted by World War II. While men went overseas to fight, women at home were called on to help the war effort by working in factories. When it was time in the minds of some for all Rosie the Riveters to quit their jobs and have babies with the returning servicemen, television and other popular culture were used to show women their place. In 1947, television was in approximately 14,000 American homes. That number quickly grew to more than 1 million, or 9 percent of American homes by 1950, and by 1960 almost 90 percent of households had television. As the popularity of television grew, so did American families and the idyllic myth of the housewife.

Many popular radio programs became prevalent on television, including ethnic comedies with female leads. But America quickly would learn to love Lucy and laugh at her struggles to become more than a housewife as television replaced radio and movies as the most popular pastime. Other television sitcoms would reinforce the cultural message that women were happier married and at home, despite the growing numbers of women in the workforce.

CULTURAL/HISTORICAL CONTEXT

After the "great" depression of the 1930s and wartime rationing in the early 1940s, Americans were ready for post-war prosperity. As people in the armed forces returned to civilian life, many women were fired from jobs they held during wartime that were now considered more rightfully men's work. Numerous companies had a policy of not hiring married women, which also meant that a woman would lose her job upon marriage. The dominant ideology for at least the middle class was that women's work was to have babies and become major consumers in establishing a pleasant household. Political activism would return in the 1960s, but as feminist historian Toni Carabillo described it, most of the 1950s had a "peculiarly passive obsession with security as the ultimate happiness" with a compulsive conformity of lifestyles and a pervasive apathy.[1]

While there was no active, popular national women's movement in the 1950s, there were still a number of noteworthy achievements. In 1953, Jacqueline Cochrane, the first woman to ferry a bomb to England during World War II, became the first woman to pilot a plane that moved faster than the speed of sound. Also that year, playwright and former member of Congress Clare Boothe Luce was appointed ambassador to Italy, the first woman to represent the United States in a major diplomatic office, and Ovata Culp Hobby, director of the Women's Auxiliary Army Corps during World War II, became the first secretary of Health, Education, and Welfare. Former First Lady Eleanor Roosevelt, long a campaigner for progressive social causes, publicly allied herself with the National Federation of Business and Professional Women in 1953 by changing her initial negative stand on an Equal Rights Amendment to favor complete equality. In 1955, women were accepted as ministers in the U.S. Presbyterian Church and Judaism allowed its first female cantor. In 1958, Marion E. Kenworthy became the first woman president of the American Psychoanalytic Association, after starting her career in 1930 as Columbia University's first female psychiatry professor. During his two terms as president in the 1950s, General Dwight D. Eisenhower named twenty-eight women to Senate-confirmed posts, topping his predecessor, Harry Truman, by eight.[2]

If people were to use television situation comedies as their guideline to what the 1950s were like, they would miss the paranoia of communism and war as well as the struggle for civil rights and integration that pervaded the decade. The "cold war" with the Soviet Union began after World War II, as it spread communism throughout Eastern Europe and paranoia in the United States. The House Committee on Un-American Activities in 1948 investigated about 2 million federal employees for communist endeavors, leading to 526 resignations and 98 firings.[3] The "red scare" escalated throughout the early 1950s, led by fanatical Senator Joseph R. McCarthy from Wisconsin. Many people were blacklisted—including hundreds in the entertainment industry—and unable to find employment. The Army-McCarthy hearings in 1954, given considerable television and newspaper coverage, did much to help end McCarthy's anticommunist witch hunt as he made accusations against the U.S. Army. From 1950 to 1953, the United States was heavily involved in the Korean War, but it was the cold war that grew between the United States and the U.S.S.R. Children were taught to "duck and cover" in school, and families were encouraged to build bomb shelters in anticipation of an attack from the Russians. The launch of the first Earth satellite, *Sputnik I,* by the Soviet Union in 1957 unnerved many leaders in the United States, who began a "space race" to beat the Soviets in future technological developments.

Racial segregation in public schools was declared unconstitutional by the Supreme Court in 1954, and a year later the Interstate Commerce Commission banned segregation on interstate trains and buses. In 1955, Rosa Parks refused to give up her seat in the front of a bus in Montgomery, Alabama, and she was arrested. When her trial began, African Americans launched a boycott of the city's buses that lasted over a year. In 1957, racial violence erupted in Little Rock, Arkansas, over the desegregation of Central High School. Many African Americans in the South also were continually denied their right to vote; the Civil Rights Act of 1957 established the Civil Rights Commission, allowing the Justice Department to file suit when that right was denied.

Immediately after World War II, inflation spiraled upward, as did crime. There were bitter labor disputes and a shortage of housing. The "baby boom," a surge in the population that had started during the war, continued and led to a shortage of schools and teachers. Many suburbs were created as families moved out of big cities and purchased homes. Thanks to the G.I. Bill, not only could families afford homes because of low-interest loans, money received for college helped to create an educated middle class with disposable income. Some of that income went to burgeoning automobile sales and family vacations, made possible by the construction of thousands of miles of interstate highway. While salaries and wages increased, unemployment fluctuated from a low of 3.2 percent in 1950 to a high of 7.7 percent in 1958. In 1956, almost 13 million women were in the workforce, compared to 8.5 million in 1947. That same year, however, *Life* magazine published interviews with five male psychiatrists who believed female ambition was the root of mental illness in wives, emotional upsets in husbands, and homosexuality in boys.[4]

In 1946, a decade before the "space race" with the Soviet Union began, the first electronic digital computer, Eniac, was introduced. It weighed thirty tons and occupied a 1,800-square-foot room. Baby boomer children twirled hula hoops around their waists in the late 1950s and played with Barbie dolls, which had impossibly thin waistlines designed for fashionable outfits that sometimes cost more than real children's clothing. Fashions for real kids included poodle skirts, saddle oxfords, and blue jeans with white socks. Children of all ages benefited greatly from the polio vaccine developed by Dr. Jonas Salk in the mid-1950s; doses were often administered in schools via sugar cubes. By the end of the 1950s, there were fifty stars on the American flag, and children learned about the new states of Alaska and Hawaii. Ignored by many women during these baby boom years, birth control was finally officially sanctioned by the American Medical Association in 1959.

In popular media, many "women's" magazines gave advice on housekeeping and how to keep one's husband happy with good cooking, but *Playboy* in 1953 introduced another way to a man's heart. Also in 1953, *TV Guide* made its debut; on its cover was the baby of the stars of television's number one show, *I Love Lucy*. Destined to become an international favorite for decades, the *Peanuts* comic strip, with Charlie Brown, Lucy, and Snoopy, made its debut in eight newspapers in 1950, appealing to both children and adults. A standard in what was then known as the "women's" section, the advice column by "Ann Landers" debuted in 1955 and continued into the twenty-first century in newspaper sections no longer considered for women only. Violence in comic books and rising juvenile delinquency led to Senate hearings in 1954 to determine if there was a connection, an experience similar to what most media, particularly television, would endure throughout the century whenever politicians became particularly concerned about crime.

The book industry enjoyed prosperity, especially because of the introduction of paperback books during World War II. Popular fiction included James Michener's Pulitzer Prize–winning *Tales of the South Pacific* in 1950 and the oft-banned (in high schools) story of Holden Caulfield in *The Catcher in the Rye* in 1951. J.R.R. Tolkien's cult classic trilogy *Lord of the Rings,* a movie sensation in the early twenty-first century, was published in 1955, and Grace Metalious's *Peyton Place,* a 1960s hit on television, in 1956. Reflecting an emphasis on domesticity, the best-selling nonfiction book in 1950 was *Betty Crocker's Picture Cook Book,* and for two years at the end of the decade television personality Art Linkletter's *Kids Say the Darndest Things!* was number one. In 1953, French feminist writer Simone De Beauvoir's book *The Second Sex* was published in the United States, introducing the phrase, "women's liberation." Alfred Kinsey's book on *Sexual Behavior in the Human Female* outraged many who had conservative notions of female sexuality.

The big band sound was popular in the 1940s, along with Frank Sinatra, who had teenage girls swooning and screaming at his concerts. The mellow sounds of Rosemary Clooney ("Come On-a My House"), Perry Como ("Catch a Falling Star"), Patti Page ("Tennessee Waltz"), and Nat "King" Cole ("Mona Lisa") were typical of the popular music played on radio and television throughout the early 1950s. But the music industry and popular culture were dramatically changed by the mass introduction of rock 'n' roll in 1955. With its roots in gospel, blues, jazz, and "hillbilly," the wild, suggestive movements it seemed to inspire with its heavy beat had adults concerned that it would encourage juvenile delinquency and premarital sex.[5] A 1955 movie about juvenile delinquents in high school, *The Blackboard Jungle,* introduced the country to what would become the first number one rock 'n' roll record, "Rock around the Clock," by Bill Haley and His Comets. But it would be a truck driver from Tennessee who would really strike terror in the hearts of parents and community leaders: Elvis "the Pelvis" Presley, whose swiveling hips suggested more than the lyrics of his hit songs, such as "Hound Dog" and "Love Me Tender." By 1957, two-thirds of the sixty best-selling records in the United States were rock.

The movie industry in 1946 enjoyed its biggest box office ever, with 82 million people attending each week. Although not immediately a big success in 1947, the upbeat *It's a Wonderful Life* with Jimmy Stewart and Donna Reed would become an annual television favorite around Christmas. Disney released several animated films in the 1950s that would become classics, including *Cinderella* in 1950, a movie that perhaps has taught many little girls that someday a Prince Charming will rescue them. *Sleeping Beauty* at the end of the decade also featured a damsel in distress rescued by a prince, and both films had evil stepmothers. In competition with television, the film industry attempted to do what television couldn't to get its audience back, including the introduction of three-dimensional (3D) movies, which required moviegoers to wear cardboard glasses. Wide-screen "cinemascope" and big budget movies like *Ben Hur* were critical and popular successes, and film stars from previous years, such as Humphrey Bogart and Katherine Hepburn in *The African Queen,* continued to attract viewers. A new film star was born when Marilyn Monroe appeared in *Gentlemen Prefer Blondes* in 1953. The sex symbol of the decade, Monroe became an icon for the beautiful but dumb blonde, often oozing sex and little-girl innocence simultaneously, offering men both the virgin and the whore. James Dean, the symbol for youthful rebellion, died in a car crash at the age of twenty-four just a few days before the now classic *Rebel Without a Cause* was released in 1955. Elvis Presley, who symbolized both rebellion and sexuality himself in his persona as a rock star, began his successful movie career in 1956 with *Love Me Tender.* Sandra Dee portrayed the innocent teenager in both *Gidget* and *A Summer Place* in 1959, going from innocent "beach bunny" to pregnant teenager. While movies remained popular, particularly with young people who could also view them at the increasingly prolific drive-in theaters, television had cut attendance drastically as more people stayed home and were entertained for free.

THE TELEVISION INDUSTRY

In 1946, as the country was recovering from World War II, television networks began broadcasting a few offerings of regularly scheduled programs in the evening. By 1948, CBS, NBC, and ABC, all veteran radio broadcasters, and Dumont, a television manufacturer, had a fairly complete lineup of programs.[6] Since most people did not have television in their homes, viewing sometimes took place at a local bar, and the many sports programs were a perfect match for that audience. The schedule also was full of musical programs and some anthology dramas, including *Philco TV Playhouse, Texaco Star Theater,* and *Chevrolet Tele-Theater.* The year also saw the debut of *Toast of the Town,* later named *The Ed Sullivan Show* after its host. A variety show that would remain a family favorite on CBS until 1971, it featured acts that ranged through the decades from the Russian ballet to standup comics to Elvis Presley and the Beatles. In the early years, however, most programming was broadcast live, lost forever for future audiences, or it was filmed directly from a television monitor while broadcast, resulting in poorly preserved "kinescopes," a reference to the television picture tube that was filmed.

The 1950s often have been referred to as the "golden years" of television, primarily because of the live television dramas originating from New York City, but also because of the immense growth of the medium, financially and in people's homes. Many radio programs migrated to television during those early years, including such family comedies as *The Aldrich Family* and *The Goldbergs.* Known under various names, *Walt Disney* began its thirty-four-year prime-time run in 1954. An anthology series, it offered a variety of cartoons, adventure dramas, and documentary-type programs sometimes connected to Disney's theatrical films and its theme park, Disneyland. By far its biggest success, and a cultural phenomenon, was the three dramatic episodes about Davy Crockett. Children through-out the country began wearing coonskin caps like Davy, and "The Ballad of Davy Crockett" was the number two hit of 1955. Big-money quiz shows, such as *$64,000 Question* and *Twenty-One,* were also popular, but when a former contestant in 1958 revealed the games were rigged, the public felt cheated and a congressional hearing was held. Such games dis-appeared for many years. *Dragnet* was a popular police drama, purport-edly based on real Los Angeles police stories, but by the end of the decade westerns ruled the airwaves, led by *Gunsmoke,* another former radio show.

Comedy was also popular in the 1950s, from the sketch comedy/variety found in *The Milton Berle Show* (known as "Mr. Television" for his great popularity and versatility) and *Your Show of Shows* with Sid Caesar and Imogene Coca to a variety of situation comedies. In the early years a diver-sity of people could be seen in sitcoms: an immigrant/first generation American Norwegian family in the popular *Mama,* a Jewish family in *The Goldbergs,* an African American woman in *Beulah,* African Americans in *Amos 'n' Andy,* and an Italian immigrant in *Life with Luigi.* By the end of the decade, however, sitcoms were basically filled with white, middle-class families. The exception would be the Cuban Ricky Ricardo on *I Love Lucy.*

SIGNIFICANT COMEDY SERIES

Undoubtedly the most popular situation comedy in the 1950s, still seen in syndication around the world fifty years later, was *I Love Lucy.* While many real women were treated as second-class citizens at home and in public, a handful were starring in their own sitcoms. Because of their pop-ularity and cultural significance, the following series are highlighted: *I Love Lucy, Mama, Beulah, Our Miss Brooks, Private Secretary,* and *The Donna Reed Show.*

I Love Lucy

Many of the 193 episodes of *I Love Lucy* have become classics, seen in constant syndication for more than forty years. During its six years of orig-inal half-hour episodes between 1951 and 1957 (thirteen hour-long episodes also were made as specials between 1957 and 1961), the series never ranked below third in the ratings.[7] People still laugh at the absurd, slapstick situations in which Lucy Ricardo finds herself, including stuffing candy in her mouth to keep up with an assembly line and fighting with another woman in a grape vat in Italy. To Lucy fans it is legendary that

CBS did not want Lucille Ball's real husband, Cuban bandleader Desi Arnaz, to play her husband on the series; CBS brass thought nobody would believe them as a couple. Ball was determined to work with Arnaz to keep her marriage together (he had been touring with his band while she worked in movies and radio), so they put together a series of slapstick routines about a movie star who tried to join her bandleader husband's act.[8] Their vaudeville tour was a popular and critical success. CBS still took some convincing, but finally agreed to a pilot (sample) episode.

The writers for the pilot as well as most of the series—Jess Oppenheimer, Madelyn Pugh, and Bob Carroll Jr.—had worked with Ball on her radio show, *My Favorite Husband,* the series CBS initially had intended to bring her to television. The program was about Liz Cooper, a housewife whose schemes always got her into trouble, and her patient, banker husband, George. Liz's best friend was Iris, the wife of George's boss. Oppenheimer says that of the first forty shows of *I Love Lucy,* about half were based on the radio show.[9] One could argue that the differences between the radio show and *I Love Lucy* were slight—Ricky Ricardo is a singer and bandleader from Cuba, and Lucy is his showbiz-struck wife. Their best friends are Fred and Ethel Mertz, their landlords and neighbors. Of the *Lucy* show itself, Oppenheimer wrote that they were never trying to manufacture something funny, "instead we were looking for a situation where Lucy's and Ricky's problems and differences of opinion were the same ones that most of our audience had encountered. We called it 'holding up the mirror.'"[10] While situations would often get outlandish and silly, Oppenheimer insisted on a logical foundation for every story.[11]

The basic premise of *I Love Lucy* involves a battle of the sexes, usually with Ricky forbidding Lucy to do something (often involving her desire to work in show business) and Lucy defying his wishes. Despite the dominant ideology for gender roles at the time, Lucy is not content to be just a housewife and mother. In Diana Meehan's analysis and categorization of female characters in prime-time television, Lucy is defined as an imp who conflicted with society's expectations of her. Meehan wrote of the imp that "like a tomboy, she rejected the frills and fancies of her sex for the hardier advantages of the boys. Her figure and dress were boyish. She was active but awkward and graceless. In addition she was curious, imaginative, independent, adventuresome—and asexual."[12] Sexuality was certainly downplayed for all sitcom characters in the 1950s, and married couples slept apart in twin beds. In the episode where Lucy reveals to Ricky that she is expecting a baby, CBS objected to the use of the word "pregnant," and to appease the network the writers engaged a Catholic priest, a Protestant minister, and a rabbi to review scripts dealing with her pregnancy. Romance was allowed, however, with chaste kisses and hugs, and the Ricardos could be romantic at times. At the end of each episode, Lucy would learn her lesson and return to her role as housewife, making peace with Ricky.

Two episodes in particular address the roles of men and women, "Job Switching" and "Equal Rights." As "Job Switching" begins, Ricky is angry at Lucy for bouncing checks and complains to her and the Mertzes. Immediately forming gender-based battle lines, the men accuse the women of spending their time lying around the house and playing canasta while the men earn the money. The women argue that they also work hard, and Lucy challenges the men to swap roles with her and Ethel for a week. In parallel scenes we see Lucy and Ethel struggle to find and keep a job (at the employment agency it seems they are not qualified for much of anything) and Ricky and Fred fail at several household duties. As the women cycle through several tasks at a candy factory to find one at which they are competent, their working career ends with them at a conveyer belt where they are to wrap candy. The classic slapstick scene ensues with them putting candy in their mouths and clothing as they struggle to keep up. When Lucy and Ethel return to the Ricardo apartment in defeat, they discover a terrible mess in the kitchen; the men have failed at yet another household task. The obvious lesson learned by all is finalized when Ricky and Fred enter and admit they are "lousy housewives." The women admit they are not so good at bringing home the bacon and that they got fired from their first job. Ricky suggests they go back to the way they were: "We'll make the money, and you spend it." It is perhaps significant that he mentions the women's roles as consumers, not as housekeepers and cooks. In this way, not only are advertisers happy, but the men come across as providers and the women as dependents, not competent managers of households, except perhaps through consumption.

In "Equal Rights" again battle lines are drawn between the women and men as Lucy and Ethel insist on being treated equally. When the couples go out to dinner together, the men finally agree that the women should be treated equally and each pay their own dinner check. Neither Lucy nor Ethel have enough money, so Ricky arranges with the restaurant manager for the women to wash dishes in lieu of payment. Angry at their husbands and tired after washing so many dishes, Lucy decides to call Ricky and pretend they are being robbed, expecting him and Fred to panic and feel bad that they put their wives in such a situation. When Ricky and Fred rush over to help their wives after calling the police, they secretly see that Lucy and Ethel are playing a trick and decide to teach them a lesson. Masquerading as robbers, they scare the women and the police arrive to assume Ricky and Fred are actually robbing the women. Lucy and Ethel refuse to identify their husbands until they go to the police station. With the women clearly having the upper hand, the men agree to "equal rights" and Lucy and Ethel get them released from jail. Unfortunately, it would appear that the only equal rights to which they have agreed involve tricking each other—and the women clearly won this round.

Feminist critic Lori Landay sees Lucy Ricardo as a female trickster who violates the boundaries between male and female spheres, a liminal figure who

> always sees opportunity in ordinary, everyday situations; despite Ricky's dictates and any other rules or restrictions, she creates new roles for herself that bend and warp the social institutions she subverts. No social space is off-limits to her; just as she moves freely between social spaces, she performs impersonations that cross the boundaries demarcating gender, race, age, and class.[13]

Landay says that Lucy's incompetence, however, "undercuts her subversiveness, reinforcing the home and the social role of the housewife as the only option for women."[14] In at least three episodes, however, Lucy is successful in obtaining a job, but it is she who decides to not work outside the home. In the first season's "The Audition," Lucy sneaks into Ricky's nightclub and does a vigorous slapstick routine for network executives there to see Ricky. When Lucy is offered a contract and not Ricky, she happily turns it down to remain a housewife. In the fifth season (1955–1956) in "Lucy and the Dummy," Lucy uses a replica of Ricky to perform a dance at a studio party in Hollywood. After her unwittingly hilarious attempts at getting the dummy off her costume, she is offered a contract as a comedienne. Not wanting to stay in California without Ricky and the baby, she declines. In "Lucy Wants a Career," an hour-long special originally broadcast in 1959, Lucy is successful on an early morning television show where her credentials as a housewife impress both the sponsors and the audience. Unable to spend much time with Ricky and the baby, however, she gladly gives up the job to stay home. It would seem that, despite Lucy's unrest at being "just a housewife," the recurring lesson is that, ultimately, that is what makes her most happy and she cannot successfully have both a career and a family life.

While it is easy to interpret *I Love Lucy* as merely another program that reinforced gender stereotypes, there are other ways to read it. Lori Landay in some ways saw the program as an inspiration for future generations: "When Lucy, like her tricky predecessors, looks around in search of the opening in the system that seems to enclose her, she presents a model of female ambition that is relentless in its craving for freedom, participation, and equality. This is the kind of prefeminist scrutiny of the sex-gender system that resulted in the second wave of feminism in America."[15] British media critic Paul Wells also sees Lucy Ricardo as somewhat feminist:

> Lucy's comic antics are essentially a symbolic mode of empowerment in which she controls and reconstructs her body in terms which give her complete physical freedoms and/or parody patriarchal codes. Though this is seemingly contained by the closed context of the established gender order, the open conviction of Lucy's position is the comic narrational device which carries the most social and moral certainty. Her invention, imagination and initiative essentially redefine every previously "male" space. Her anarchy is something laughed with by women, laughed at by men, the latter naively assuming that the social order will inevitably stay the same when it is changing before their very eyes. It is probably one of the key reasons why *I Love Lucy* endures in syndicated reruns worldwide.[16]

While Lucy may seem at least prefeminist, if not feminist, in her rebellion against Ricky and patriarchal culture, there are elements of their relationship beyond any battle of the sexes that are disturbing. Primarily, Lucy is afraid of Ricky. In several episodes Lucy is shown wincing and backing away from Ricky when he is angry. In at least two episodes he spanks her on screen. In "Lucy Plays Cupid," Ricky spanks Lucy when she disobeys him and attempts to play cupid for a single woman in their apartment building. Not one to quit, in the next scene we see Lucy rubbing her sore bottom as she continues her attempt at matchmaking at the woman's apartment. In another episode, Lucy is spanked in front of the Mertzes for yet another transgression according to Ricky. The Mertzes look on in what seems like approval. Lucy is treated as the child who must be punished by her husband/father. In an episode that takes place soon after the Ricardos have moved to Connecticut, "Lucy Gets Chummy with the Neighbors," Lucy calls the Mertzes in New York to come protect her from Ricky's temper after she has overspent on furniture. Despite her fear of Ricky's temper, Lucy certainly is not afraid to make fun of his Cuban accent, even though he is clearly bilingual and she is not. Feminist critic Patricia Mellencamp interprets Ricky's role as secondary and that he as a "slapstick foil for Lucy's pies in the face suggests that Lucy's resistance to patriarchy might be more palatable because it is mediated by a racism which views

Ricky as inferior."[17] One also must wonder about their relationship when, in an early episode, "The Girls Want to Go to a Nightclub," Ricky and Fred arrange to bring other women to a boxing match when their wives refuse to go. Even though Lucy and Ethel end up disguising themselves as dates for their husbands, the idea of the husbands openly arranging for a date with other women is rather mind-boggling.

Although the title of the series suggests that the primary relationship is that of the Ricardos (the "I" in the title is Ricky who loves Lucy), it is the strong bond of friendship and love between Lucy and Ethel Mertz that is the most pleasurable and dominates at least as much screen time. Ethel is always involved by Lucy in her schemes against Ricky (and often Fred, who is Ricky's cohort in the gender battles). In several episodes, Lucy and Ethel cry at the prospect of being separated; thus, the Mertzes accompany the Ricardos to California, Europe, Florida, and ultimately their move to a Connecticut suburb. In squabbles between the couples, such as "The Court-room" where they fight over a television set and "Never Do Business with Friends" where they fight over a washing machine, it is Lucy and Ethel who end up crying in each other's arms. It is Ethel who first guesses Lucy is pregnant before she does in "Lucy is Enceinte," and she is very excited about the prospect of being a godmother. When the Ricardos first move to Connecticut, first Ethel and then Lucy become jealous of the other's friend-ship with a neighbor woman in the suburb, and each woman fears she will be forgotten. Unfortunately, one episode in particular illustrates a stereo-typical viewpoint of women's relationships and depicts them as catty and jealous of each other. In "Lucy and Ethel Buy the Same Dress," each prom-ises to return the dress she found for a charity event, but neither does. When they subsequently appear on stage together to sing, ironically, "Friend-ship," they proceed to systematically tear each other's dress.

The only social issues addressed in *I Love Lucy* were those concerning gender roles, with public space the domain of men and private space, the home, the province of women. While Lucy's relationship with Ricky was a little frightening at times, the bond of friendship she had with Ethel, despite their occasional squabbles, was equal and strong, based on love, not fear. It is Lucy's relationship with Ethel, and not her occasional successful forays into public life, that were perhaps the most liberating aspect of the series. When Lucy returned home after turning down jobs, she also returned to Ethel.

Mama

Framed as a memory of a grown daughter, *Mama* was a favorite for most of its 1949–1956 run on CBS and was one of several ethnic comedies in the early years of television. Each episode began with a closeup of a photo album with daughter Katrin's voice reminiscing about her father, brother, and sister, but "most of all, when I remember that San Francisco of long ago, I remember Mama." In this series Mama, Marta Hansen, was the nucleus of the family, a housewife who centered her world around her husband, Lars, a carpenter, and their three children, Nels, Katrin, and Dagmar. Presented live throughout its entire run, only a handful of kinescopes remain of it, but it was significant to those who watched it and arguably a predecessor of gentle family comedies in the latter half of the 1950s.

Mama is based on a book by Kathryn Forbes, *Mama's Bank Account*, and in the 1940s it became a stage play and a film, both titled *I Remember Mama*. The television series took some liberties in its version from the book. According to ethnic studies critic George Lipsitz, "Mama represents a traditional mother raising independent daughters—using her traditional cooking skills to make social connections that allow Katrin to pursue an untraditional career as a writer. On television, tradition reigns as Mama instructs Katrin about cooking to help her land a husband, and Katrin becomes a secretary rather than a writer."[18] Author Forbes complained that the television Hansen family had too much wealth to accurately represent the circumstances she wrote about, with four children in a house shared with relatives and boarders. On television the family lives alone, although relatives and friends visit frequently, and there are only three children. The TV version certainly fits with the 1950s ideal of the nuclear family in their own home.

Episodes of *Mama* were not interrupted by commercials. For approximately twenty-seven minutes viewers would follow the main story line focusing on any one of the family members, but it is with Mama in her kitchen where problems eventually are solved. In the last two minutes of each show, the sponsor's product, Maxwell House coffee, would be served by Mama over conversation, a denouement that ritualized resolution to problems in connection with the product served.

Both Marta (Mama) and Lars (Papa) immigrated from Norway and are determined to raise their children to be honest, loving, and hard-working, traditional values to be assimilated with whatever direction the children decide to take. While Marta and Lars speak with Norwegian accents, the children do not—they are first-generation Americans who want to fit in with dominant American culture while still retaining their parents' values. It is Marta who spends the most time with the children, nagging them to practice piano, do their homework, and so on. Lars is called on for the bigger issues, such as speaking to Nels about his smoking cigarettes, but he is a reluctant disciplinarian who would prefer that Marta do it. In a particularly interesting episode, Marta becomes overwhelmed with her household problems and making sure that the children are doing what they should. In exasperation she says, "Everyone wants something for nothing in this house" and "Why do I have to make everyone do everything?"

What is implied is a strong work ethic that includes people working together to achieve goals. What is also clear is that Marta does not feel appreciated, a theme that appears in many situation comedies with housewives. She laments that "What does a family mean? Work. And no one appreciates it." She tells her sister that she wishes she were an old maid. The final straw is when she spends hours making a new meatloaf recipe for her family, and no one compliments her. Lars dominates the dinner conversation when the children ask excitedly about his lunch at a restaurant with his boss. Marta leaves in a huff to go play cards, an activity she had earlier turned down because she had too much to do. As the women are playing cards and gossiping, one of them mentions a sick child. This immediately makes Marta feel guilty. Earlier in the day, Dagmar had complained of feeling ill and Marta had attributed it to her having a spelling test at school; she calls her daughter's bluff and scoots her off to school. Marta quickly leaves the card party, but when she gets home she finds that her family has done everything she had been nagging them to do. Lars proudly shows Marta the kitchen drawer he finally fixed, but gets irritated when Marta asks him about speaking to Nels about smoking. When Lars exclaims, "heavens, Marta, do I have to do everything around here?" she laughs in recognition.

The lesson for 1950s housewives, of course, is that their role is important, even though it is hard and often unappreciated. Another meaning could be read in this episode: anyone can do housework and raise children. Mama's family relies on her because they don't want to perform her tasks, yet Mama's dreams for her daughters would put them in the same situation. In an episode about her birthday, when Katrin asks her what she would like, Marta says: "Well, I think a fine new job for your Papa. You and Dagmar to marry nice young men and have a lot of wonderful children—just like I have. And Nels, well, Nels to become president of the United States."[19] Her wishes made clear a perpetuation of stereotyped gender roles.

Marta's role in her family occasionally got her out of the house to do tasks other than household-related work. When Lars wishes to become an American citizen, he is embarrassed to go to school for it, so Marta goes and learns everything a citizen must know. Instead of using that knowledge to become a citizen herself, however, she teaches Lars at home. He passes the test to become an American citizen. She's not interested because that is for "menfolk."[20] Certainly voting was for "menfolk" only in the early part of the twentieth century, and Marta seems content with the status quo. Marta is often the mediator among family members and even in the public sphere. In one episode, Lars has forbidden Katrin to read a controversial romance novel, even though, as his daughter points out, he has never read it. Marta reads the book herself and loves it. When a friend of Lars tells him that women read romances when they are restless, Marta must assure him that she loves him as much as ever. In another episode, the children are disappointed in their father when he loses his job promotion as a foreman. When Marta explains that he lost the position because he could not bring himself to fire a man, the children are once again proud of him for his gentleness.

Marta is surrounded by a network of women who share in her trials and tribulations as a housewife and mother. Of particular importance is one of her two sisters, Jenny, who frequently visits and offers advice when Marta complains. In the "Mama's Birthday" episode, Jenny asks Marta to a fashion show, but Marta says she can't go because she has to cook dinner for Papa's guest. Jenny thinks it is a disgrace that Marta cannot have time to herself and "can't call her soul her own."[21] Jenny's solution is a new cooking stove to save Mama time, and her children decide to buy it for her. When Marta learns that her husband intends to build her one, rather than hurt his feelings, she persuades the children to get her another gift. The children buy her dishes, and once again Marta is the selfless mother rewarded on her special day by more household items that will benefit her entire family. Jenny's prefeminist arguments with her sister's family have only partially been resolved. However, feminist writer and activist Robin Morgan, who played younger daughter Dagmar for six years, interprets the series in retrospect as stronger for women than one might initially think: "Dagmar did routinely thrash the neighborhood bully whenever he tried to cramp her assertive style. Not coincidentally, the Hansen family was matriarchal less in structure than in affirming that its primary source of wisdom and strength was the title character."[22]

A far cry from the slapstick comedy and battle of the sexes in *I Love Lucy*, *Mama*'s humor and story lines were gentle and usually about the everyday trials and tribulations in working-class families. Certainly Mama (Marta) was generally content with her roles as housewife and mother, and her surrounding network of female friends helped her get through the day.

Beulah

The character of Beulah, a nurturing African American maid, began as a supporting role in several radio series, including the very popular *Fibber*

McGee and Molly.[23] In 1945, Beulah got her own radio show on CBS; in 1950, the series made its debut on television on ABC. Until 1947, the character of Beulah was played by a Caucasian male whose thick accent contributed to the buffoonish stereotype of this domestic servant.[24] Media critic Robin Coleman calls this a double-erasure because it is not only "culturally disturbing, as it pertains to the demolition of Black identity, but it evidenced an oppressive racial and gender deletion."[25] *Beulah* was the first narrative form of entertainment on television to star an African American woman, and the only one until 1968; her image mattered to African Americans and to those for whom she was the only contact with people of color.

Beulah is the maid for Harry and Alice Henderson and their young son, Donnie. The Hendersons are a white, middle-class family in the suburbs who always need Beulah to get them out of a crisis. Her character is a stereotype found in popular culture for centuries, "the large, often dowdy, usually darker, all-knowing, all-seeing, all-hearing, all-understanding mammy figure, whose life is built around nurturing and nourishing those in the Big House."[26] In the three years the series was in its original network television run, three different renowned African American actresses played Beulah, all with their own variation, however slight, on her character. The first to play her on television, Ethel Waters, was an accomplished film and stage actress as well as singer who, according to media critic Donald Bogle, "transformed Beulah into a knowing earth mother, able to unravel life's tangled (albeit trivial) difficulties and to make everything right. Waters portrayed Beulah as a relaxed, older southern Black woman, aware of the racial codes of the household in which she works—and fond of the family—yet not all-sacrificing for them."[27] Oscar-winner Hattie McDaniel (Mammy in *Gone with the Wind*), according to Bogle, played the character too broadly, keeping audiences at a distance. Illness forced her to quit after six episodes. The last to play Beulah, this time as a cheery woman who often came across as childlike, was film actress Louise Beavers.[28] Regardless of who played Beulah, however, there was no getting around the stereotype of the maid/mammy character.

The television episodes typically begin with Beulah facing the camera and making a witty comment about herself, sometimes about her lack of a husband, a fact that bothered her very much. For example, in one episode she begins with, "Don't let anyone tell you I'm in the market for a husband. 'Course I would be, but they don't sell husbands in a market." Beulah does have a steady boyfriend, Bill Jackson, another stereotyped character. While Bill has his own fix-it shop, he is always avoiding work and freeloading meals from Beulah. He is loath to marry, much to Beulah's constant frustration. He is willing, however, to help Beulah solve the Henderson family problems. For example, when ten-year-old Donnie Henderson has to attend a dance class party and is worried about his dancing ability, Bill and Beulah teach him how to dance to boogie-woogie type music. After the conservative dance instructor is predictably scandalized when Donnie dances that way instead of waltzing, the boy becomes a hit with the girls, and Bill allows Donnie to offer his own dance lessons to them in his fix-it shop.

Occasionally Beulah is the cause of problems that have to be solved. In one episode, she mistakenly assumes that a baby carriage delivered to the house was ordered because Mrs. Henderson is pregnant; when it disappears, she assumes Mrs. Henderson wants to hide the fact that she is pregnant. Swearing Bill and another maid to secrecy, of course the rumor gets all around the neighborhood. When the good-humored Mrs. Henderson denies that she is pregnant, the neighbors who brought her presents all have a good laugh too. The image of gossipy servants in this episode is clear, as is the eagerness of mammy Beulah to take care of a new, white baby while being denied the chance to have her own. Interestingly, Bill is excited about the new baby too, but he is not willing to commit to a family himself. In another episode, Beulah's concern for the Hendersons' marriage (they seem to take each other for granted) almost backfires when she orders a book on how to make a marriage work and Mr. Henderson gets angry at his wife. Beulah somehow gets them to make up, and the two renew their vows with their young son, Donnie, serving as minister. Bill is willing to let Donnie marry him and Beulah, and he's willing to wait until he is old enough.

Beulah also has a close woman friend in whom to confide, although deep secrets and character depth were hardly part of the series. Oriole (played for two years by Butterfly "I don't know nothin' 'bout birthin' no babies" McQueen) is yet another stereotype—the shrill scatterbrain she played in *Gone with the Wind* and also a single woman desperate for a man. Oriole is the maid for the white family next door to the Hendersons, and frequently stops by to chat with Beulah. She eagerly volunteers to help Beulah with her white family's problems, but it sometimes backfires, as it does when she finds a substitute date for Donnie at his dance class party. The new girl with whom she sets him up is sixteen years old, but it all works out well. As a teenager, his "date" is quite pleased with the fast dancing style Donnie has learned from Beulah and Bill.

It is not surprising that, with all its stereotypes, *Beulah* came under heavy criticism, despite its early popularity. Both newspaper television critics and the National Association for the Advancement of Colored People (NAACP) lamented what they considered hurtful images in this series as well as *Amos 'n' Andy,* another radio series about African Americans (again created and played by Caucasians!) transported to television with the usual stereotypes. NAACP executive secretary Walter White remarked in 1951 that such series could be taken in stride if only there were previously produced shows that "portrayed Negroes as normal human beings and an integral part of the scene."[29] When *Beulah* went off the air in 1953 because Beavers decided to leave the role (and the series had never reached the top 30 programs in ratings), it would take fifteen years before another African American actress would star in her own situation comedy (Diahann Carroll in *Julia*). Critics would again have a field day, but for different reasons.

Our Miss Brooks

Making its television debut in 1952, *Our Miss Brooks* began on radio in 1948 and was simultaneously broadcast on both media until the mid-1950s. Connie Brooks is an English teacher at Madison High School. She evidently appeared quite competent because during its run Eve Arden, the actress who played her, was in much demand to speak to educational groups and was offered positions as an English teacher in real high schools.[30] Energetic and wisecracking, Connie Brooks is always getting into trouble with the conservative principal, Mr. Conklin, but her heart is in the right place. Several episodes involve her helping students and other people with whom she comes into contact. Connie rents a room from a kind, older woman, Mrs. Davis, who sometimes gets involved in her schemes and likes to listen in to her phone conversations. Connie is driven to school each day by a student, Walter Denton, who is not particularly bright and the cause for some of her troubles, but he also helps her. He clearly admires her and considers her a friend.

Like many single women in 1950s television, Connie has her mind set on getting married. She is obsessed with Philip Boynton, a handsome but very shy biology teacher, and in several episodes she schemes to be with him. Even though they appear to have gone to several social events together, they address each other formally as Mr. Boynton and Miss Brooks. This formality does not stop Connie from flirting with him at every opportunity, however, and putting a sexual or romantic spin on the conversation. As a result, he often gets embarrassed. For example, in the Christmas show of 1954, she goes to see him in his biology lab to bring him the gift she bought for him by exchanging the perfume he bought for her (throughout the series, she is always scraping for money). She, of course, acts like she didn't open his present and comments that he couldn't possibly know what she wanted—and she says the name of the perfume he had bought her.

Philip: I've never heard of such a coincidence.

Connie: Neither have I. Kiss me. (She leans toward him.)

Philip: (He laughs and backs away.) I know you're fooling now, Miss Brooks. But when I go to your house Christmas morning you better not be standing under any mistletoe.

Connie: Oh, don't be silly, Mr. Boynton, I threw the mistletoe away in the closet. Now don't forget...Christmas breakfast is at 10 o'clock.

Philip: Good. I'll be looking for you.

Connie: Good, I'll be in the closet.

Philip: (Laughs) There you go kidding again.

One gets the distinct impression that, if she is kidding, it is only half-heartedly. Connie Brooks is definitely interested in Philip Boynton sexually. In another episode where Connie complains to him that Walter accused her of stealing his newspaper article about her, Philip says she has been known for stealing—she stole a kiss from him last New Year's Eve when they were parked on Outpost Road. As usual, she always has a comeback: "That wasn't stealing. It was petting larceny." Earlier she told Walter if he wanted proof that she didn't steal his paper, Mr. Boynton could search her. Connie is not shy about who knows of her lust for Philip. When the principal's daughter tells Connie that Mr. Boynton has a new stove with four burners, Connie complains that she has four burners too, but he never turns them on.

The battle of the sexes in this series is primarily Connie's battle to get a man (particularly Philip Boynton) to marry her while he clings to his bachelorhood. However, sometimes gender lines are drawn, as in "The Big Jump" when Connie and Philip are talking on the phone about Principal Conklin's planned jump off the high school roof in some sort of Civil Defense demonstration. When Connie remarks that Conklin will do anything for publicity, Philip chastises her for belittling Conklin's courage. He also remarks that "in matters of bravery, it's only natural that men should rate above the weaker sex." Both Connie and Mrs. Davis (who had been listening on the extension) are insulted, and Connie hangs up on him. After Principal Conklin changes his mind about jumping and all the other male teachers also claim injuries, Connie is drafted into the jump. She decides to hire a circus man who, she discovers, is really afraid of heights and whose wife jumps into a net in their act. Both Conklin and Boynton end up on the roof to check out what's going on and say that the crowds are waiting. When Walter rushes up to tell them there is a fire and they can't go down the stairs, the smoke pouring through the door convinces the adult men to jump. Before Connie is about to take her turn, Walter tells her she doesn't need to jump—he was just burning smudge pots so someone else would jump for her. Connie calls him brilliant and says he settled something conclusively: "Men are always braver than women as soon as they get panicky enough." Yet Connie is still desperate for a man.

Other single women are Connie's rivals for Philip Boynton's affections. When she is upset about another teacher knitting things for Philip, Walter says, "Well, you just listen to old Dr. Cupid. Now I ask you, who is the handy, little potential housewife who's going to volunteer to cook the first meal on Mr. Boynton's new stove?" When Connie goes to Philip's lab to invite him, her current rival, Daisy Enright, is there, having him try on the sweater she knitted for him (it is much too small and lopsided). A stereotypical verbal cat fight ensues. When Daisy insincerely remarks that they should see each other more often, Connie retorts that there's no reason they shouldn't, "after all, science has discovered antidotes for everything these days." When Daisy brags to Boynton about her domestic skills saying that she knitted everything for him with her own little needles, Connie retorts, "Oh, you use a needle? I thought maybe you just threaded your own claws." When Philip begins to protest the remark, Daisy replies, "Don't pay any attention to her, Mr. Boynton. She probably got up on the wrong side of her broom this morning."

Neither woman is evidently very competent in the housewifely skills they claim, but they are willing to pretend and deceive to get their man. Connie convinces Mrs. Davis to cook the meal at Philip's apartment, but then to leave before he returns so he will think Connie made it. Mrs. Davis doesn't mind because "After marriage, all a girl needs is a lipstick and a good can opener." Lusty Connie remarks that "and if she has the right lipstick, she doesn't even need a can opener." She proclaims to Philip, however, that "Some day I'd just like to have a baby and cook. Not on the same day, of course." In his study of situation comedy in relationship to liberal democratic ideology, Darrell Hamamoto wrote that "being denied love seemed almost a form of 'punishment' for Connie Brooks, a cautionary warning perhaps to women intrigued by the notion of independence."[31] One could also question how independent she really was. Renting a room from Mrs. Davis was rather like having a house mother instead of living on her own in an apartment. Her principal was the strict father figure, always trying to put a damper on her spirit and independent ideas. And her primary goal was to go from these mother and father figures to married life with a man who seemed to have no special affection for her.

In an attempt to improve ratings in the fall of 1955 (the show's ratings had fallen out of the top 30 after its first two years), Connie got a new job at a private elementary school and a new love interest—a young physical education teacher, Gene Talbot, who chased her. Connie continued to make a poor salary and sometimes worked extra jobs. Philip Boynton was brought back in a last attempt to save the show in spring 1956, but ratings didn't improve and the show was canceled. Perhaps to placate frustrated fans, Connie finally got her man in a 1956 Warner Bros. movie based on the series, but she remained a frustrated spinster on television.

Private Secretary

Actress Ann Sothern portrayed two single working women on television in the 1950s, starting with *Private Secretary* (called *Susie* in syndication) from 1953 until 1957, then the self-titled *The Ann Sothern Show* from 1958 until 1961. Sothern co-produced the latter series with Desi Arnaz. Both were among the top 25 rated programs through the 1950s, with *Private Secretary* reaching a high of 12 in 1955.

In *Private Secretary,* Sothern plays Susie MacNamara, secretary to Peter Sands, a successful talent agent and owner of International Artists in New York City. Susie is an attractive woman, probably in her 30s, and with what some might call a "full figure," particularly in her hips. Her weight is not an issue, however, because several episodes indicate men are attracted to her. In at least one episode it is her boss who decides he needs to lose weight, not her. Susie is a woman who is not ashamed of what she eats. In one episode she complains that someone is keeping her from going to lunch where she will have steak, shrimp cocktail, and maybe a piece of pie. Susie also wears glasses, primarily to read, and it is her boss who is too vain to admit he needs them (she eventually gets the glasses for him). She dresses very nicely, usually a dress with a full petticoat. Her weakness, as a matter of fact, is clothes shopping. In "Dollars and Sense," both receptionist Vi and Sands respectively try to help her control her spending by keeping her paycheck and giving her an allowance. Susie wants to save money, but she can't with her penchant for shopping. By the end of the episode, however, in typical sitcom fashion, she seems to have learned her lesson, after being caught lying and spending money that wasn't hers to spend.

Susie is very smart and savvy, sometimes saving her boss from bad business decisions. For example, in "Efficiency Expert," Sands considers merging with a larger company that is renowned for its efficient operation. Susie is concerned about the unscrupulous reputation of the owner, Sherman, and does some research of her own (she plies one of his employees with martinis at dinner and questions him about working for Sherman). While Sands signs the merger contract, Susie asks pertinent questions of Sherman that make Sands realize he has made a mistake. Fortunately, Susie purposely put the carbon in backwards when she typed the contract, and Sands can call off the deal. Susie often works behind her boss's back to help him, and sometimes she lets him think it was his accomplishment. In "What Every Secretary Wants," Sands tells Susie of a business deal he'd like to propose to a prominent theatrical producer, Mr. Hugo. When Susie offers to call Hugo's secretary, Sands says it's an important deal "and can't be done by secretaries." He also disregards her information that Hugo's wife influences his decisions. Despite Sands' dismissal of her helpful suggestions, Susie proceeds to meet Mrs. Hugo and the two women bond in their conspiracy to get Hugo to hire two of Sands' singers. In the end, Sands naively chastises Susie for "still looking for the woman behind the man. Who's behind me? (he scoffs) You?" While women have been stereotyped as being manipulative to have their way with men (often to buy a new dress), Susie's manipulations are of a clever businesswoman who knows how to succeed.

Susie is obviously quite educated in matters other than business. She is shown to speak fluent French and easily answers difficult crossword puzzle questions. She is also smart about people, understanding individuals from all walks of life. In "Elusive," Susie is able to convince an aging and reclusive actress to star in a new Broadway play. In "Cats in a Hot Tin File," she reasons that an actress's cat allergy is psychosomatic and arranges for her to see a psychiatrist that Susie used to date. Susie turns out to be right (although the psychiatrist takes the credit), and the actress is able to star in a play with a cat. In "Thy Name is Sands," Susie points out problems with a contract and remarks to Sands about the lawyer who drew up the contract, "gorgeous he is, honest he ain't." She continually outwits her shady nemesis, Cagey Calhoun, a low-class talent agent who tries to steal Sands's clients. Although he admits she has brains and beauty, Cagey claims she doesn't have a heart and he has scars to prove it. In "Little Caesar of Bleeker," Susie helps turn around the life of a street-smart kid who poses as a shoeshine boy to steal from offices. Interestingly, she credits her faith in the boy to her grandmother, who used to say, "if you don't trust other people, you don't trust yourself." Her affection and understanding of children is further evidenced in "Old Dog New," where she teaches a ten-year-old star of Broadway both manners and humility.

Susie's best friend is Vi Praskins, the receptionist/switchboard operator at International Artists, although it is clear Susie is also friends with other secretaries and receptionists in the building.[32] Vi and Susie go to movies, play Scrabble, and do other things together, and Susie is protective of Vi. Although Vi is competent at her job, she is easily upset and afraid, sometimes fainting in the middle of a predicament. Vi lives with her Aunt Martha in Brooklyn, and Susie has been there on several occasions to visit. In "Not Quite Paradise," Sands has accepted a dinner invitation to Vi's house, and it is the first time he will have been there in the five years Vi has worked for him. Her Aunt Martha is convinced by a neighbor that there must be a romantic connection between Vi and Sands. The friend also convinces Martha that Susie is competition and they must make her look bad in front of Sands. Although Martha protests that she hates to do that because "Susie is such a sweet girl," she reasons that it is okay and she'll explain it to Susie after Vi and Sands are married. Susie catches on to what the two older women are doing and warns them to stop. Martha accuses her of being jealous and claims that, because Vi is not a fighter, she must do it for her. When Martha discusses Vi with Sands, he thinks that Vi invited him to dinner because she has designs on him, and he fires her. Vi, of course, is innocent in what is going on and terribly embarrassed. Despite the treachery of the older women, Susie is not angry with them and develops a plan to get back Vi's job. While the behavior of the older women is disturbing, they express a long-held idea that women are rivals for the affection of men, to the detriment of any kind of friendships among them. Neither Susie nor Vi indicate any rivalry, however, and Susie does not let the older women's behavior disrupt her affection for them. It is indicated that Vi would like a husband (she reluctantly admits in one episode that she attended a "lonely hearts club" meeting), but she is insecure about her looks and not about to compete with Susie.

As mentioned earlier, Susie has many men vying for her affection, but none of them suit her. In "Not Quite Paradise," she admits that she can't cook (an old-fashioned notion of the way to a man's heart) and that "when the right man comes along for me he'll have to bring a nurse with him." Susie is not alone because she can't find a man, however. In "Three's Company," she has both a successful producer and a new playwright vying for her affections. She happily dates both until it interferes with business and the men refuse to work with each other. The producer offers her anything she could possibly want, including the chance to be a movie star, while the young writer is willing to give up his chance for fame if she would agree to go back to his small town with him. She turns down both, saying she loves her job and her apartment—she is happy as she is. She pretends to have a lot of other men in her life so that her two suitors will unite against her and reconcile. It works. Sands accuses Susie of "vamping" and flirting with his clients, thus being at fault for their refusal to work together. Susie, of course, rightly denies it. In many episodes she has to do nothing but be herself and men ask her out.

Social issues that appear in *Private Secretary* are dealt with in a personal way and not labeled as social problems. For example, in "Little Caesar of Bleeker," juvenile delinquency is connected to the abandonment of a child by his parents and solved by Susie's trust in him. In "Susie's Crusade," the wrongful firing of a cleaning lady is not a labor or class problem, but the fault of a mean, new building manager who Susie eventually outsmarts to get the woman's job back. Interestingly, the opening credits of *Private Secretary* start with a line drawing of Susie with big eyes and no mouth, then it cuts to live action with Susie thoughtfully putting her glasses in her mouth. While one might interpret these credits as stifling Susie's speech, it is perhaps better interpreted as marks of Susie's astute observations and problem solving, albeit on a personal, rather than social, level.

Although Susie attracts men and solves many problems, she is not without fault. As discussed earlier, she has a weakness for clothes to the detriment of her bank account. When Sands finally puts on his glasses, he notices some typing mistakes of hers. She sometimes lies to get out of trouble and when the IRS audits her, she confuses the auditor with long, convoluted explanations. Nevertheless, even when her plans backfire, Susie usually manages to make things right by the end of the episode, as has been typical in most sitcoms. As Sands tells her in one episode, she has a good salary, sick leave, and vacation with pay. She has friends and her choice of men, despite the fact that she is not slender, but marriage does not seem to be on her mind. Susie MacNamara is quite an anomaly in the sitcom world, particularly in the 1950s, and perhaps an inspiration for girls who dreamed of careers in the big city.

Ann Sothern moved almost seamlessly into *The Ann Sothern Show,* where she played Katy O'Connor, an assistant manager of the Bartley House hotel in New York City. When her first boss is transferred in 1959, Katy's hopes of succeeding him are dashed when another white male arrives to take his place, an early demonstration of the "glass ceiling" that real women would continue to experience into the twenty-first century. In this series, however, Katy has her own secretary instead of being one. Katy's best friend in *The Ann Sothern Show* is Olive Smith, who is also her secretary and roommate, blurring the lines of public and private life and indicating a workplace family as substitute for a more traditional nuclear one.[33] Katy even has a child she helps to take care of, nine-year-old Donald Carpenter who is a permanent guest at the hotel. Katy's new boss, James Devery, is an attractive, single man, but she isn't out to trap him into marriage. In "Three Loves Has Katy," it is clear that she has been "playing the field" for quite awhile when three of her old boyfriends come for a college reunion at the Bartley House. Occasionally plots revolve around Katy's dissatisfaction with her job, although these are treated on a personal level rather than as a stance for all poorly treated female employees. For example, in "Springtime for Katy" she feels taken for granted by her boss, and in "Katy's New Career" she expresses disgust for her long hours with little pay and seeks another job. While there are some minor differences between *The Ann Sothern Show* and *Private Secretary,* for the most part Susie MacNamara and Katy O'Connor are essentially the same strong, competent, and caring women seemingly happy with their single status.

The Donna Reed Show

For many people, the 1950s invokes television images of the happy, white, middle-class family in suburbia as depicted in several sitcoms of the time, including *The Donna Reed Show.* What sets this series apart from other suburban family comedies, such as *Father Knows Best* and *Ozzie and Harriet,* is that the primary focus is ostensibly on the female star of the show and her character, a housewife and mother. Furthermore, Donna Reed had much creative input, including decisions made about casting and scripts, and coworkers have described her as feminist.[34] The series debuted on ABC in 1958 and ended its original run of episodes in 1966, when the couple's biological children had been grown and gone for some time and they had an adopted eleven-year-old daughter still to raise.

In her excellent study of the suburban family comedies of the 1950s, Nina Leibman argued that, in fact, they are not comedies at all, but when "shorn of their laugh tracks and the critical assertion that these programs are indeed 'funny'—these series bear the unmistakable generic markers of domestic family melodrama, characterized by the same familial strife and reconciliation that form the foundation of the feature-film domestic melodrama."[35] In these television series, including *The Donna Reed Show,* she found several elements that helped to define and reinforce the ideal consuming family:

> Speeches in every episode underscore one or more of the following points: the superiority of the middle class, the required subjugation of housewives, the omnipotence of fathers and father-love, the fairness of the American system of capitalism, and the necessity of gender-bound roles and attributes. At the same time, characters actively suppress any interests which might interfere with the successful functioning of these value systems.[36]

When the series begins in 1958, the family on *The Donna Reed Show* consisted of Donna Stone, a housewife; her husband, Alex, a pediatrician whose office is conveniently located in their home; daughter Mary, about fourteen years old; and son Jeff, two years younger. Donna clearly is an attractive, loving, intelligent woman, but details about her background as revealed in different episodes are incongruous. Various episodes reveal that "Donna Stone—who graduated from college after four years, during which time she had a roommate and wanted to be an actress—is supposed to have married Alex at eighteen and to have been a nurse (just two years out of high school) at the time of their marriage, but didn't work after the marriage; [and] she gave birth to Mary when she was 19."[37] Regardless of the confusing aspects of her background, this series presents clear messages about the proper role of women. In the several episodes where Donna attempts to be more than "just a housewife," by the end of the story she has learned she is better off to focus on the running of her household. In Mary Ann Watson's cultural study of television since 1945, she wrote about how women's aspirations were something to be stifled in television. In an example from *The Donna Reed Show* where Donna is a candidate for town council, she concluded that "the moral of the story is that a woman has no business trying to make a difference in the world and that a man is justified in feeling diminished by the success of his spouse."[38] Her husband, Alex, surely loves Donna, but, rather than encourage her, he is threatened by her in additional episodes, including when she demonstrates skill in running his home office. While the children often go to Donna for advice and help related to interpersonal considerations and clothing, they all defer to Alex in other matters. It has been noted that Donna Reed herself was concerned about the writers not offending any man, as a cautionary memo from her to the writers indicates concerning an episode where daughter Mary runs for class president.[39]

While Donna Stone occasionally participates in volunteer activities that put her in contact with other women, she has no consistent women friends until the appearance in 1963 of Midge Kelsey as the family's next-door neighbor and wife of Alex's colleague. The two do many things together, such as take French lessons and Donna teaches Midge to drive a car, but they fight over who gets the mink coat when one of their shared lottery tickets wins it. In one episode, Donna explains to Alex that "women are only nice to other women when they feel sorry for them. When they envy them, they slander them."[40] Donna does occasionally find herself in situations where she has to advise a woman how to land a man or create a domestic lifestyle, including "teaching intellectual women to hide their scholarly prowess, wear makeup, and entice the males."[41] Interestingly enough, however, she feels that it is important that her daughter go to college. Donna's household is always clean and she is immaculate in a shirt-waist dress, with a ready smile and immediate attention to the needs of her family. Fans would write to the show for advice from her, and the series won many awards from youth, women's, and educational groups. Donna Stone is a good example of why some feminists have expressed that they would like a wife too.

WOMEN IN 1940s AND 1950s TELEVISION COMEDY

The first network television sitcom was *Mary Kay and Johnny,* a series with elements very similar to *I Love Lucy.* Broadcast live on the Dumont Network from 1947 to 1950, this domestic comedy revolved around young newlyweds, Mary Kay and Johnny Stearns, played by real-life marrieds using their own names. While Johnny doesn't have the more exotic ethnicity and job that Cuban bandleader Ricky Ricardo has (he was a banker), both couples have a baby boy in real life who is worked into their series. Mary Kay is described as "pretty, pert and something of a screwball, while [Johnny] was more serious and always getting her out of various dilemmas."[42] On the lower end of the social scale, however, personalities often are reversed. For example, *The Life of Riley* (NBC, 1949–1950, 1953–1958), first heard on radio in 1943, featured a bumbling husband full of malapropisms whose long-suffering wife, Peg, stands by him.

Vying for lead screwball wife of the 1950s with Lucy Ricardo in *I Love Lucy* was Gracie Allen of *The George Burns and Gracie Allen Show,* on CBS from 1950 to 1958. With another real-life couple playing themselves, this series had an interesting, self-reflexive twist. George occasionally faced the audience and commented on the action, even viewing a scene in another room of the house on a television set in the den. But he played "straight man" to Gracie, whether it was in scenes from the story line or in the standup routine they did at the end of each episode. Gracie lived by her own rules, perhaps in her own world. As feminist critic Patricia Mellencamp wrote, "despite being burdened by all the cliches applied to women—illogical, crazy, nonsensical, possessing their own, peculiar biologic and patronized accordingly—in certain ways, she seemed to be out of (or beyond) men's control."[43] Her improbable stories and schemes baffle both her husband and most of the other characters on the show, but they are "invariably true in amazing circumlocutions which became that week's 'plot.'"[44] Susan Douglas described Gracie Allen as "the master of linguistic slapstick, using puns, malapropisms, and a willful misunderstanding of language to turn male logic on its head. She refused to be contained by the conventions of male language that seemed to leave women no positions from which to speak honestly about their lives."[45]

Gracie Allen both loved, and was loved by, her husband in the series and in real life. Despite the confusion Gracie causes, she is never threatened by George. Since she is playing herself, she is also playing a working woman who is in show business, a fact that never bothers George. Their real-life son, Ronnie, also played their son on television its last three years. Gracie seems to have smoothly integrated her family life with a career. While she certainly may have come across "ditzier" than Lucy Ricardo, she manages to do what Lucy Ricardo could not, and she has the support of her husband. Gracie also has a best friend to support her, next-door neighbor Blanche Morton. Blanche's accountant husband, Harry, gets furious at the chaos the two women cause, but Blanche continues to support Gracie, even when she doesn't understand everything Gracie says.

A number of other "screwball" and "kookie" women were around in television sitcoms of the 1950s with titles that framed them through the perspective of a significant other in their lives. *I Married Joan* (NBC, 1952–1955) is about the wife of a domestic court judge. Each episode opens with Judge Bradley Stevens in court explaining how he dealt with a similar problem with his own wife, Joan. Like Lucy and Gracie, Joan has close friends to help her in her schemes. *My Friend Irma* (CBS, 1952–1954) is the story of an illogical, but sexy and friendly secretary whose level-headed friend and roommate, Jane, gets involved in her predicaments and narrates the story. In the second year of the series, Jane is replaced with newspaper reporter Kay Foster as a roommate, and Irma's seven-year-old nephew also comes to live with them. *My Little Margie* (CBS/NBC, 1952–1955) is about a twenty-one-year-old woman who lives with her widowed father and is always either scheming to save him from the clutches of a woman or trying to circumvent his control over her. In a type of intergenerational bonding, their older neighbor, Mrs. Odetts, is always helping Margie in her schemes. Gale Storm, who played Margie, would later star in her own series, *The Gale Storm Show* (CBS, 1956–1959; ABC, 1959–1960), as the social director of a luxury liner. Episodes usually revolved around her and her best friend, Esmerelda "Nugey" Nugent, operator of the ship's beauty salon, in some scheme that would annoy the ship's conservative captain.

A number of series highlighted single people, and, of course, many of the episodes would be devoted to dating and the pursuit of marriage. The title character in *Meet Millie* (CBS, 1952–1956) is Millie Bronson, "a young, attractive, middle-class secretary working in Manhattan."[46] Her mother is always looking for eligible men as a potential spouse for her, but throughout most of the series her boyfriend is her boss's son. *Dear Phoebe* (NBC, 1954–1956) is the title of an advice-to-the-lovelorn column written by former college instructor Bill Hastings. In a switch from stereotypical roles, the newspaper has a female sportswriter, Mickey Riley, who likes Bill but "tried to hide her affection by being extremely competitive"[47] Bill is open about his affection for Mickey, however, and many episodes dealt with their rocky romance. In a refreshing focus on a nice mother-in-law, *December Bride* (CBS, 1954–1959), senior citizen Lily Ruskin lives happily with her daughter and son-in-law. An attractive widow, she has an active social life and a best friend in peer Hilda Crocker.

While striving to be middle class was certainly the ideal depicted in 1950s television, other working-class families beyond the "ethni-coms" discussed earlier were featured in sitcoms. The best known are the battling Kramdens on *The Honeymooners* (CBS, 1955–1956), initiated as a skit on the Dumont network's *Cavalcade of Stars* in 1951 and revived on *The Jackie Gleason Show* in the 1960s after its initial run. The title of the series, of course, is ironic—Ralph and Alice Kramden have been married for many years and their constant fights with each other are anything but romantic. Like Ricky, Ralph often threatens his wife with physical violence—with fist up and ready to strike, he threatens to "send her to the moon" on many occasions. Unlike Lucy, however, Alice is not intimidated by her husband, as she faces him, annoyed, with arms crossed. She also does not hesitate to tell him off when she is angry and frequently makes sarcastic comments about his weight. Ralph is often jealous of Alice and detests the idea of her working outside the home. When he finally lets her work at home after he loses his job as bus driver, he is consumed with jealousy of her handsome boss who comes to the apartment. As soon as he gets his job back, Ralph kicks Alice's boss out of the apartment and insists she quit. In their shabby, poorly furnished two-room flat, Alice evidently spends the day with little to do and even less to spend. At night Ralph often goes bowling or to a lodge meeting with his best buddy, Ed Norton. Trixie Norton is Alice's best friend, but the two never scheme together as did Lucy and Ethel, and they do not seem to even spend much time together. Alice is obviously the stronger and smarter of the couple, yet she stays with Ralph in a very lonely, boring, stress-filled existence. Despite the arguments during each episode, Ralph always ends up apologizing to Alice, taking her in his arms, and saying, "Baby, you're the greatest." This is evidently enough for Alice, a bad message to women watching. Feminists Andrea Press and Terry Strathman see Alice Kramden as the real boss in her family and think the series illustrates the tendency of television to romanticize working-class women by exaggerating their power and the respect they receive.[48] As a strong, smart woman in New York City, however, Alice's decision to stay with Ralph or to not fight him about her working defy logic. Perhaps the title *The Honeymooners* implies she loves him so much that she is willing to sacrifice her own sense of self for him, a message that is plausible for 1950s culture.

When *Amos 'n' Andy* made the transition to television from its long, very popular run on radio, it brought with it a history of protest by many African Americans for its offensive characterizations. Although at least this time the characters were portrayed by black, not white, actors, stereotypes were still in evidence, and the NAACP denounced it, as well as *Beulah,* discussed earlier.[49] Of particular concern was that white children who had no direct contact with African Americans would "learn" what a whole race of people were like through this series. Amos is depicted as a fairly respectable middle-class man who drives a taxi to support his wife, Ruby, and three children, but they all appear relatively infrequently. Despite the title of the program, the central character is really shiftless George "Kingfish" Stevens, with many episodes revolving around his attempts to con Andy, who is very gullible and not very bright. The two women who appear most in the series are Kingfish's wife, Sapphire, and "Mama," her mother. Sapphire is depicted as bright and, unlike the men on the series, she often speaks general American English. Although her scolding of her lazy and dishonest husband is understandable, she takes it to another, unflattering, level. As researcher Melvin Ely described Sapphire, "her assertiveness often took on the shrill tone of the shrew, and the couple's relationship conformed closely to the stereotype of the female-dominated black family—sans children in this case. 'Sapphire,' in fact, had already become a generic folk term among Afro-Americans for a domineering wife."[50] Her mother is a stereotypical interfering mother-in-law, who constantly nags and "epitomized both the race-transcending battle-ax and the hard-edged version of the familiar black 'mammy.' "[51] The series was on CBS from 1951 to 1953, but was in syndication for another decade. According to program experts Brooks and Marsh, when a Chicago station announced it was resuming reruns, there were widespread and bitter protests; by 1966 the program was withdrawn from sale.[52]

Another "ethni-com," *The Goldbergs* concerns a middle-class Jewish family in the Bronx and was a popular series on radio for about twenty years before its 1949 CBS television debut. Central to the family is housewife and mother of two teenagers, Molly, whose good heart always gets her mixed up in everyone's business. Molly's Uncle David also lives with the family. Gertrude Berg, who played Molly, wrote for the series. Like many early programs, commercials for the often single sponsor were interwoven into the story. Molly would talk directly into the camera about RCA Victor television sets, for example, and then turn from the window into her apartment where the story would begin. At the end of the episode she would return to the window for another sponsor plug. Her credibility as a housewife was assumed for the household items presented during the show. Molly's husband, Jake, is in the clothing business, and the two seem to have a comfortable relationship. It is clear that their teenage daughter, Rosalie, has learned cleaning and cooking skills from her mother, and she is expected to help on a regular basis. However, Molly also pushes her daughter to have culture, symbolized by piano lessons, and says to her when Rosalie rebels, "Is it wrong I want you to be more than me?"

After its original network run, the Goldbergs moved to the suburbs, as much of the country was doing, for one year of syndicated shows. Critic George Lipsitz wrote how the insecurities and anxieties among consumers who grew up during the Great Depression of the 1930s and World War II in the 1940s compelled the television networks to address related issues in order to promote consumption in the 1950s.[53] Consequently, Molly Goldberg is seen to change her philosophy about buying only what one can pay for in cash and she buys new furniture on an installment plan. Molly had become a good consumer.

In the suburbs, high school daughter Rosalie thrives with many boyfriends, thanks to her then college-age brother, Sammy. Her parents both encourage her to date several boys, but when she is pressed by three to go steady in "The Boyfriend," each adult has a favorite. Molly's favorite is a boy who will be a college professor and, she explains to her daughter, "to share such a life is a privilege." She does not mention or ask what her daughter's own goals are, and one can assume from this that it is to marry well. In "Rosie's Nose," however, Molly and Jake are curious when Rosalie tells them she wants to be "financially independent" and therefore wants money for her birthday, not presents. She also turns down social events to babysit and tutor to earn more money. When brother Sammy explains to the adults that Rosalie is unhappy with her looks and wants to have plastic surgery on her nose, they are upset and try to build up her confidence. Psychology terms are abundant in this episode as they discuss her inferiority complex, her ego, and Freud. Rosalie knows what they are up to, but is convinced by a woman in the doctor's office that her nose looks fine and she will regret having the surgery. Molly had previously asked the doctor to talk Rosalie out of surgery, but, instead of doing it himself, he had his former actress wife pretend to be unhappy, fooling both Molly and Rosalie. In the end, Rosalie is satisfied with her nose, but now wants to cut her hair. Ever understanding of teenage angst, Molly tells Rosalie to cut her hair to her heart's content, despite Jake forbidding it; her hair will grow back. Molly's penchant for getting involved in people's lives is taken to another level in "Nurse's Aid" where she becomes a volunteer and starts bringing people home to convalesce under her care once they are released from the hospital. No matter how much husband Jake protests (and his protests are generally neither loud nor long), Molly always gets her way.

Little did Molly Goldberg know that, as middle class as she was, her ethnicity, if not her gender as the headlining star of a series, would be disappearing from television in an array of generic family sitcoms that would mark the latter half of the 1950s and early 1960s. Also gone would be the zany and rebellious women of the early 1950s who pushed at the ever-increasing gender boundaries perpetuated by television and who offered a catharsis. As Patricia Mellencamp wrote:

> For Lucie, Gracie, and their audiences, humour was a "rare and precious gift." Given the repressive conditions of the 1950s, humour might have been women's weapon and tactic of survival, ensuring sanity, the triumph of the ego, and pleasure; after all, Gracie and Lucy were narcissistically rebellious, refusing "to be hurt." On the other hand, comedy replaced anger, if not rage, with pleasure.[54]

Pleasure, of course, can make one complacent and content. The second wave of feminism was yet to come.

NOTES

1. Toni Carabillo, "'A Passion for the Possible,'" *Feminist Chronicles 1953–1993,* by Toni Carabillo, Judith Meuli, and June Bundy Csida (Los Angeles: Women's Graphics, 1993), 1.

2. Toni Carbillo, Judith Meuli, and June Bundy Csida, *Feminist Chronicles 1953–1993* (Los Angeles: Women's Graphics, 1993), 41.

3. Gorton Carruth, *What Happened When: A Chronology of Life & Events in America* (New York: Harper & Row, 1989), 813.

4. Carabillo, Meuli, and Csida, 40.

5. Sarah Brash and Loretta Britten, eds., *Rock & Roll Generation: Teen Life in the 50s,* Our American Century (Alexandria, VA: Time-Life, 1998), 23.

6. Dumont, unable to afford the initial losses in establishing a television network as the three radio-based networks could, folded its network in 1955, leaving CBS, NBC, and ABC to dominate the industry for more than two decades.

7. Tim Brooks and Earle Marsh, *The Complete Directory to Prime-Time Network and Cable Shows 1946-Present,* 7th ed. (New York: Ballantine, 1999), 479.

8. Bart Andrews, *The "I Love Lucy" Book* (Garden City, NY: Doubleday, 1985), 12–15.

9. Andrews, 47.

10. Jess Oppenheimer with Gregg Oppenheimer, *Laughs, Luck...and Lucy: How I Came to Write the Most Popular Sitcom of All Time* (Syracuse, NY: Syracuse University Press, 1996), 180.

11. Oppenheimer, 186.

12. Diana Meehan, *Ladies of the Evening: Women Characters of Prime-Time Television* (Metuchen, NJ: Scarecrow, 1983), 21.

13. Lori Landay, *Madcaps, Screwballs, & Con Women: The Female Trickster in American Culture* (Philadelphia: University of Pennsylvania Press, 1998), 161.

14. Landay, 173.

15. Landay, 193.

16. Paul Wells, "'Where Everybody Knows Your Name': Open Convictions and Closed Contexts in the American Situation Comedy," *Because I Tell a Joke or Two: Comedy, Politics, and Social Difference,* ed. Stephen Wagg (London: Routledge, 1998), 189.

17. Patricia Mellencamp, "Situation Comedy, Feminism, and Freud: Discourses of Gracie and Lucy," *Feminist Television Criticism: A Reader,* ed. Charlotte Brunsdon, Julie D'Acci, and Lynn Spigel (New York: Oxford University Press, 1997), 70.

18. George Lipsitz, "The Meaning of Memory: Family, Class, and Ethnicity in Early Network Television Programs," *Private Screenings: Television and the*

Female Consumer, ed. Lynn Spigel and Denise Mann (Minneapolis, MN: University of Minnesota Press, 1992), 91–92.

19. Lipsitz 81. Quoted from a script in the Theatre Art's Collection at the University of California, Los Angeles.

20. Gerard Jones, *Honey, I'm Home! Sitcoms: Selling the American Dream* (New York: St. Martin's Press, 1992), 43.

21. Jones, 43.

22. R.D. Heldenfels, *Television's Greatest Year: 1954* (New York: Continuum, 1994), 38.

23. Donald Bogle, *Prime Time Television: African Americans on Network Television* (New York: Farrar, Straus and Giroux, 2001), 19.

24. Bogle, 19.

25. Robin R. Means Coleman, *African American Viewers and the Black Situation Comedy: Situating Racial Humor* (New York: Garland, 2000), 59.

26. Bogle, 22.

27. Bogle, 25–26.

28. Bogle, 26.

29. Quoted in Coleman, p. 61, from Walter White, "Negro Leaders Look at TV Race Problem," *Printer's Ink* 236 (1951, August 24): 31.

30. Brooks and Marsh, 768.

31. Darrell Y. Hamamoto, *Nervous Laughter: Television Situation Comedy and Liberal Democratic Ideology* (New York: Praeger, 1989), 33.

32. In 1957, when the characters of *I Love Lucy* were in hour-long episodes of *The Lucille Ball-Desi Arnaz Show,* it was revealed that Susie MacNamara was a friend of Lucy's when they were both stenographers in New York City. In "Lucy Takes a Cruise to Havana," the two women take a trip to Cuba to meet men. Lucy hooks up with Desi, and Susie gets involved with his friend, played by Cesar Romero, when they meet through the men's taxi-touring business. In another crossover episode at Desilu Studios, only this time with *The Ann Sothern Show,* "The Lucy Story" has Lucy Ricardo checking into the Bartley House and loudly denouncing marriage because Ricky has gone skin-diving without her. Naturally, Katy gets involved.

33. The workplace family would become a common theme in sitcoms of the 1970s as the traditional nuclear family became less the norm and there was more emphasis on career women, such as Mary Richards in *The Mary Tyler Moore Show.*

34. Nina Leibman, *Living Room Lectures: The Fifties Family in Film and Television* (Austin: University of Texas Press 1995), 182. Leibman learned of the identification of Donna Reed as a feminist through interviews with several people associated with her show, including Shelley Fabares, who played her teenage daughter from 1958–1963. These statements were also made in interviews for the Arts & Entertainment cable channel's *Biography* series in an episode about Donna Reed.

35. Leibman, 5. In a comparison with filmic melodrama of the time, Leibman analyzed more than 100 episodes each of *The Adventures of Ozzie and Harriet, Father Knows Best, Leave It to Beaver, The Donna Reed Show,* and *My Three Sons.*

36. Leibman, 34.

37. Leibman, 47.

38. Mary Ann Watson, *Defining Visions: Television and the American Experience Since 1945* (Fort Worth, TX: Harcourt Brace, 1998), 61.

39. Leibman, 182.

40. Leibman, 175.

41. Leibman, 182.

42. Brooks and Marsh, 636.

43. Mellencamp, 63.

44. Mellencamp, 63.

45. Susan J. Douglas, *Where the Girls Are: Growing up Female with the Mass Media* (New York: Times Books, 1994, 1995), 50.

46. Brooks and Marsh, 651.

47. Brooks and Marsh, 246.

48. Andrea Press and Terry Strathman, "Work, Family, and Social Class in Television Images of Women: Prime-Time Television and the Construction of Postfeminism," *Women and Language* 16.2 (1993): 7(9), http://lib.newpaltz.edu, in Expanded Academic ASAP.

49. Freeman Gosden and Charles Correll were the two white men who created and starred in the radio version, starting in 1929 on NBC. For an excellent history of the controversy both the radio and television versions created, see Melvin Patrick Ely, *The Adventures of Amos 'n' Andy: A Social History of an American Phenomenon* (New York: Macmillan, 1991).

50. Ely, 208.

51. Ely, 208.

52. Brooks and Marsh, 44.

53. Lipsitz, 77.

54. Mellencamp, 73.

Chapter 3

1960s: WAR AND WITCHES

The 1960s began much like the 1950s ended, with the ideal of the suburban, nuclear family intact and mom at home. But like any nuclear object, it was subject to violent explosion. By the end of the decade, there was a full-blown feminist movement and the nation was divided not only over women's rights but also the Vietnam War. While men walked on the moon by the end of the 1960s with the freedom of little gravitation, the gravity of racism on Earth for black people led to many riots and deaths throughout U.S. cities.

One gets a very different view of the world through situation comedies of the 1960s. The Kennedyesque young, white, suburban Petrie family of *The Dick Van Dyke Show* was quite idyllic compared to the reality of most people's lives. Television news, however, was instrumental in raising the consciousness of the American people by showing startling images of war overseas and racism in the deep South. Young people found new freedom in rock 'n' roll with the arrival of the Beatles and a subsequent British Invasion in both music and fashion.

CULTURAL/HISTORICAL CONTEXT

In 1960, John F. Kennedy was elected president. His victory was attributed by many to television and a landmark series of debates in which Kennedy appeared more relaxed and confident than opponent Richard M. Nixon. In 1961, the President's Commission on the Status of Women was established, publishing its report, *American Women*, two years later. Although the document called for important reforms, including equal pay for equal work, more flexible job-related weight-lifting limitations, and child care, it was somewhat conservative and proposed that women already had constitutional equality; it said what was needed was judicial clarification through test cases.[1] That same year, Betty Friedan's *The Feminine Mystique* was published and became a best-seller. A suburban wife and mother of three, Friedan wrote that women who sought fulfillment exclusively through their homes and families had lost their own identity. Her book was inspired by interviews she had conducted with former classmates at her 15-year reunion at Smith College in 1957.

While a new women's movement was beginning to stir, desegregation of schools and civil rights activities were escalating, along with related violence. For example, in 1963, four black girls were killed during a church bombing in Birmingham, Alabama, the same city where television viewers saw fire hoses and attack dogs turned on civil rights marchers. In "the long, hot summer" of 1967, the United States suffered the worst race riots in its history, with trouble in more than 100 cities (Detroit was the worst, with forty-three people dead over five days). In 1963, at a civil rights rally in Washington, D.C., Reverend Martin Luther King Jr. had given his famous "I Have a Dream" speech, where he described a country free of racial hatred and injustice. While Dr. King had been a strong advocate of nonviolent means to civil rights, others disagreed. He was assassinated in 1968.

Perhaps the most devastating violence to the nation as a whole was the assassination of President Kennedy on November 22, 1963. At forty-three, he had been the second youngest man to take the office, and with his beautiful wife, Jacqueline, and two young children, there was a romantic aura about them. Jackie Kennedy had been instrumental in restoring the White House and its treasure, while many women copied her bouffant hairstyle and elegant fashion sense. During his short tenure as president, Kennedy had brought the nation through the Cuban missile crisis as the U.S.S.R. attempted to help Cuba establish nuclear weapons just off U.S. shores. In 1963, he signed into law the Equal Pay Act, which required equal pay for equal work. Hearts broke as we watched his funeral on television and young John F. Kennedy Jr. saluted his father in his coffin. The sad saga of the Kennedys would continue with the assassination of Robert Kennedy in 1968 on the night he won the California democratic presidential primary.

Vice President Lyndon Johnson succeeded as president shortly after Kennedy's death. He signed into law the Civil Rights Act of 1964, which prohibited discrimination on the basis of race in employment, public accommodations, publicly owned facilities, union membership, and federally funded programs. President Johnson appointed five people to the Equal Employment Opportunity Commission (EEOC), the agency charged with enforcing the prohibition against sex discrimination in Title VII of the act.[2] Frustration with the failure of the EEOC to do its job, however, led to the formation of the National Organization for Women (NOW) in 1966, with Betty Friedan as its first president. NOW's "Bill of Rights for Women," adopted in 1967, included the following goals: the passage of the Equal Rights Amendment to the Constitution, the repeal of all abortion laws, and publicly funded child care.[3] That same year, a radical women's group in New York was formed, which introduced "consciousness raising" techniques to further women's liberation and the concept of "sisterhood is powerful."[4]

While the struggle for equal rights had a long way to go, there were many positive achievements for women as individuals and as a group in the 1960s. For example, Margaret Leech became the first woman to win the Pulitzer Prize in history in 1960, and Harper Lee's novel on Southern bigotry, To Kill a Mockingbird, also won a Pulitzer. Marie Goeppert-Mayer was the first American woman to win a Nobel Prize for physics in 1963. In 1964, Margaret Chase Smith, the first woman to be elected to both the United States House and Senate, became the first woman to run for the presidential nomination of a major party (Republican). In 1968, Shirley Chisholm became the first black woman elected to the House of Representatives. That same year, the Equal Employment Opportunity Commission ruled that sex (gender) was not a bona fide occupational qualification for airline flight attendants and that it violated the Civil Rights Act for employers to place help wanted ads divided by gender. In 1969, the U.S. Court of Appeals ruled that the weight-lifting restriction for women that kept them from certain jobs also violated Title VII of the Civil Rights Act. The 1960s were primarily quite prosperous for most people, although employment rates would rise and fall. In 1960, while female employment was increasing at a rate four times faster than that of men, women's average earnings were less than 60 percent.[5] One of the most liberating achievements for women of the 1960s, however, happened near the beginning of the decade when birth control pills became available.

The cold war with the U.S.S.R. continued from the 1950s, but the devastating war we would end up fighting was in Vietnam. What started during Eisenhower's presidency as an advisory role escalated to a war in 1965 when the first U.S. combat forces were sent to South Vietnam. Protests escalated, sometimes getting violent, and it wasn't just coming from the protesters. In 1968, at the Democratic National Convention in Chicago, television viewers saw police forces out of control and injuring more than a thousand antiwar demonstrators and bystanders, including some members of the press.

The unprecedented number of babies born after World War II ("baby boomers") were in their teens and twenties in the 1960s, and youth began to dominate popular culture. With their youthful unrest, it was music that spoke both for and to young people. In the early 1960s much of the music centered on the age-old concerns of love and having fun. The Beach Boys sang of surfer girls and teenagers danced to Chubby Checker's "The Twist." Detroit's Motown records offered a number of hits by black artists such as Smokey Robinson and the Miracles ("Shop Around") and Marvin Gaye ("Can I Get a Witness"). But perhaps it was the "girl groups" who spoke best for girls coming of age. In 1960, the Shirelles became the first girl group to hit number one on record-sales charts with "Will You Love Me Tomorrow." Dozens of songs followed by other groups, the most successful being the Supremes ("Baby Love," "Where Did Our Love Go?").

In early 1964, there was a revolution in rock 'n' roll music—the Beatles. They made two appearances on *The Ed Sullivan Show* and had a very successful tour of concerts around the United States, singing hits such as "I Wanna Hold Your Hand" and "She Loves You." Many adults were upset by the group's long hair (which was actually not much longer than a Beach Boy might wear his hair, but the Beatles had long bangs). The Beatles began the "British Invasion," paving the way for groups such as the Rolling Stones and the Who. A fashion invasion also came from Britain, which included miniskirts, white go-go boots and white lipstick. For both genders, long straight hair, bell-bottom pants, paisley shirts, and colorful tie-dyed shirts became popular. In discotheques around the country, "go-go girls" would dance on platforms or in cages, as others did the Monkey and the Frug on the dance floor. The Who sang of youthful rebellion in "My Generation." No longer were young people striving to obtain the goals their parents had.

With the youth culture came the drug culture, with former Harvard professor Timothy Leary urging young people to "tune in, turn on, drop out." While health warnings were required on cigarette packages starting in 1965, smoking marijuana became popular with both college students and "hippies," the name given to young people who spoke of peace and free love, often living in communes. "Psychedelic" drugs, such as LSD, also were popular and often associated with musicians. While some youth were tuning out, others were tuning in on their radios in their sporty-looking new Mustangs, introduced by Ford in 1964. Eight-track cassettes were how much music would be played in these cars and homes later in the 1960s. In 1969, all youth became part of the "Woodstock" generation—named after the three-day "Music and Art Fair" in Bethel, New York, that would be the epitome of sex, drugs, and rock 'n' roll.

Music was also popular in movies. Four of the ten Academy Award winners for best film in the 1960s were musicals, including *West Side Story*, a Romeo and Juliet saga set in modern New York City with rival gangs instead of rival families. Hitchcock films were popular, such as *Psycho* and *The Birds*, as were James Bond spy films with Sean Connery. Westerns did well too, with John Wayne winning an Oscar for best actor in *True Grit*, and Paul Newman and Robert Redford glamorizing real-life bad boys *Butch Cassidy and the Sundance Kid. The Graduate* used the music of Simon and Garfunkle to help tell a timely story of a disillusioned college graduate who has an affair with an older woman then falls in love with her daughter. Popular female stars included Elizabeth Taylor *(Cleopatra, Butterfield 8, Who's Afraid of Virginia Woolf?)* and Barbra Streisand *(Funny Girl)*. Bigger-than-life movie star Marilyn Monroe was found dead of an apparent drug overdose in 1962 at the age of thirty-six, although her legend as a sex goddess and troubled woman would continue.

In print, new books of the 1960s included Joseph Heller's antiwar novel *Catch-22;* Rachel Carson's *Silent Spring,* an indictment of the use of pesticides and other chemicals; Sylvia Plath's *The Bell Jar;* Jacqueline Susann's story of three glamorous working women, drugs, and sex in *Valley of the Dolls;* Eldridge Cleaver's *Soul on Ice;* Maya Angelou's *I Know Why the Caged Bird Sings;* and Mario Puzo's *The Godfather.* New magazines debuting in the 1960s included *Penthouse* and *Rolling Stone.*

THE TELEVISION INDUSTRY

In 1961, when Federal Communications Commission chair Newton Minow declared programming on television to be a "vast wasteland," the most prevalent programs were still westerns, such as *Gunsmoke, Wagon Train,* and *Bonanza.* Courtroom dramas were also popular, including *Perry Mason* and *The Defenders.* Two popular medical dramas began in 1961 and became known for their serious subjects as well as their handsome lead doctors, *Dr. Kildare* and *Ben Casey.* A variety of police/detective dramas also did well, including *Hawaii Five-0* and *77 Sunset Strip.* On the other side of the law was *The Fugitive,* a man being sought for the murder of his wife as he pursues the real killer. By the late 1960s, *The Mod Squad* appealed to a younger audience, with its three young, "hippie" cops. The big breakthrough in drama, however, had come in 1965 when Bill Cosby became the first African American to costar in a dramatic show, *I Spy.* Another breakthrough came the following year, when virtually all prime-time television programming was in color.

Soap opera also made its way into prime time, with the television version of Grace Metalious's *Peyton Place* on twice a week from 1964 to 1969. In the mid-1960s, two science fiction programs debuted, *Lost in Space,* with its nuclear family of space travelers, and the venerable *Star Trek.* Some game shows survived the quiz scandals of the 1950s, such as *What's My Line?* and *The Price Is Right.* Variety shows were popular during the decade, including those headed by Ed Sullivan, Red Skelton, Jackie Gleason, Lawrence Welk, Dean Martin, Glen Campbell, and Carol Burnett. The first Super Bowl took place in 1967, an event that would attract the largest television audience each year (and display the most expensive commercials).

The 1960s was a great time for television documentaries that addressed social ills, such as Edward R. Murrow's *Harvest of Shame,* about the dire circumstances of migrant farm workers. But it was television news that reached more people and exposed the everyday injustices of racial prejudice, social unrest, and the horrors of war. When CBS news anchor Walter Cronkite in 1968 reported from Vietnam that we could not win there, President Johnson was duly upset and assumed he had thus lost the support of "middle America" for the war. He soon declared he would not seek reelection and was succeeded by Richard Nixon. Technology improved dramatically throughout the 1960s, including the use of communications satellites. When Neil Armstrong took his first historic steps on the moon, people watched worldwide and heard his words: "That's one small step for man, one giant leap for mankind." Women and girls were thrilled too; they just were not deemed fit by the National Aeronautics and Space Administration (NASA) for space travel.

The highest rated program in the United States for the 1968–1969 and 1969–1970 seasons was *Rowan & Martin's Laugh-In* (NBC, 1968–1973). A topical comedy/variety show, it "crystallized a kind of contemporary, fast-paced, unstructured comedy 'happening' that was exactly what an agitated America wanted in 1968."[6] In it, Goldie Hawn became famous as a giggling, bikini-clad dumb blonde with glib sayings written all over her body. Lily Tomlin became known for her portrayal of a sarcastic and nasal telephone operator as well as Ruth-Ann, a clever little girl who sat in a big rocking chair. *The Smothers Brothers Comedy Hour* was another comedy/ variety show that debuted a year earlier but became much more controversial because of its choice of guests who were "predominantly antiwar, left-wing, and outspoken."[7] Situation comedy, of course, was popular on television in the 1960s, but many of the characters were of the fantastic variety. Television news brought stressful realities into our living rooms; sitcoms offered escape and some new roles for women.

SIGNIFICANT COMEDY SERIES

The Dick Van Dyke Show portrayed perhaps the closest to a traditional, nuclear family in the 1960s, while another sitcom featured a wife who was a witch. Single women also abounded in sitcoms, including one who wanted nothing more than to take care of her "critters" and another who took pleasure in serving her "master." Two groundbreaking series also debuted that focused on both family and careers of women, one featuring the struggles of a young actress in New York City and the other the first series to star an African American woman as someone other than a servant. Because of their combination of popularity and social significance, the following series will be highlighted: *The Dick Van Dyke Show, The Beverly Hillbillies, Bewitched, I Dream of Jeannie, That Girl,* and *Julia.*

The Dick Van Dyke Show

Considered by many to be a quality, classic situation comedy, *The Dick Van Dyke Show* (CBS, 1961–1966) rated eightieth its first season. Once placed after the very popular *The Beverly Hillbillies,* however, it never rated below the top 20 prime-time television programs again. During its run, it garnered several awards, including fifteen Emmys. However idealistic the series may appear in its stories about a television comedy writer, his family, and his coworkers, the roots of *The Dick Van Dyke Show* are based on the life of creator/writer/actor Carl Reiner, played by Van Dyke. Mary Tyler Moore's natural talent for comedy and the chemistry with her costar inspired Reiner to expand the role of wife Laura Petrie to more than just the "ear" for her hard-working husband's laments, placing the sitcom fairly equally, perhaps for the first time, in both the home and workplace.[8]

It's not until the third season that it is revealed (to both the audience and Rob) that the former Laura Meehan was a child bride—a mere seventeen years old when she and Rob Petrie married. Through flashbacks throughout the series run, we learn that Laura was a dancer in the USO at the army base where Rob was stationed. In "Oh How We Met the Night That We Danced," their meeting and early courtship is revealed. For Rob, it seems to be love at first sight, and he clumsily pursues her, breaking her toe in a soft-shoe routine in which he conspires to join her. Rob soon wins Laura's love, and later episodes flashback to their wedding and early married years, including the birth of their son, Ritchie.

Laura Petrie seems quite content to be a housewife and mother who willingly gave up her dancing career to focus on domestic life. Mary Tyler Moore says she "wanted to establish her as a woman who had her own point of view and who would fight with her husband—a good fight, if necessary. She wasn't a 'yes' wife, nor did she focus everything on him. But that's about as liberated as Laura Petrie was. I think she truly believed that her only choice was to be a wife and mother and couldn't combine [that with] a career."[9] On a couple occasions, Laura is given the opportunity to work for *The Alan Brady Show,* to Rob's great distress. In "My Part-Time Wife," Rob reluctantly agrees to hire Laura as an interim secretary during cowriter Sally's unexpected absence. He is worried not only about the awkwardness of working together, but also about how this might affect his comforts at home. When Laura is hired as a replacement dancer in "To Tell or Not to Tell," she does very well and is offered a permanent job. Much to Rob's relief, she turns it down because the dancing is too strenuous and she prefers to be a housewife. She reminds Rob of what she said to him when he proposed: "Take me away from all this. I don't want to be a dancer—I want to be your wife." In Laura's mind, reflecting the dominant middle-class culture, it was an either/or position. But Laura's talents are seen throughout the series, particularly as a song-and-dance partner with Rob when the writers perform in various venues, such as a resort in the Catskills, a prison, and for a Christmas episode of *The Alan Brady Show.* Like then–First Lady Jacqueline Kennedy who once was a respectable photographer, Laura opts for the domestic life and motherhood, but she supports her husband's career in several ways.

The characters of Rob and Laura Petrie have been compared to their contemporaries in the White House in other ways, but sitcom critic Gerard Jones claims the resemblance to the Kennedys is actually restricted to a few physical details, such as their youthful good looks. As he points out, however, the differences between the sitcom couple and the couple in the White House say much about each:

> Where the Kennedys set styles, the Petries nervously tried to adopt them.
> Rob filled his house with bourgeois modern decor and then promptly

tripped over the ottoman. Kennedy was groomed to play the role of an American aristocrat; Rob was self-created—through imitation—and never quite seemed to know what he should do. Jackie was socially infallible; Laura did her hair like Jackie's and dressed like Jackie and tried her best to play the sophisticated hostess, but she was a quaver-voiced nerve case who constantly battled her own insecurities and jealousies.[10]

In other words, the Petries were more like the rest of us struggling to fit in.

While Carl Reiner enjoyed the comedy of *I Love Lucy,* he did not want his series to be a battle of the sexes; he wondered how Lucy and Ricky could really love each other with her always fooling him and him never catering to her.[11] He said his show was "based on a mutually respecting husband and wife. It was two against the world. And even when it was one-against-one, it was the kind of one-against-one you have in a family that loves each other."[12] What Reiner was looking for as the producer and creator of *The Dick Van Dyke Show* were what he called "realies" in the scripts—carefully observed realities from his own life or others that gave a feeling of reality to the show.[13] Although he wrote dozens of the 158 episodes and carefully trained the other writers for the series, he was occasionally upset with an episode because it didn't fit with his idea of the characters or the series. One show he particularly didn't like was "The Curious Thing about Women," where Laura gets mad about Rob for depicting her as an incurable snoop. To prove his point, Rob has a package delivered to himself at home and Laura can't resist opening it—a large rubber raft, which immediately inflates. Reiner objected to the fact that it made Laura look silly; he couldn't imagine his own wife doing such a thing, and Laura was modeled after his own wife.[14]

Dick Van Dyke's least favorite show was "The Bad Old Days," an episode where his coworker Buddy tries to convince Rob that modern American males are being systematically emasculated as they help their wives around the house. Rob has a dream of living in the 1890s and insisting on being master of his household as his submissive wife waits on him hand and foot. While Rob ends up defending his willingness to help Laura at home, Van Dyke seemed to think the premise was old and did not work.[15] But Rob's speech to Buddy, Sally, neighbors Millie and Jerry Helper, and Laura at the end of the episode is an important message in the early days of the second wave of feminism. Although he claims everyone should decide what they are going to do and where they will draw the line, Rob does say, "I don't think doing things around the house is gonna hurt your masculinity if you like to save a few bucks or if you just enjoy doing things." That is a message some men still need to hear. But Rob does revert to the notion of "women's work" when it suits him. For example, in "How to Spank a Star," Rob brings home flowers to Laura and she asks if he would put them in water while she finishes setting the table. He refuses, calling it "women's work," and says he'll do the men's work of taking out the garbage.

Laura and Rob do have many squabbles, but they are usually disagreements that most couples might have, such as Laura being upset with Rob because he always picks up the check when they are out with others. In "The Night the Roof Fell In," the two recount (her to her friend Millie and he to his coworkers, Sally and Buddy) very different versions of a fight they had where Rob ends up storming out of the house. In a particularly interesting episode, "My Mother Can Beat Up My Father," it is revealed that Laura knows judo when she defends Rob from an abusive drunk in a bar. Rob is proud of her ability until the joking from others becomes too much. He learns some judo moves so he knows she can't flip him. In demonstrating his skills to assuage his ego, however, he hurts himself and ends up in the hospital. Laura and Rob are occasionally jealous of another man or woman they feel is a threat to their marriage, including female stars that Rob works with and Laura's old boyfriends. In the end, however, it seems that there is nothing that can break apart their marriage—they love each other too much.

Although the Petries, in requisite 1950s TV fashion, sleep in separate twin beds, it is obvious they are physically attracted to each other, as indicated by both the onscreen chemistry of the two stars as well as the scripts. In the pilot episode, "The Sick Boy and the Sitter," Laura reluctantly goes with Rob to a party given by his boss, Alan Brady, even though she is sure their six-year-old son, Ritchie, is sick. At the party, Laura finally convinces Rob that they need to go home to take care of their son; it turns out she is right. When asked how she knew, she says, "Darling," and continues after lightly kissing him, "I'm a woman" (a phrase she will use several times throughout the series when Rob wonders how she knew something). She then unhooks her string of pearls, and as they slip from her neck, she heads toward their bedroom. Rob's very appreciative "yeah" makes it clear what is on his mind as he follows her. *Van Dyke* expert Vince Waldron says this scene can also be interpreted on another level, one that immediately distinguishes Laura Petrie from the housewives of the 1950s: "In casting off the ubiquitous string of pearls that had symbolically condemned so many earlier prime-time wives to a life of sexless domesticity, Laura Petrie and her creators seem to be offering their own long overdue farewell to the era of June Cleaver and her perfectly matched jewelry, tasteful coiffures, and sensible pastel dresses."[16] Mary Tyler Moore, in her insistence that Laura be allowed to wear capri pants occasionally, also helped to distinguish Laura from her predecessors. Moore argued to the reluctant producers and sponsors that she wore pants every day to do her chores and run errands; it would be realistic for Laura to do the same.

Laura Petrie could usually hold her own in fights with Rob, but sometimes the insecurities of her youth got the better of her and she would break into a sobbing monologue, occasionally precipitated by her trademark "Oh, Rob." While Rob has his office coworkers as his sounding board for problems at home, Laura has Millie Helper as her best friend and next-door neighbor. Many times, however, Millie would cause more problems than she would solve. In "My Blonde-Haired Brunette" it is Millie who suggests Laura dye her hair blonde when Laura thinks the spark has gone out of her marriage. When Rob says something to Laura on the phone about her beautiful brown hair, Laura, in a panic, tries to dye it back before he gets home. She ends up with half blonde/half brown hair, and tearfully explains to Rob how and why she did it. Millie tries to talk Laura into lying "for women drivers everywhere" in "Scratch My Car and Die" when Laura is trying to figure out how to tell Rob she got a scratch on his new sports car. Millie is Laura's "ear," her faithful friend at least since the days when they were in the USO together. They listen to each other's troubles, borrow things from each other, and help each other with their kids in their comfortable middle-class suburban lives.

Sally Rogers is the single career woman on the show, and she is quite unhappy about it. She sometimes leaves work early to get ready for a date, and her friends are always trying to find suitable husband material for her. Culture critic David Marc describes her as

a bull in a china shop. Too assertive, too aggressive, too willing to use her "unfeminine" powers, Sally is the career woman whom Laura wisely chose not to be.... The only men who can accept her are her co-workers; they know how to harness her sexually ambiguous eccentricities for productive purposes. Some of the single men Sally encounters are emasculated by her verbal powers; others can only see her as a source of the valued commodity of humor. None can accept her as a woman.[17]

Several episodes, however, contradict the notion that no man can accept her as a woman. Reliable boyfriend Herman Glimsher already has been emasculated by his doting mother; Sally's strength perhaps is an attraction,

Freudian as it may be. But there are other men who find her attractive on her own, including a very handsome guest star singer.

It is a shame that Sally is portrayed as being so desperate for a husband—she is attractive, funny, strong, smart, and a great friend to her coworkers, Rob and Buddy, as well as to Laura. One can't help but wonder if she is desperate only because she feels it is expected of her. In one episode, "Dear Sally Rogers," she delights audiences on a talk show when she advertises for a husband. She gets lots of letters, including a heartfelt one from her reliable "momma's boy" boyfriend, Herman, the butt of many of her jokes. But perhaps Sally's constant comments about wanting a husband are really only jokes, to be taken as she means them—only half seriously. Sally indicates on many occasions that she'd take a marriage proposal from anybody, that she'd even be happy to marry a dull, poor guy, but there are episodes where she rejects men, despite her claims to the contrary.

Several episodes focus on Sally and her disastrous relationships, many of them actually quite touching. Sometimes her heart is broken, and sometimes she breaks a heart. In the compelling episode "Romance, Roses, and Rye Bread," it is clearly established that Sally is not willing to just settle into any marriage, even with a man who is crazy about her. The program begins with Sally discovering a rose on her desk and fantasizing who might have left it for her. The owner of the delicatessen where they get lunch, Bert, tells her it came from him, and she is disappointed. He tells her that it marks their anniversary—of when she first came into his deli. He then gives her one theater ticket that he claims he got from a customer and can't use. Rob and Buddy are convinced that Bert has a crush on Sally, but she doesn't think he means his lighthearted words of love. When Laura takes Sally's place at the theater because the writers have to work on a script, she discovers a very unhappy man next to her who is expecting his girlfriend. When Laura complains to Rob at home, he figures out that the disgruntled man was Bert. The next day when Sally goes home from work at lunchtime rather than face Bert, he brings her hot soup and the truth finally comes out, albeit in a subtle, awkward way. Bert admits he is in his fifties and lonely. He tells Sally her problem is that she never stumbles—in the movies the girl stumbles, the guy catches her, and they get married. Sally replies that she doesn't want to stumble—she wants a nice, clean fall into love. When Bert leaves, she picks up her cat, Mr. Henderson, and tells him she wishes she had nine lives like him—then she would give one to Bert. Sally believes in the ideal of marrying for love—romantic love—and would rather continue being alone than to settle for anything less.

Rob and Buddy are particularly protective of Sally and worry about the various men she dates. Sally usually is quite open about her feelings and rather trusting, despite her jokes and occasional cynicism. In "Jilting the Jilter," Sally's latest heartthrob is Fred, a standup comic who badly needs a writer. Sally supplies him with new material, and the guy wants her to marry him. Of course, Rob and Buddy suspect his motives, and they are right—he wants Sally for her brains and talent, not because he loves her. Buddy and Rob write Fred a great new act, assuming that he will then no longer want Sally. Their plan does not work, and the couple continue with their marriage plans. Sally calls it off, however, when Fred tells her that their marriage will prove to the show-biz industry that he is not a welsher. Again, Sally is not willing to settle, although she does go home to cry for "at least two hours."

Rob and Buddy are Sally's best friends, and their relationship is platonic and respectful, although filled with jokes. It is Buddy and Sally who attend events together, and not Buddy with his wife, Pickles. Explanations aren't usually given—that is just the way it is. In the office, Sally usually does the typing, but she is their equal in every way. When Sally takes a leave of absence to work on a talk show in "The Pen Is Mightier Than the Mouth," Rob and Buddy have a hard time working without her. In the end, she gives up the glamour of the performing life to return as an integral part of *The Alan Brady Show* writing staff. In "Sally Is a Girl," Laura gets angry at Rob for treating Sally like one of the guys, telling her new date at a dinner party that Sally is "strong as a bull" while Laura tries to tell the date that Sally is a good cook. Rob decides to start treating Sally like a "girl" (primarily by showing good manners, such as holding out her chair). Although at first Sally is suspicious, she begins to enjoy it while Buddy and producer Mel suspect they are having an affair. When Buddy tells Sally she has to discourage Rob, she suddenly understands and kisses Rob on the cheek when he returns to their office. She shows up at the Petries later that night with her date from the night before. This time the man is smitten with her—Sally's car had supposedly broken down in front of his house and she needed him to rescue her. Her lesson is that to catch a man she has to act helpless, not strong like a bull.

But that is not always the case. Laura decides to play matchmaker once again for Sally in "Sally and the Lab Technician." When Laura complains to Rob that she can't understand why Sally is not married—"she's a comedy writer, she'd be fun to be with, she's an attractive girl"—Rob tells her that Sally scares guys off, that she's too quick with answers and guys hate girls who make jokes of everything. Rob would seem to be right—Sally seems to overwhelm the shy lab technician, Thomas, at dinner, and he hardly says a word. The next day Sally comes to work depressed, disappointed she hasn't heard from Thomas and chastising herself for her behavior. At home that night, Rob tells Laura that "the next time you want to get Sally a date, invite Milton Berle and have them meet in Madison Square Garden." Much to their surprise, however, Thomas stops by to thank them for what a wonderful time he had. He is crazy about Sally and wants to ask her out again; he is just shy.

In addition to mixed dating lessons, the "Sally Is a Girl" episode in particular raises interesting questions about gender and sex in the workplace that still plague people today. Should a woman be treated "like a man"? Does a woman need to act "like a man" in order to function well at work? Sally certainly doesn't hide the fact that she is a woman—she frequently talks about dating men and fixes her nails and hair at work. She often wears a bow in her hair. But Sally is aggressive and independent in ways that some may not consider feminine, thus making it easier to regard her as one of the "boys." Interestingly enough, several of Sally's romantic relationships do seem successful, but we never find out what happens to them, other than they clearly don't end in marriage.

Like other sitcoms of the times, *The Dick Van Dyke Show* was not touched by the turmoil outside its own reality—the Cuban missile crisis, Kennedy's assassination, and violence against blacks were not part of any stories. African Americans did have some presence on the show, however, and were integrated as army buddies, secret agents, and the like. In "A Show of Hands," Rob and Laura attend a dinner where Rob is to accept an award for racial tolerance on behalf of *The Alan Brady Show*. Both have accidentally dyed their hands black while preparing a costume for Ritchie, and, concerned that they will be misunderstood, they wear white gloves to the dinner. As Rob accepts the award for racial tolerance, he decides to take the gloves off, literally and figuratively, and asks for the audience's understanding, which their laughter indicates he's got. In a heartfelt speech he says he can't wait for the day when understanding is common and no awards have to be given for it. Laura's role in all this is primarily to sit there and support her husband by embarrassed giggles and showing her black hands. The growing women's movement also did not touch the series; women chose to be either housewives and mothers (Laura) or career "girls" (Sally). Despite this fact, Laura Petrie and Sally Rogers are basically strong and delightful characters.

The Beverly Hillbillies

After the first few episodes of its debut in 1962, *The Beverly Hillbillies* (CBS, 1962–1971) became the number one rated series in the United

States. As the country dealt with near nuclear warfare with the U.S.S.R. and the fight for civil rights in the South, millions of people each week watched the adventures of the Clampetts, a hillbilly family from the Ozarks who became instant oil millionaires and subsequently moved to a mansion in Beverly Hills. When the oil company, which found the "black gold" in the Clampett swamp, made contact with the Clampetts, it might also have notified anthropologists for here was a family seemingly untouched by civilization. They didn't know what a phone was, and they thought a helicopter was a big bird in the sky. Filled with vastly exaggerated "fish out of water" stories, the series focuses on how the family has to contend not only with new appliances and technology but also with a culture that seems to have vastly different, capitalistic values.

Jed Clampett is the patriarch, a gentle widower who thinks the word "million" is just another kind of dollar, like gold or silver, and he's receiving 25 to 100 of them for his swamp. Also in his household is his mother-in-law, Granny, who specializes in backwoods medicine and moonshine. Elly May is Jed's beautiful, innocent "tomboy" daughter whose body may be developing into a woman's, but who still has the mind of a child. Jethro is the big, energetic, but stupid son of Jed's cousin, Pearl, who drives his family out to Beverly Hills and decides to stay. Pearl is the one who had to explain to Jed that being a millionaire meant he was rich. Awaiting them in Beverly Hills is Milburn Drysdale, who takes a personal interest in the Clampetts because they are the largest depositors in his bank and they are also his next-door neighbors. Mrs. Drysdale is the stereotypical rich snob who becomes determined to get rid of the Clampetts. Jane Hathaway is Drysdale's plain, but devoted secretary whose job it becomes to keep the Clampetts happy.

Donna Douglas as Elly May became quite a sensation through this series. As the beautiful, but innocent daughter, she was perhaps a fantasy virgin for many male viewers but she was also someone who needed to be tamed. Within the first few minutes of the pilot episode, "The Clampetts Strike Oil," before the audience even sees Elly May, we hear Granny complaining about Elly's wildness as she sews her clothes torn by a fight with a bobcat. Granny tells Jed that it's time Elly May started wearing dresses and acting like a woman: "Girl runnin' around and wild as a cougar, rasslin', fightin' and huntin'. She oughtta be doin' women's work, helping me with the still." Our first encounter with Elly May is when she comes into the tiny cabin with a man over her shoulder. She plops him on the table and asks her "paw" if she can keep him, as if he were a pet. If she is attracted to him as a man, she doesn't know it but might sense it. On the other hand, throughout the series it is clear that Elly May has a special relationship with "critters" and collects a variety of animals as pets, indicating a mothering instinct as well as an instinct for healing. A logical next step in the minds of many would be for her to transfer those feelings to mating and having her own children. Finding Elly May a husband is indeed a goal set by her family that will continue throughout the nine years of the series.

In the second episode, "Getting Settled," Jed has a little talk with Elly May after she beats up her big cousin Jethro over who is tougher and who should get to chop down the firewood. He says, "You gotta start minding your manners, fixing yourself up real nice, and wearin' dresses." When Elly May complains that people would call her a sissy, her paw says it's not sissy for girls to "act like girls." In a touching scene with soulful harmonica music in the background, Jed explains that he raised her as a boy after her maw died because "every man'd like to have a son, and you was my only youngin'." He continues that he was wrong, that it is not right for folks to go against nature. And so the setting is established for an anticipated transition from tomboy to debutante, in the great tradition of Eliza Doolittle and even the movies' backwoods darling from the 1950s, Tammy. The first man Elly May dates is Mr. Drysdale's snobby stepson, Sonny. There are other attempts now and then to fix her up with someone from "home." Inevitably a number of men want her primarily because of her money, and many of her dates are disastrous. Dash Riprock (who sounds like a character out of the *Flintstones*) is a handsome actor Elly May dates in several episodes, however. The series ends with her still unmarried and dating navy lieutenant Mark Templeton.

Unlike her cousin Jethro, Elly May does not avidly pursue a career. She spends much of her time taking care of her "critters," a collection of monkeys, chickens, skunks, and other animals that wander around the mansion grounds as if it were a farm. While Jethro attends sixth grade, Elly May goes to a finishing school for spoiled rich girls. In a wry comment on fashion trends, the other girls at the school think Elly May is setting a fashion trend in her blue jeans and flannel shirt, and copy her style. Elly May is also subject to trends, however, and on one occasion she and Jethro join a bunch of beatniks; in another episode she joins a group of hippies. She works in one episode as secretary to her dad when he sets up an office in Drysdale's bank. Elly May's skills, however, lie with her care of animals as well as the "tomboy" or athletic skills she learned in the backwoods of the Ozarks.

Elly May's grandmother and Jed's mother-in-law, Granny, might be revered in a primitive culture as a wise elder and healer. It is easy in the

Beverly Hills of the 1960s, however, to interpret her as a silly, superstitious old woman. Granny is the caretaker of the family, cooking family meals of "possum innards," mustard greens, and the like as well as giving them tonics for illness. Granny's "rheumatiz" medicine is her illegally distilled whiskey (moonshine) that she admits won't cure it, "but it'll make ya happy ya got it!"[18] In "Brewster's Baby" she is determined to go back to the Ozarks to "fetch" a baby into the world. In another episode, "The Common Cold," she opens her own doctor's office when a real M.D. refuses to believe Granny has a cure for the common cold. In an era of new age and alternative medicine that involves more natural cures, Granny's healing ways might fit right in.

Granny might be old, but she certainly doesn't act it. She gets involved in women's wrestling and is part of a tag team match after defeating one woman in "The Rass-lin Clampetts" and "The Great Tag-Team Match." Although she may not be the size of what one might envision as a "mountain woman" (she is quite small and slender), she is feisty and strong. She also is confident that she has the capability of attracting men on her charms alone, although a few episodes indicate she is pursued because of her money. When Sam Drucker from Hooterville (in another of producer Paul Henning's creations, *Petticoat Junction*) wins a trip to Hollywood and visits the Clampetts, Granny assumes he has come to propose to her. Granny often plays matchmaker herself, particularly for Elly May, her only granddaughter. In "The Courtship of Elly," she even distills a "love potion" to get a husband for her. Granny believes that a girl over fourteen who is not married is a "spinster" and needs all the help she can get.

Granny gets terribly confused by anything outside of her limited experience in the Ozarks. Soon after her arrival in Beverly Hills, she is convinced that it must get awfully cold at night because the food in the "storage bins" in the kitchen is frozen; of course, the audience knows she is referring to the freezer. In the most watched episode of the series, and one of the top watched programs of all time of any kind, "The Giant Jackrabbit," Granny sees a kangaroo and thinks she has discovered a five-foot jackrabbit. When Elly dates a navy frogman, Granny is convinced over several episodes that the man is really half frog/half human. Needless to say, Granny has a hard time adapting to new ways and ideas, and she often wishes to go back home. It is a wish that on some level has been felt probably by most people. In the violence of the 1960s and in the vast changes in technology that were taking place, including in space exploration, a journey back to simpler times might have been welcomed by the viewing audience and, in a way, the Clampetts gave them that.

When Granny and Elly May get fed up with all their household chores, they join the women's liberation movement in "Women's Lib" and move in with Jane Hathaway. In a plot reminiscent of an old *I Love Lucy* episode, the men are left in charge of the house and make a mess of it. Jed and Jethro's solution, however, is to hire a trio of beautiful Japanese women. By the third episode on this theme, Granny and Elly May are assured of their equal rights and return to the Clampett mansion. The episode is reminiscent of many of the popular misconceptions about women's liberation. If only it just concerned housework!

Jane Hathaway, the very efficient college-educated secretary to banker Drysdale and assistant to the Clampetts, is a model of the stereotypical plain career "girl." There is no doubt that she is smart, yet she has a crush on Jethro, a very stupid but handsome man-child. If nothing else, however, it shows that Jane has an active libido even if she is willing to forego an intellectual equal. But with all the beautiful women around Beverly Hills, she does not stand much of a chance to attract any man. Jane is always quite willing to do whatever it takes to keep her job. She suffers many indignities as she involves herself in the Clampetts' lives, but she develops a friendship with them that seems to go beyond the duties of her job. Perhaps more important, she voices liberal middle-class sensibilities that speak up for the lower-class Clampetts and act as the conscience of the upper-class Drysdales. As critic David Marc said, "of the city folk, she is clearly the moral paragon, berating Mr. Drysdale for his greediness, even at the risk of her job, and clearly opposing Mrs. Drysdale's blind snobbery, often with lofty speeches on the theoretical virtues of democratic attitudes."[19]

In their nine years on the air, The Clampetts never seemed to grow much, and the "fish out of water" theme was continued on occasional trips to places such as England, New York City, and Washington, D.C. Despite the fact that most critics hated *The Beverly Hillbillies* and even some viewers complained that no one could be as stupid as the Clampetts, the show was the number one rated program its first two years and in the top 20 its first eight. The humor was primarily slapstick, but the Clampett hillbilly lingo and verbal misunderstandings were also an integral part of the characters. With the idea that comic strips were the most-read part of a newspaper, Paul Henning reportedly "created characters that were very much like those in cartoons—only they would be animated in live form."[20] Certainly there are some parallels with the characters in the popular cartoon strip "L'il Abner," with the beautiful Daisy Mae (Elly May) and Mammy Slocum (Granny).

Henning has been quoted as saying he is surprised "when the program is fitted with cultural symbolism. The show was simply meant to entertain."[21]

But a creator cannot control how people "read" his or her work, and the fact that millions of people watched *The Beverly Hillbillies* makes it likely that the show must have touched some people on some level beyond entertainment. Cultural critic Gerard Jones called *The Beverly Hillbillies* a synthetic sitcom that juggled and refused to resolve contradictory messages: "Were viewers asked to laugh at the dumb hicks or at the phony slickers? Were the Clampetts demonstrating that we can preserve simple values in the modern world or that there's just no place for provincials in mainstream culture? Was their sudden wealth a wish fulfillment or a cautionary lesson?"[22] One might also add to these questions how the characters of Elly May, Granny, and Jane Hathaway should be interpreted and how they may have influenced young girls watching them. Elly May certainly makes a case for beauty, but she is also strong and athletic. Granny and Jane may make a case for not getting old and being "plain," but they also have their own brand of common sense and usefulness.

Bewitched

Samantha Stephens is a beautiful young woman who confesses to her husband, Darrin, on their wedding night that she is a witch. Mortal that he is, he is upset and makes her promise to not use her witchcraft; thus the premise of most episodes of *Bewitched* (ABC, 1964–1972) are established as Samantha struggles to keep that promise. Samantha's family, particularly her mother, Endora, is not happy with her choice of a mortal husband and complicates Samantha's often futile attempts to not use witchcraft. Nosy neighbor Gladys Kravitz notices the sometimes strange activities at the Stephens's household and confounds Samantha's life even more.

The biggest hit in the subgenre of comedy that critic David Marc calls "magicom,"[23] *Bewitched* rated second only to the western adventure *Bonanza* during its first year on the air (1964–1965) and averaged a 35 percent share of the television audience throughout its eight-year run on ABC.[24] It was also recognized with twenty-two Emmy nominations, winning three. Despite the twist of magic in the domestic scene, Marc points out that Darrin Stephens is a typical sitcom husband who goes out into the world to earn the family income while his wife "is treated as little more than a contractual housekeeper who is to be kept safely locked away at home, be that a tenement in a Brooklyn slum, an Upper East Side apartment, a ranchburger in New Rochelle, or a fine substantial house in the Springfield vortex."[25] But why would a strong, smart, powerful witch like Samantha settle for the suburban housewife life her husband wishes, actually demands, of her? She has options that the women in 1950s sitcoms like Lucy Ricardo did not. Samantha had to have loved Darrin so much that she chose to give up her magical world for the love of her man, a sacrifice that has been asked of women from various backgrounds since time eternal. Samantha claims in several episodes that she enjoys what she is doing. In "Darrin the Warlock" she says, "I happen to think cooking on a stove is a lot more fun than using witchcraft...and I also enjoy taking care of my husband and children in the everyday mortal way."[26] Writer Gerard Jones calls *Bewitched* "a concession and a plea from American men to American women—or girls. 'We know you'd be happier if you broke from domesticity and led the lives you secretly desire,' said the men, 'but we'd be lost without you. Stay in this life and take care of us poor inferior fellows...not for your sake but for ours.' It flattered women and played on maternal guilt."[27] But the moral to this series is not that women should stay in their place; as a matter of fact, Samantha shows that it is impossible, indeed against nature, to keep women confined in any role.

Series writer and feminist Barbara Avedon says the Stephenses' marriage "may even have been the basic metaphor for the male-female relationship of the 1960s—when women really kept their own strengths hidden within the prescribed boundaries of marriage."[28] But Samantha could not keep her strengths hidden. In all 254 episodes, Samantha uses her magic, sometimes as a convenience to herself but more often to help someone in trouble. Darrin is the stereotypical middle-class husband who struggles to achieve the status quo through a very competitive and stressful career in advertising. His job is showcased in several episodes where something, often magic by one of Samantha's relatives or associates, threatens one of Darrin's accounts, and Samantha must resolve the issue. Darrin's ego is quite fragile, and it is important to him most of the time that his wife doesn't help him. He can also be jealous of her. In at least two episodes Samantha comes up with a better idea for an advertising campaign than he, and Darrin accuses her of using witchcraft. Of course, she is insulted that he doesn't think she can be creative on her own and that he thinks she is lying. Darrin can be quick-tempered, particularly when he is convinced that Samantha has used magic against his wishes. Whenever Darrin wrongly accuses Samantha of witchcraft, it leads to a big fight; Samantha is not about to let him get away with calling her a liar and not trusting her. Inevitably Darrin offers some sort of apology, and the two kiss and make up.

Despite Darrin's periodic insistence that Samantha give up witchcraft, in the end he realizes it is part of who she is and he accepts it. For example, Samantha is made head witch in "Long Live the Queen," but has promised Darrin she will hold court only after midnight. When subjects, including chairs and animals, start showing up at their front door during the day, Darrin insists she must abdicate. When she says she can't for at least a year, he goes off to a bar. As has happened in several episodes, someone at the bar tells Darrin about his own sad situation and makes Darrin realize the importance of what he has. When Darrin gets home, several people are walking out and one, who had been turned back into a man from a crow, tells Darrin how good his wife is. Samantha is so delighted to see Darrin that she tells him he is more important than any crown and, though it has never been done before, she will find a way to abdicate. He replies, "The thing I realized is that your being queen is part of what you are, and if I love you enough I have to accept that. Just the way you accept certain things about my world. So (he kneels)...I'm at your disposal, your majesty." In this timeless love scene, they are each ready to sacrifice for the other.

The couple struggles on throughout other episodes to accept each other for who and what they are—she a powerful, talented, modern woman and he an egocentric, insecure, and traditional man. But they love each other and, as the saying goes, "love conquers all." And it is not a chaste love of which we speak—many episodes indicate their lust for each other, starting with the pilot, "I, Darrin, Take This Witch, Samantha." A voiceover tells us how they met when they kept bumping into each other at a store and decided to have drinks together. A montage shows them kissing on several locations. In the last minutes of the episode, Darrin is kissing Samantha in their kitchen and whispers, "It's bedtime." When she says that she has to get the kitchen cleaned up, he whispers in her ear, "tomorrow," and she reminds him that this is what he said the night before. After he leaves, she "zaps" the kitchen clean, obviously eager to join her husband in the bedroom. Unlike the Petries of *The Dick Van Dyke* show, this couple is not hindered by twin beds; they share a double.

Elizabeth Montgomery, who played Samantha Stephens, initially thought her character was wimpy in succumbing to Darrin's wishes and not using her powers at will. Her husband and director of the series, William Asher, however, offered Montgomery a different interpretation, comparing Samantha's restraint to that of former gunfighter and hero in the movie *Shane*. Said Montgomery, "The guns shouldn't be pulled off the wall indiscriminately because someone could get hurt...And also, it just implies good manners. Something we're all brought up with...that you don't take advantage of other people."[29] In addition, despite Darrin's angry protests to the contrary, Samantha knows that Darrin loves her enough to "forgive" her occasional use of witchcraft. In "Allergy to Ancient Macedonian Dodo Birds," Endora has lost her powers temporarily, which leads Samantha to ask Darrin if he would be happy if she lost her power. He replies, "It's a very difficult question—with a very simple answer. I love you and I don't want you to change one bit. You just stay as wonderful as you are."

Several episodes indicate that Samantha's power lies not just in her witchcraft (often indicated by a wiggle of her nose or wave of her hands) but also in her intelligence. She speaks several languages and seemingly knows all about any historical figures that her befuddled Aunt Clara accidentally conjures up. In "My Friend Ben," she speaks French with Benjamin Franklin and discusses his innovations with him, including a volunteer fire department. But it is her great powers of persuasion and logic that are demonstrated in episodes such as "Samantha's Thanksgiving to Remember," where she defends Darrin against witchcraft in seventeenth-century Salem. At the end of a rousing civics lesson and plea for a tolerance of differences, Samantha points out to the court, which includes John Alden, that "If one examineth one's neighbors closely, he will find differences enough so that no one is safe from the charge of witchery. But is that what we seek in this new world? Methinks not. The hope of this world lyeth in our acceptance of all differences and a recognition of our common humanity."

Writer Barbara Avedon assisted a class of high school students in writing an episode that dealt specifically with racial prejudice. In "Sisters at Heart," Samantha's daughter Tabitha becomes close friends with a black girl, Lisa, the daughter of one of Darrin's coworkers. In this episode, Darrin is removed from an important account when the bigoted client thinks Lisa is his daughter. Tabitha wishes she and Lisa could be sisters, but a playmate in the park tells her that it is impossible because they are not the same color. In the end, Samantha tells the girls that "You can be sisters without looking alike...Sisters are girls who share something. Actually, 'all' men are brothers...even if they're girls."[30] Sisterhood is powerful, even beyond the coven or witches' council.

Several other episodes demonstrate that Samantha is socially conscious and active in the mortal community, as she helps to save a park, raise money for UNICEF, and campaign for a sympathetic town councilman. As author Susan Douglas wrote, "the repeated combination of magic, diplomacy (her forte), and good common sense made Samantha's solutions to problems the ones that were clearly the most viable and sensible. Here was a housewife with logical and creative ideas about how to make the world better, and with an ability to act on those ideas and get them a fair hearing, even if she had to do so through her bumbling surrogate, Darrin."[31]

Danny Arnold, the coproducer of *Bewitched,* said the conflict of the show "was divided into two main sections: (1) the power of a woman versus the ego of a man, and (2) a mother's objection to her daughter's marrying an unsophisticated man."[32] Actually, Samantha's mother, Endora, was mortified that her daughter had married a mere mortal and could not understand why she would choose to give up her life of witchery. The role Endora plays is shown metaphorically in the animated opening credits. As Darrin holds Samantha in the kitchen, smoke suddenly comes from a frying pan on the stove, turning into a black cloud with the credit for Agnes Moorehead as Endora. She is the epitome of the stereotypical, interfering mother-in-law who pops in at will. While she clearly loves her daughter, Endora finds it difficult to accept Darrin and the two frequently fight. Refusing to call him by his right name, she often casts spells on him during confrontations, and he is variously shown as a chimp, mule, werewolf, goose, pony, parrot, goat, crow, dog, and statue. While at times the two have a truce, such as when they hug and cry together after daughter Tabitha is born, many episodes show Endora intent on breaking up her daughter's marriage, sometimes by introducing a handsome warlock into the scene. But Samantha always forgives her mother, and so Endora continues her attempts to separate her daughter from Darrin, even after the couple have two children.

Endora has a marriage of her own, to Samantha's father, Maurice, but theirs is an "informal marriage," he declares in "Samantha's Good News." Although the couple don't see each other for months at a time, Endora is still capable of jealousy, as she threatens to disintegrate Maurice's beautiful new female assistant. She may not want him, but he is still hers, and she has the power to keep it that way. In Susan Douglas's media autobiography, she claims that the older women in this show, including Endora, were grotesque in comparison to Samantha, but that "Endora got to say what many women wished they could say, and her complete indifference to the approval of men was a joy and relief to watch, even as we knew we did not want to be like her."[33] Or maybe we did—occasional jealousy and temper aside, Endora was powerful.

Gladys Kravitz, on the other hand, was an older woman one did not want to be. She was the Stephenses' nosy neighbor who not only watched their activities through her window, but she even spied on them through their own windows. When she would hysterically call for her retired husband, Abner, to observe something strange, such as the street suddenly being turned into a lake or Benjamin Franklin visiting, he would invariably just miss it. Seemingly bored with her, he would encourage her to take her nerve medicine and indicate he wanted to be left alone. Despite her hysterical complaints to police and in court on occasion, the Stephenses still managed to be nice to her.

Other female characters that appeared on the show included Samantha's various relatives, such as her beloved but befuddled Aunt Clara. Clara is an older witch who is losing her powers and often accidentally conjures up characters into the Stephenses' living room. Despite the messes that Clara gets them into, Samantha defends her and treats her kindly, insisting that others do the same. A variety of women also pass through the advertising agency as clients. Perhaps the most interesting is one of Darrin's former girlfriends, whom he says promised to get even with him for dumping her. Darrin is surprised when she signs a lucrative contract after seeing him, but she later tells him she is no longer that vengeful girl. When he remarks that she has come a long way in the business world, she says, "For a woman, you mean. Oh, it's alright. Ladies who work in what's considered a man's job get used to that. What we don't get used to is keeping up in the business world and taking care of our children at the same time." When this highly successful businesswoman who is married with children complains about how difficult it is, it could be read as a warning. It also could be read simply as an important recognition of the difficulties in having both a career and a family.

I Dream of Jeannie

Another magicom, *I Dream of Jeannie,* debuted the year after *Bewitched,* obviously hoping to attract as large an audience with its similar theme of a magical lead female character. In its five years on NBC, however, its highest rating at number 27 was achieved during its first year, and it never received any Emmys. Nevertheless, the series stands out as being a long-running show with a female lead that touched the popular culture of the day. Actress Barbara Eden is still associated with the genie she played years ago in harem pants, and the show itself is often compared to *Bewitched.* Eden has argued that Jeannie was more powerful than Samantha: "I think they could both do the same things magically. There was one big difference: Samantha was inhibited by her husband. Jeannie was never inhibited by her master, and absolutely glorified in her magic. So I think that is an empowerment and I think that she would be more powerful."[34]

The pilot episode, "The Lady in the Bottle," depicts how astronaut Tony Nelson met Jeannie on a deserted island when he had to parachute onto it during a failed mission. After saying to him in Persian, "Your wish is my command, master," she immediately seems love struck, walks over to him, and kisses him. It is evident from the beginning that she is sexually attracted to him. When he says he doesn't know how to thank her for saving him, she says, "I will teach thee, master." Although he sets her free (it would seem primarily because he doesn't know how to explain her to the folks at NASA), she hides in his pack. When Tony's fiancée brings him home, out comes Jeannie, fresh from a shower, wearing only a shirt of his. Naturally, the fiancée is upset and leaves. Jeannie refers to her as a "black-haired demon" for no other reason than she is jealous. Despite Tony's attempts to get rid of her, she is determined to stay. At the end of the episode, he goes into his bedroom. She follows as a puff of smoke, pouring herself under his door. He yells at her and the puff of smoke returns as Jeannie smiles into the camera, letting the audience know she will never give up pursuing him. This episode sets up important characteristics about Jeannie that last throughout the series: she is sexual, she is obsessed with Tony, she is jealous, and she follows only those commands that please her. Media critic Susan Douglas described Jeannie as

> the dumb, shapely, ditzy blonde with too much power, which she often used impetuously. Hyperfeminized, Jeannie was unreasonably jealous and possessive, giggled a lot, and was overly enthusiastic about whatever her master did: in fact, she often behaved and was treated like a child. Although she got her master into embarrassing situations, unlike Samantha [of *Bewitched*] she left him to explain his own way out.[35]

In this "kiddified male sex fantasy," as critic Gerard Jones called it, Tony plays hard to get despite the fact that this beautiful woman who lives in his house is willing to "please him very much" as she says in the pilot.[36] But why doesn't Tony give in? Perhaps as an astronaut during a time of intense space exploration he feels he has an image to uphold. But his dignity is lost time and again as Jeannie gets him into embarrassing situations, refusing to leave him alone. She soon gets rid of his fiancée by making a former boyfriend fall in love with her, and Jeannie ruins all of Tony's dates. If she wasn't a genie, some might consider her a stalker. Jeannie tries everything in her power to get Tony to ask her to marry him. In "The Americanization of Jeannie," she reads an article in a magazine called "The Emancipation of Modern Woman," which includes the following advice: (1) you must learn to challenge his masculine arrogance, (2) you must be independent, self-reliant, and unpredictable, and (3) you must learn to cope with him on his own ground. With instructions that sound like a mixture of both feminism and subjugation, Jeannie decides to no longer clean house nor cook, and she buys very expensive clothing. Tony is enchanted with how she looks in her new dress and takes her out to an expensive dinner where she gets jealous of a harem dancer and makes a scene. In the end, he tells her that she is everything a man could want—she's warm, considerate, and affectionate—but she needs an outlet. His solution? A pet. In another episode, "What House across the Street?" she conjures up her mom for advice on how to get Tony to marry her. Her mother suggests she say yes to Roger Healy (Tony's coworker and best friend) who'd like to marry her. When Jeannie says that is not honest, her mother replies, "Show me a woman who is honest and I will show you an old maid." In another episode, "How Do You Beat Superman?" Tony is jealous of a man to whom Jeannie is evidently engaged and is encouraged by a colonel on the base to go after her. He plans to ask her to marry him until he sees that his rival was conjured up by Jeannie.

While Tony has a best friend—fellow astronaut Roger Healy—Jeannie has no women friends. As a matter of fact, she sees other women as rivals. Her own sister attempts to steal Tony from Jeannie after they are married. Amanda Bellows, wife of the air force base psychiatrist who appears in most episodes, is Jeannie's matron of honor and yet in one episode Amanda glee-fully tries to catch Tony in a breach of ethics that could get him fired.[37] In other episodes she also is judgmental, showing little warmth toward anyone.

It is difficult to find redemption for a series where the lead female character insists on calling the lead male character "master," and even harder to fathom its audience during the growing second wave of feminism. However, Barbara Eden (Jeannie herself) has a reasonable explanation:

> It really didn't have anything to do with women's lib or subjugation of women either.... She was very independent. But she wasn't real. She was smoke and, not only that, she was smoke from three thousand years ago. And that was our comedy. She was a fish out of water.... And her "yes, master"—she was doing her job, that's all. She's a very powerful woman or entity. And so, she'd say "yes master," but if she thought it was better for him, she'd do what she wanted to do.[38]

Sidney Sheldon, creator of *I Dream of Jeannie* and writer of dozens of its episodes, claimed the series "was symbolic of the relationship between 'masterful man and his supposedly servile woman that exists in real life.... They may both claim that he's the boss, but in practice it doesn't usually work that way.' "[39] Others claim the series was simply meant to make people laugh, that it was escapism. Regardless of how it was intended, audiences could read *I Dream of Jeannie* in a number of ways.

That Girl

Hailed as the prototype series about independent career women, *That Girl* debuted on ABC in 1966 and its star, Marlo Thomas, was clearly in control from the beginning. Although she was the daughter of the successful producer and entertainer Danny Thomas, Marlo had to prove herself to become an actress on her own. The head of ABC, Edgar Scherick, was impressed with her talent and wanted to find a series for her. After reading many scripts that she considered old fashioned, Thomas suggested doing a series about a girl like her, "a young, struggling actress who yearned for independence."[40] She described the character as "a girl who had graduated as a teacher from college, which I had, who wanted to be an actress, as I did. Whose parents didn't want her to move out, as my parents didn't want me to move out. Whose father was terrified she was going to lose her virginity and who was always concerned [about] whether or not there were men in her apartment, which was what my father was like."[41] She had a hard time convincing Scherick, however, that the character should be completely independent—no husband and no steady boss. Finally, she gave him a copy of Betty Friedan's *The Feminine Mystique,* which he read. She told him that experience was happening to young women, and if he wanted to reach them, then "you need to tell this."[42] He agreed, and Sam Denoff and Bill Persky, former writers on *The Dick Van Dyke Show,* were hired as creators, writers, and executive producers. When ABC offered a five-year contract, however, they were not willing to commit to that length of time, so Marlo Thomas became the series producer to assure continuity, forming Daisy Productions as her production company.

The series begins with Ann Marie, a pretty, intelligent young woman in her early twenties, moving from her parents' home in Brewster, New York, to New York City, forty miles away. It is revealed in various episodes that Ann had been a grade-school teacher for awhile as well as a meter maid, but now she is going to pursue her dream of becoming an actress. Her mother, although on the verge of tears, is supportive of her daughter's move, but her father is quite upset.

When Ann walks into her nice apartment in Manhattan, we see a stack of her belongings already there, waiting to be unpacked and placed. Ann pulls out an ottoman with wheels and rolls around her living room, with the realistic delight of any young person in their first apartment on their own. Throughout the five-year run of the series, Ann has a number of "survival" jobs to help her get by as she pursues her acting career, including salesperson and waitress. Some of her jobs are quite embarrassing, including one where she wears a chicken costume and another where she portrays a mop. She is in a number of silly situations as she seeks stardom, including her own schemes to reach a Broadway producer (she hires men to wheel her into his office on a platform so she can audition). Professionally she has some short-lived successes, including a stint on Broadway with Ethel Merman, a number of roles in plays around the country, and a variety of commercials. She seems to be competent in her roles, except for her national television debut where she plays a dead person and opens her eyes. One of her most interesting jobs is for the Air Force as the spokesperson and poster model for recruiting women into the space program in "Fly Me to the Moon." At a time when NASA in reality had thought women to be unqualified for space flight, this episode could be considered feminist in tone. In a contrast of old roles with new, Ann is flying around the country in a jet fighter plane for personal appearances, while neglecting to finish redecorating her boyfriend's apartment.

Ann Marie may have lost her dignity occasionally in the jobs she had to take, but she never lost her style. As author Stephen Cole described her, she "was an idealized character who needed to look beautiful and glamorous on every show."[43] Although her character realistically could not have afforded the clothes she wore, Marlo Thomas decided to dress her fashionably anyway, in the miniskirts, hats, oversized earrings, fishnet stockings, white boots, and dresses of the time. It was also important to Thomas that Ann's makeup was perfect. Even in scenes where Ann is in bed, her makeup is flawless. A potentially negative message to the women who made up the bulk of the audience, such standards of beauty and fashion are not only hard to follow, but also questionable. Nevertheless, female viewers undoubtedly took pleasure in her wardrobe. Ann's looks as a whole are considered "fresh scrubbed" and wholesome. In "Call of the Wild," Ann is hired for a soap commercial because she is "every mother's child, a girl scout who stays a girl scout." This upsets her; she wants to have sex appeal and suddenly becomes insecure about it. As it turns out, the producer who told her how wholesome she looks makes a pass at her in her apartment, and in a strange sort of way, Ann is assured she can excite men. Ann finds herself in a number of compromising positions throughout the series where she has to fend off the unwelcome advances of men, usually involved in entertainment, but she is able to do so on her own, notwithstanding the occasional rescue attempts by the men in her life.

Despite the fact that Marlo Thomas wanted Ann to be independent, she agreed to her character, Ann Marie, having a steady boyfriend, actually calling her series a "relationship show" and adding that he (Donald Hollinger, played by Ted Bessell) was half of its success.[44] Cocreator Sam Denoff said they were sure she should have a significant other; they had learned from geniuses like Sheldon Leonard and Carl Reiner (of *The Dick Van Dyke Show*) "that if a main character has responsibility to someone, they're funnier. They're just funnier. Because if you just go off by yourself and do what you want, there are no consequences."[45] In the first episode of the series, the couple "meet cute" in the building where Donald works as a writer for the weekly magazine, *Newsview*.[46] Ann is working at the candy counter in the lobby where she is recruited by a producer to appear in a commercial to be filmed in the building. Donald buys gum from her, and later they meet again at a shop where they squabble over a roll-top desk. During the filming of the commercial, Donald walks into the scene after working late and thinks Ann is really being kidnapped by a couple of actors. He "rescues" her and, of course, the two have a fight. Other misunderstandings ensue over the lecherous owner of the desk they both want, but in the final scene the two end up at dinner where they share a dessert instead of fight over it.

There are predictable episodes where one or the other is jealous, but for the most part, they have a mutually respectful relationship. Donald is supportive of Ann's career and even gives up some of his own opportunities in order to stay with her (for example, in "Fly Me to the Moon" he opts to do a series of articles on Manhattan rather than on another country because it would have taken him away from her for too long). Interestingly, Ann feels Donald is challenging her femininity when he cooks and cleans her kitchen while she recovers from a sprained ankle in "A Friend in Need." Their fights are believable, but the chasteness of their relationship is not. During the time of a so-called sexual revolution, spurred by the availability of birth control pills, Donald is shown at the end of their dates, after just a few kisses, to leave her apartment.

In the beginning of the fifth season, the couple gets engaged. When Ann opens the ring box and Donald asks her to marry him, there is a moment frozen in time where we see her jump high into the air in slow motion, as if this is what she had been waiting for all her life. But by the end of the series the couple are still not married, a conscious decision on the part of

Marlo Thomas, who said, "I really felt that That Girl getting married sent a wrong message to the girls of America. They had really counted on her for a certain stand. If her story ended with a marriage they might think that it meant that that was the only way to have a happy ending."[47] As a matter of fact, the last episode of the series has Ann taking Donald to a women's liberation meeting after he had written what she felt was a condescending article on the movement.

The other significant person in Ann's life is her father, Lou Marie, who frequently stops by his daughter's apartment from forty miles away. Obsessed with her keeping her virginity (although, of course, that is never mentioned), he sometimes finds her in innocent but compromising situations and gets angry. On many occasions, Ann needs to remind both of her parents, but particularly her father, that "You did a wonderful job of raising me and helping me grow up, but now I'm up!"[48] Ann's mother, Helen Marie, is rather low key, but she is the conciliatory voice in the family and indicates every confidence that Ann can indeed make it on her own.

With the intense involvement of both her father and her boyfriend in her life, however, just how independent Ann Marie was is questionable. But there is no question about how *That Girl* affected many of its viewers. Renowned feminist Gloria Steinem said it's clear the series was influential "because young women wrote her [Marlo Thomas] with enormous gratitude. They saw possibilities for themselves, besides immediate marriage or staying home with their parents, which had not been on television before."[49] The show received between 3,000 and 5,000 letters per week, with many of them asking Marlo Thomas/Ann Marie for advice on serious problems. Thomas hired secretaries to answer all the letters, instructing them to find out how to help the ones who asked for advice on problems such as teenage pregnancy and wife abuse. At a *That Girl* seminar at the Museum of Television and Radio in 1996, Thomas claimed that it was this mail that made her an activist when she discovered that there was no place for these women to turn.[50]

Some of the episodes in this series were somewhat socially conscious, particularly in the third season after a press release announced the intention to be more realistic with episodes on topics such as voting, jury duty, hijacking, and violence. But the messages were on a personal level, such as when first-time voter Ann gets upset at her father for voting strictly by party line, rather than researching the issues himself, and he gets angry at her for not telling him in which political party she registered. Ann's pursuit of her career and her relationships with both Donald and her father, however, were the primary focus of the series throughout its five years.

Nominated for several Emmys and garnishing respectable ratings in its pairing with *Bewitched, That Girl* ended in 1971, despite ABC's wish to continue it for another three years. It was Marlo Thomas's decision to quit, saying that the series was "really about that time in a young girl's life when she's trying to figure out who she is."[51] It was time for both Ann Marie and Marlo Thomas to move on. The last year it was on was the first year for another breakthrough series about a single career woman to begin, *The Mary Tyler Moore Show.* Mary Tyler Moore is quoted as saying that "Ann Marie opened the door and Mary Richards walked through."[52] But in contrast to that girl, this girl, as we would learn, was not a virgin, had truly bonded with other women, and did not have a father spying on her.

Julia

The first television series to star an African American woman as someone other than a domestic, *Julia* debuted in 1968 on NBC. Julia Baker, played by Diahann Caroll, is the widow of an air force captain killed in Vietnam and left to raise their six-year-old son alone. She is a nurse, and the two are able to live a nice, middle-class existence in an integrated apartment building in Los Angeles. Before the series even aired, critics complained that the main character was totally out of touch with the realities of most African Americans. In a response to one of the critics, Diahann Carroll said that "because I am black that doesn't mean I have to deal with problems of all black people. That's not my sole responsibility...all TV is divorced from reality."[53] But the news was in touch with reality, and it told a very different story—of riots and poverty and abuse of civil rights. It was unfair to put such a burden of representation on one series, but the roles of blacks on TV were minimal, making the few black characters that existed very important—to members of the African American community as well as to white communities that had little or no exposure to blacks in real life. Many in the black press supported the show, including *Ebony* magazine, which wrote, "To the ghetto Negro who, despite his poverty, has vast television reception, this may not be telling it like it is. But for television it is showing it like it has never been shown before."[54]

Julia was undoubtedly a beautiful and competent nurse. In the first two episodes, she applies for a job at Astrospace Industries and immediately is subjected to sexism, not racism. In the pilot, "Mama's Man," the personnel interviewer is not upset that she is "Negro" but that she is too pretty: "When we employ nurses far less attractive than you, we find that we lose many man-hours. Malingerers, would-be Romeos, that sort of thing. In your case, you might provoke a complete work stoppage."[55] In the next episode, "The Interview," Julia calls the doctor with whom she would work, Dr. Chegley, and he asks her if she is pretty because he is tired of working with ugly nurses. When she arrives at his office, he asks her to walk around and tells her she has a very well-formed fantail. Researcher Aniko Bodroghkozy argued that the series was not as sensitive to sexism as it was to racism because at the time the white male creators of the series "did not yet have to contend with the oppositional voices of the women's movement. On the other hand, the producers were quite concerned with the highly visible civil rights and black power movements, and were well aware of the fact that representations of racial discrimination and harassment were now socially and politically unacceptable."[56]

Racial difference was acknowledged readily in different scenes, but racism was not a serious threat to Julia, a major criticism of the series. When she first speaks to Dr. Chegley on the phone, she tells him she is colored, and he asks her what color. When she replies that she is a Negro, he says, "Have you always been a Negro? Or are you just trying to be fashionable?" Her son Corey runs into at least one racist classmate at school who calls him a derogatory name. When Julia discusses the situation with her neighbor, she tells her that she was first exposed to racism at the high school prom when no one asked her to dance. Actress Diahann Carroll says she fought with producer Hal Kanter over this, "saying it was completely unrealistic that Julia hadn't experienced bigotry before then."[57] In another episode, Julia addresses prejudice in a very confrontational and more realistic manner when she is denied a security clearance at her job. When a supervisor accuses her of belonging to a suspicious organization called ANTI, she angrily tells him that it is a nonprofit group of volunteers who teach professions to underprivileged children of all races, and then she quits. Julia also gets angry in another episode when she hears an older neighbor lady, Mrs. Bennett, tell her husband that their building is turning into a ghetto, adding, "it always happens when those people move in." Mrs. Bennett had wrongly blamed Corey for coloring on a wall in the hallway. Julia explains to Corey that Mrs. Bennett is a sad lady who thinks they are different because they have dark skin. Julia tells him that "it's up to you and me and all of us to help teach her and other prejudiced people how wrong they are."[58] Mrs. Bennett's prejudice is quickly turned around when Julia saves her granddaughter's life as she is choking on a crayon, and it's revealed that her granddaughter had drawn on the hallway wall. Racism, like sexism, is approached not as systemic, but as a problem with individuals that must be solved individually.

Many critics referred to Julia as a "white Negro," the overly good, overly integrated fantasy projection of white writers acting, they felt, in a manner sensitive to decades of TV prejudice."[59] Researcher Donald Bogle pointed out that, had the series appeared at the start of the integrationist movement in the late 1950s it would have been seen as forward looking and daring, but "*Julia*'s integrationist-style heroine arrived during an era when a segment of Black America—young Black America in particular— was loudly calling for cultural/racial separatism."[60] Nevertheless, according to Bogle, Diahann Carroll could relate to her character as someone who also came from a middle-class background.

Another criticism of *Julia* was the fact that it portrayed a single mother, indicating a stereotypical matriarchy in the black family where the man is absent. But Julia does have strong, professional, handsome black boyfriends throughout the series in chaste and respectful relationships. For the first two years, Julia goes out primarily with Paul Cameron, played by Paul Winfield. In the last year of the series, writer Donald Bogle says the scenes Diahann Carroll had with former football star Fred Williamson who played her boyfriend, Steve Bruce, "still sparkle and resonate. Here are two gilded narcissists, each confident of her/his appeal, each recognizing the other's sexy powers, but neither willing to concede in defeat in the gender games that men and women play."[61] Julia's best friend and neighbor is Marie Waggedorn, mother to Corey's white friend. The two women help each other with child care as well as confide in each other. Marie is there for Julia when she nervously prepares for a date and listens to her frustrations about work. At Astrospace Industries, Julia works with another nurse, Hannah Yarby. Members of her family occasionally appear, including her mother and a female cousin.

Researcher J. Fred MacDonald said that to some, *Julia* "was a sellout, now that Richard M. Nixon was president, to assuage white consciences and make the curtailment of social programs and the repression of riotous ghetto dwellers palatable to white society."[62] In a study of about 150 letters kept by producer Hal Kanter, Aniko Bodroghkozy found "remarkably conflicted, diverse, and contradictory responses among audience members."[63] The majority of the letters were from whites, who would self-consciously identify their race as they praised the show, many stating that they liked how it depicted African Americans as "just people." Some white viewers were not happy with the show simply because it starred a black person and depicted integration, while some self-identified housewives found Marie Waggedorn's depiction as a housewife insulting, finding her stupid in comparison to Julia. A crucial distinction Bodroghkozy found between black and white viewer letters was that many "black viewers displayed a participatory quality in their engagement with the program," some asking if they could write episodes or play parts on the show.[64] The realness of *Julia* and, in particular, the depiction of the black family was a concern, with many black women critical of the lack of a strong male head of the family. As Bodroghkozy pointed out, the history of black women, who often had to work in menial jobs outside the home, is in stark contrast to white women:

> Unlike middle-class white women, who may have seen work outside the home as potentially liberating, the history of work for black women had no such emancipatory connotations. The viewer who wanted Julia taken out of the white doctor's office was thus making sense of Julia's labor from within this larger history of black women's work. That Julia resorted to leaving Corey locked up alone in their apartment while she went off to her job interview may have had deeper meanings for black women who historically had been forced to leave their children to fend for themselves while they cared for the children of either white owners or white employers.[65]

Regardless of the criticism of *Julia,* the series was number seven in the Nielsen ratings its first year and was nominated for an Emmy as Outstanding Comedy Series. By the third year, however, the series disappeared from the top 30 programs, and Diahann Carroll said the daily grind of shooting the series had exhausted her. She also said she was worn to a frazzle because of the unending criticism and the battles with producer Hal Kanter.[66] She refused to renew her contract for a fourth season.

WOMEN IN TELEVISION SITCOMS OF THE 1960s

While the 1960s ended with *That Girl* as the prototype single career woman, the decade began with a more traditional one. *Hazel* (NBC, 1961–1965; CBS, 1965–1966) starred veteran stage and screen actress Shirley Booth as a maid/housekeeper. Like Beulah before her, Hazel is always helping the family out of trouble, but her personality is quite different from that of the African American maid of the early 1950s. In this comedy, Hazel is in charge, oftentimes doing more bossing than her boss.

A handful of shows in the 1960s focused on teenage girls. For example, *The Patty Duke Show* (ABC, 1963–1966) is about a modern teenager in Brooklyn Heights, New York, whose look-alike cousin comes to live with her family. Patty Lane is trendy, popular, and more interested in boys than her studies. Her cousin Cathy, also played by Patty Duke, is well-traveled and worldly wise, a scholar with a British accent, and reserved. Although the girls are close, there are occasional jealousies and rivalries. *Gidget* (ABC, 1965–1966), based on the movie of the same name, also stars a boy-crazy girl, fifteen-year-old Gidget Lawrence. Gidget's best friend is Larue, a girl somewhat like Cathy Lane, who has other interests besides boys and fashion. In a particularly interesting episode, "My Ever Faithful Friend," Gidget defends Larue against a sexy high school girl who invites Gidget to a party but makes snide remarks about Larue and her lack of fashion and dating. Larue prefers to spend time with a horse rather than at a party, and Gidget gets concerned that her friend will wind up alone. She decides to do a "makeover" of Larue, and Larue reluctantly agrees. While Gidget is out purchasing cosmetics for Larue, her father, a widowed English professor, comes home to find Larue waiting. He listens sympathetically as Larue tells him that she really doesn't care what others think of her, but she does care about the concern for her of people she loves. She is willing to go through the makeover for them, although she'd rather be spending time with her horse. Gidget eventually understands Larue's point of view, and tells her "feel beautiful and you are beautiful." Each episode is framed by Gidget speaking to the audience, either through a diary-like voiceover or looking directly at the camera. In this episode, she explains at the end, "It just shows you, doesn't it, as long as a girl's got something to love, all's right with the world." As Moya Luckett pointed out in her study of "teen television" in the 1960s, dealing with the sexuality of teenage girls was a problem then, so the subject was negotiated in series "by placing their heroines in innocent relationships with suitable boys whom they would probably marry at a much later date; by establishing their very close relationships with their families; and finally, and most importantly, by privileging female friendship above heterosexual relationships."[67]

The Brady Bunch (ABC, 1969–1974) is about the combined household that results when a widow with three daughters and a widower with three sons marry. Some of the episodes deal with this reconstituted family adjusting to each other, but many involve the typical middle-class problems of the teens and preteens in the family, including dating and wanting to be popular. Marcia, the eldest daughter, is cheerleader pretty and talented, but she still has to deal with the trauma of wearing braces in one episode and having a swollen nose in another. Jan is Marcia's slightly younger sister, who sometimes feels she is in Marcia's shadow. Cindy is the sister in grade school. Mrs. Brady is the pretty, stay-at-home mom who get help from the housekeeper, Alice, an easy-going woman with good advice who is in love with the butcher. Some episodes directly address gender roles, including "The Liberation of Marcia Brady," where a television reporter outside of her junior high school asks Marcia if she thinks girls are the equal of boys in every respect. She says yes, but her brothers tease her with sexist remarks after they see the newscast. To prove a point to her brothers, Marcia joins the previously all-male Frontier Scouts and successfully joins them in their campout activities. In the requisite sex-role reversal episode, parents Mike and Carol switch roles after a debate on who has it the hardest. After Mike spends time cooking with the girls and Carol plays baseball with the boys, the two are exhausted and decide, as did Lucy and Ricky Ricardo in the 1950s, that they are most suited for their gender-specific roles. With its wholesomeness and hip language of the day, *The Brady Bunch* remains a cult hit with baby boomers and their children.

Lucille Ball returned to sitcom television with various incarnations of her own series, this time without a husband. When *The Lucy Show* debuted on CBS in 1962, she played a widow with two children, living with her divorced friend, played by Vivian Vance, and her son. Lucy eventually works in a bank part-time, getting into her usual slapstick problems, with Gale Gordon playing her cranky boss. In 1968, her series was retitled *Here's Lucy*. Again, she is a widow with two children. Vivian Vance was gone, but Gale Gordon continued to play the blustery foil, in the guise of her brother-in-law. Ricky may not have been around to chastise her, but another man is. Singer and film star Doris Day also plays a widow with two children in *The Doris Day Show* (1968–1973) and, like Lucy, the formula for her show kept changing. In the beginning of the series, Doris Martin has moved from a big city with her children back to the family ranch and lives with her father. In the second season, she starts to commute to San Francisco to work on a magazine, and by the third season, she and her boys move to the city. By the fourth season, Doris has completed her transition to single career woman in touch with the times—she still works at the magazine, but the children and entire previous cast are gone.

Besides Gidget's dad, other widowers and bachelor fathers were popular in the 1960s. *My Three Sons* (ABC, 1960–1965; CBS, 1967–1972) is the story of Steve Douglas, played by the popular Disney star Fred Mac-Murray, a consulting aviation engineer, who was widowed and has to raise his three sons. Steve fends off many attractive women in the series, but he eventually marries a widow with a young daughter. All three sons are married by the end of the series as well, including the youngest at seventeen years old, indicating that the matrimonial state is best. The title of *The Courtship of Eddie's Father* (ABC, 1969–1972) made the goal of this series clear. To help raise his son, Tom Corbett has the help of his Japanese housekeeper, Mrs. Livingston, as young Eddie seeks a series of prospective brides for his father. A mother may have been lacking in the household, but the absence is felt.

By far the "bachelor father" series with the richest text is *The Andy Griffith Show* (CBS, 1960–1968). Andy Taylor is the competent and caring sheriff of small-town Mayberry, North Carolina, whose Aunt Bee moves in with him to help care for his young son. This series is also a male-bonding show, with Andy's close friendship with his cousin and deputy, the incompetent Barney Fife, a highlight. Both men date on a regular basis, although Andy Griffith has said they had a hard time writing for women on the series and his own difficulties with women made it more difficult.[68] Nevertheless, many episodes indicate that Andy is not threatened by strong women. The women he tends to date are professionals. For example, the first steady girlfriend we see him with is Ellie Walker (Elinor Donahue, who played the elder daughter on *Father Knows Best*), a pharmacist who has moved to Mayberry to take over the drugstore while her uncle is ill. When Ellie runs against a man for city council, the town becomes divided by gender lines. Andy finally publicly supports her and she wins. Perhaps the most interesting episode, however, is "The Perfect Female," in which Andy is forced to recognize his erroneous stereotype of a woman. When Thelma Lou (Barney's girlfriend) introduces Andy to her cousin Karen, Andy asks her out and treats her like he would his other dates, assuming she is a "traditional" female and that she would enjoy watching him skeet-shoot as he practices for an upcoming contest. He is so wrapped up in himself that he doesn't question her about her interests or desires. Much to everyone's surprise but Thelma's, Karen enters the skeet-shooting contest and beats them all, including the projected winner, Andy. While the other men are upset, Andy apologizes to Karen and then asks her out.

With all the violence and social unrest of the 1960s, the American public seemed to crave escape in several sitcoms—through fantasy as well as bizarre takes on history. Both *The Munsters* (CBS, 1964–1966) and *The Addams Family* (ABC, 1964–1966) are nuclear families of monsters and eccentrics. Two sitcom families originated as prime-time cartoons in the 1960s, *The Flintstones* (ABC, 1960–1966), a takeoff of *The Honeymooners* set in the stone age, and *The Jetsons* (ABC, 1962–1963), a family of the future with a wife and daughter that seem to be stuck in the 1950s with their traditional roles. The premise of *The Flying Nun* (ABC, 1967–1970) is that young Sister Bertrille (played by former Gidget Sally Field) is so light that whenever the wind catches her head dress just right, she can fly.

Gilligan's Island (CBS, 1964–1967) is peopled with character types who are stranded together on an uncharted island after a boat tour. Frequently visited by a number of people who never manage to rescue them and having a seemingly unlimited supply of clothes and jewelry, three of the seven characters are women. Ginger is the Marilyn Monroe–type movie actress, Mary Anne is the fresh-scrubbed young woman with common sense, and Mrs. Howell is the snobby wife of a millionaire.

Paul Henning's wild success with *The Beverly Hillbillies* continued with two other creations, *Petticoat Junction* (CBS, 1963–1967) and *Green Acres* (CBS, 1965–1971). In the former, Kate Bradley is a widow with three beautiful teenage daughters. She owns the Shady Rest Hotel in Hooterville, somewhere in rural America, and the girls' lazy uncle Joe helps her manage it. Billie Jo is the eldest daughter and is sometimes interested in show business. Bobby Jo is the middle child and is concerned about acceptance. Betty Jo is initially a tomboy, but, like her sisters, becomes very interested in boys. At one point, all three girls vie for the affections of a handsome pilot who crashed near the hotel. While he initially dates Billy Jo, Steve eventually marries Bobby Jo and the two have a daughter. The plots were fairly simple, as were the characters, with occasional visits from those in the other two Henning series. Of the three, *Green Acres* (CBS, 1965–1971) is the most bizarre, with occasional surreal plot lines. In another fish-out-of-water premise, Oliver Wendell Douglas quits his job as a New York City attorney and moves onto a rundown farm with his wife, Lisa. She is an aristocratic, beautiful Hungarian immigrant who enjoys the luxury of Manhattan penthouse living and does not want to move. Nevertheless, she follows her husband to their new land and actually adapts in her own way. She is a terrible cook, yet she insists on making her specialty hotcakes in a variety of configurations. She is often seen in negligees and expensive jewelry working around the house, and she becomes a friend to all the animals she encounters, even naming the chickens. This series' token nod to feminism in "The Liberation Movement" finds Lisa's consciousness raised and she takes over the farm, leaving Oliver with the housework. In another episode, she runs against her husband for mayor. Perhaps the farm living to which Lisa objected became a venue for her to discover herself and to grow. Or perhaps she was doing the best she could in a situation forced upon her. Interestingly enough, there is an androgynous character in this series, Ralph Monroe, the sister half of two siblings who does carpentry work for the Douglasses. Ralph "looked like a man, dressed masculine...and ended up being a pretty damned good cook."[69]

From the idyllic traditional family of *The Dick Van Dyke Show* and a series of fantastic women and innocent teenagers, to career women still attached to their fathers, to a proliferation of bachelor-father sitcoms, women in 1960s sitcoms were a mixed group with conflicting messages. While sitcoms of the 1960s indicated little of what was going on in reality, that situation was about to change.

NOTES

1. Toni Carabillo, "'A Passion for the Possible,' " in *Feminist Chronicles 1953–1993,* by Toni Carabillo, Judith Meuli, and June Bundy Csida (Los Angeles: Women's Graphics, 1993), 4.

2. It has been argued that "sex" was amended to the Civil Rights Act of 1964 as a strategy by some southern congressmen to defeat the entire bill. See Toni Carabillo, "A Passion for the Possible," 8–11. Carabillo describes the hostile environment in which it passed in Congress, including Representative Martha Griffith's comment at the hearings that "the laughter of the men at the introduction of the amendment only underscored women's second class citizenship," 10.

3. Toni Carabillo, Judith Meuli, and June Bundy Csida, *Feminist Chronicles 1953–1993* (Los Angeles: Women's Graphics, 1993), 50.

4. Carabillo, Meuli, and Csida, 50, 51.

5. Carabillo, Meuli, and Csida, 42.

6. Tim Brooks and Earle Marsh, *The Complete Directory to Prime Time Network and Cable TV Shows 1946-Present,* 7th ed. (New York: Ballantine, 1999), 875.

7. Brooks and Marsh, 937.

8. Vince Waldron, *The Official Dick Van Dyke Show Book* (New York: Hyperion, 1994), 125. Director John Rich explained that an "ear" is "somebody to whom you turn at night and say, 'This is what happened at the office today, and this is what my problem is.' " When Mary Tyler Moore demonstrated great comedic talent in the early episode "My Blonde-Haired Brunette," Rich says it forced the producers to rethink her character.

9. Ginny Weissman and Coyne Steven Sanders, *The Dick Van Dyke Show: The Anatomy of a Classic* (New York: St. Martin's Press, 1983), 45.

10. Gerard Jones, *Honey, I'm Home! Sitcoms: Selling the American Dream* (New York: St. Martin's Press, 1992), 145.

11. Waldron, 95.

12. Waldron, 95.

13. Waldron, 233.

14. Waldron, 148.

15. Waldron, 153.

16. Waldron, 96.

17. David Marc, *Comic Visions: Television Comedy & American Culture,* 2nd ed. (Malden, MA: Blackwell, 1997), 95.

18. Stephen Cox, *The Beverly Hillbillies* (New York: HarperCollins, 1993), 51.

19. Marc, 53.

20. Cox, 3.

21. Cox, 154.

22. Jones, 166

23. Marc, 110.

24. Herbie J. Pilato, *The Bewitched Book* (New York: Dell, 1992), 2.

25. Marc, 111.

26. Pilato, 31.

27. Jones, 179.

28. Pilato, 109.

29. Pilato, 32.

30. Pilato, 11. Barbara Avedon, who worked with the students on this episode, is a feminist and went on to help develop the drama loved by many feminists in the 1980s, *Cagney & Lacey.*

31. Susan J. Douglas, *Where the Girls Are* (New York: Times Books, 1994, 1995), 131.

32. Pilato, 16.

33. Douglas, 132.

34. Interview clip on Nick at Nite, 1996, during Women of Television week.

35. Douglas, 134–35.

36. Jones, 180.

37. In the last episode of the series, "My Master, the Chili King," Jeannie works with Tony's distant cousin to distribute chili with Tony's name and picture on it. Unbeknownst to Jeannie, astronauts are not allowed to endorse products and he could lose his job over this. Amanda grabs a can of the chili and says it is evidence. As Tony's nemesis in many early episodes, her husband, psychiatrist Dr. Bellows, seems quite sympathetic to Tony in comparison.

38. Barbara Eden interview segment from Nick at Nite, 1996, during the Women of Television marathon.

39. Steve Cox with Howard Frank, *Dreaming of Jeannie: TV's Prime Time in a Bottle* (New York: St. Martin's Press, 2000), 19. Sidney Sheldon worked on many other television shows and was a prolific novelist, with such best-sellers as *Rage of Angels* and *The Other Side of Midnight.* In 1966, he received an Emmy nomination for his writing on *I Dream of Jeannie.*

40. Stephen Cole, *That Book about That Girl* (Los Angeles: Renaissance, 1999), 34.

41. Cole, 34.

42. Cole, 42.

43. Cole, 57.

44. Cole, 22.

45. Cole, 46.

46. To "meet cute" is the entertainment industry phrase for a usually sweet, touching, or funny first meeting between a man and a woman who become a couple.

47. Cole, 142.

48. Cole, 162.

49. Cole, 129.

50. Cole, 129.

51. Cole, 136.

52. Cole, 137.

53. Donald Bogle, *Prime Time Blues: African Americans on Network Television* (New York: Farrar, Straus and Giroux, 2001), 142.

54. Bogle, 145.

55. Aniko Bodroghkozy, "'Is This What You Mean by Color TV?' Race, Gender, and Contested Meanings in NBC's *Julia,*" *Private Screenings: Television and the Female Consumer,* ed. Lynn Spigel and Denise Mann (Minneapolis, MN: University of Minnesota Press 1992), 146–47.

56. Bodroghkozy, 147.

57. Bogle, 147.

58. Bogle, 148.

59. J. Fred MacDonald, *Blacks and White TV: African Americans in Television Since 1948,* 2nd ed. (Chicago: Nelson-Hall, 1992), 125.

60. Bogle, 150.

61. Bogle, 150.

62. MacDonald, 126.

63. Bodroghkozy, 148.

64. Bodroghkozy, 157.

65. Bodroghkozy, 161–62.

66. Bogle, 151

67. Moya Luckett, "Girl Watchers: Patty Duke and Teen TV," *The Revolution Wasn't Televised: Sixties Television and Social Conflict,* ed. Lynn Spigel & Michael Curtin (New York: Routledge, 1997), 102.

68. Richard Kelly, *The Andy Griffith Show,* rev. ed. (Winston-Salem, NC: Blair, 1989), 54–55.

69. Stephen Cox, *The Hooterville Handbook: A Viewer's Guide to Green Acres* (New York: St. Martin's Press, 1993), 62.

Chapter 4

1970s: SPUNKY GIRLS AND ANGRY WOMEN

The 1970s began much like the 1960s ended. Social unrest was rampant, with African Americans and women of all races continuing their fight for equality. Antiwar protests escalated, along with the fighting in Southeast Asia, sometimes with devastating results. People became even more disillusioned with government as the Watergate scandal was exposed and impeachment proceedings began. By the end of the decade, hippies were replaced with the "me" generation, and the entire nation was held hostage.

Television comedy in the late 1970s was more like sitcoms in the late 1960s. Any turbulence on the news rarely made it into story lines. In the early 1970s, however, a golden age of comedy began, introducing new lifestyles and social issues as never before in several prime-time series that are still critically acclaimed today. It was also a golden age for the women's movement.

CULTURAL/HISTORICAL CONTEXT

The women's movement continued to benefit from the civil rights movement. In January 1971, the Supreme Court upheld the equal hiring provisions of the 1964 Civil Rights Act by ruling that businesses could not deny employment to women with preschool children unless they applied the same hiring criterion to men. This marked the high court's first decision on sex discrimination in hiring practices.[1] The decade was also full of other firsts. In sports, Billie Jean King was the first woman athlete to win more than $100,000 a year. In a well-publicized "battle of the sexes," King later would beat Bobby Riggs three straight sets in a nationally televised tennis match. Title IX was passed in 1972, which prohibited sex discrimination in educational institutions that received federal funds; among other things, this paved the way for equal opportunities in women's sports. The first athletic scholarship given to a woman was awarded in 1973 by the University of Miami. In 1974, Little League baseball opened its teams to girls. There were also many firsts in the workforce, politics, and religion. For example, the 1970s saw the first woman FBI agent, Marine Corps general, governor, mayor of Chicago, head of the Republican National Committee, university president, network television news anchor, rabbi, and Episcopal priest.

Arguably the two most significant events in the 1970s for the women's movement were the passage of the Equal Rights Amendment (ERA) by Congress in March 1972 and the Supreme Court decision in January 1973 to strike down state laws restricting abortions during the first six months of pregnancy (*Roe* v. *Wade*). As Susan Faludi has documented, however, perceptions that women are making great strides produces backlashes.[2] In 1970, the year a liberal abortion law went into effect in Hawaii, the Catholic Church established the National Right to Life Committee, an antiabortion organization. Antifeminists gathered forces to defeat the Twenty-Seventh Amendment; historian Flora Davis said that if they had not organized, the ERA would have passed in 1973 or 1974.[3] The ERA simply stated that "Equality of Rights under the law shall not be denied or abridged by the United States or by any State on account of sex," yet mandated equality for women evidently struck terror in the hearts of many.[4]

The National Organization for Women increased its enrollments during the 1970s as thousands of women pressed to get the ERA passed. While some opponents had feared passage of the Equal Rights Amendment would require unisex bathrooms and the drafting of women into the armed forces, others felt it was unnecessary because of other laws already in place. Besides the Civil Rights Act of 1964, which prohibited sex discrimination on the job, many other laws and court decisions in the 1970s made it harder to discriminate on the basis of gender. For example, the Supreme Court in 1973 ruled that women in the armed forces were entitled to the same benefits for their spouses as those accorded to servicemen. That same year, AT&T agreed to pay $15 million to women and minority employees who had been treated unfairly and to set up job-training programs and establish hiring quotas. In 1975, Congress passed a bill authorizing admission of women to the military academies of the three major services.

Perhaps the most intense memories for most people in the early 1970s revolve around the Vietnam War, protests, and peace talks. Four months into the decade, the Strategic Arms Limitation Talks (SALT) between the United States and the U.S.S.R. resumed in Vienna, not long before U.S. and South Vietnamese troops invaded Cambodia. On May 4, 1970, four students at Kent State University were killed when the National Guard fired at antiwar protestors. Eleven days later, two students were killed at Jackson State College in Mississippi when city and state police opened fire on demonstrators. While thousands of men under twenty-one years of age had been fighting in Vietnam, the voting age was not lowered to eighteen until 1971. Although President Nixon continued to withdraw troops from Vietnam, major protests continued all over the country while bombing overseas escalated and the death toll rose. Finally, in early 1973, the United States, North and South Vietnam, and the Viet Cong signed a peace agreement in Paris. In 1975, when the last U.S. citizens were airlifted out of Saigon as the Viet Cong took over the city, the final death toll was more than 58,000 Americans. Concern over U.S. citizens in foreign lands continued in another part of the world during the latter half of the 1970s. Perhaps the most devastating event occurred when the U.S. embassy in Teheran was seized by Iranian revolutionaries in 1979 and Americans were taken hostage; most were held for more than a year.

Inflation and unemployment were also on people's minds in the 1970s, and for the first time in the twentieth century, imports exceeded exports in 1971.[5] For awhile, gas shortages and rumors of other shortages abounded. Besides the Vietnam War, the Watergate scandal contributed greatly to the discontent and loss of faith in national government. First several staff members, then Vice President Spiro Agnew (on the basis of a charge of income tax evasion), and finally President Nixon resigned from office over the two years after the break-in at the Democratic National headquarters in Washington, D.C., in 1972. Gerald Ford took over as president (earlier he had replaced Agnew as vice president), and Betty Ford became the outspoken First Lady. In 1975, she created an uproar when she said during a TV interview that she suspected all four of her children had tried marijuana, that she would not be surprised if her eighteen-year-old daughter was having an affair, and that the Supreme Court had made a great decision in legalizing abortion.[6] Later, of course, she would establish the Betty Ford Clinic to help those like herself who suffered from alcoholism and other addictions. The 1970s ended with Democrat Jimmy Carter as president and a more soft-spoken First Lady.

In popular culture, talk of a sexual revolution abounded as more women used birth control pills and people read *Everything You Always Wanted to Know about Sex but Were Afraid to Ask* by Dr. David Reuben. Joyce Carol

Oates won the National Book Award for her novel *Them* about a troubled family, and Norman Mailer's *Marilyn* was a fictionalized version of Marilyn Monroe's life that made people wonder if she was murdered because of political liaisons. Other books of note included Peter Benchley's *Jaws, Looking for Mr. Goodbar* by Judith Rossner, *Jonathan Livingston Seagull* by Richard Bach, *All the President's Men* by Carl Bernstein and Robert Woodward, *Roots* by Alex Haley, *The Thorn Birds* by Colleen McCullough, and *Sophie's Choice* by William Styron, all of which made their way to film or television. The feminist *Ms* magazine made its debut in 1972, while other women's magazines were targets of protests for stereotyping women in editorial content and their unfair treatment of female employees.

Among songs of love and longing, Helen Reddy's anthem about the women's movement, "I am Woman," hit the top of the Billboard charts in December 1972.[7] Singer/songwriter Carol King had a big hit with her *Tapestry* album, and Simon and Garfunkel brought comfort to troubled times with their *Bridge over Troubled Water*. The Beatles broke up in 1970, but individually they still did well with hits such as George Harrison's "My Sweet Lord," John Lennon's "Instant Karma," and Paul McCartney's "Maybe I'm Amazed." Mellow rock abounded with the sounds of Elton John, the Eagles, James Taylor, and Fleetwood Mac, while hard rock continued with the Who, Led Zeppelin, and Bruce Springsteen. Joni Mitchell, Carly Simon, Linda Ronstadt, and Diana Ross, now separated from the Supremes, made several popular records. Janis Joplin's "Me and Bobby Magee" became a big hit after her death from drugs and booze months earlier.[8] Many sang songs of social concern, including Marvin Gaye's "Mercy, Mercy Me" and Crosby, Stills, Nash and Young's "Ohio." In the middle of the decade disco was born, along with dance clubs, and people danced to Van McCoy's "The Hustle." Donna Summer was the disco queen with such songs as her breathy "Love to Love You, Baby" and "Bad Girls." The Bee Gees, in a major change from their 1960s style, became disco kings with "Night Fever" and "How Deep Is Your Love?" featured in the film *Saturday Night Fever*.

For people who couldn't attend the Woodstock rock festival in 1969, a documentary film about it debuted in the spring of 1970. *Saturday Night Fever* in 1977 contributed to disco fever and accompanying fashions of gold chains for men and swirling dresses for women. The 1970s also hosted many disaster films, such as *Jaws* and *The Towering Inferno*. Clint Eastwood had big hits with *Dirty Harry* and *Play Misty for Me* (about a woman who becomes obsessed with his disc jockey character). Both *Love Story* (with Ryan O'Neill and Ali McGraw) and *The Way We Were* (with

Barbra Streisand and Robert Redford) made audiences weep with their sad romances. The *Godfather* trilogy, still hailed by some as the best pictures of all time, debuted in 1972. *Rocky* was a feel-good movie in 1976 that showed how an underdog can become a winner. The most popular movie of the 1970s, however, was 1977's *Star Wars,* directed by George Lucas. Interestingly enough, an earlier film by Lucas, *American Graffiti,* in 1973, arguably started nostalgia for life in the 1950s. The roles of women in movies were quite a mix. For example, Princess Leia in *Star Wars* wore a revealing harem-like outfit, but used a weapon to protect herself. In films such as *Private Benjamin, Diary of a Mad Housewife,* and *A Woman under the Influence,* marriage was depicted as stifling for women. In *An Unmarried Woman* and *Alice Doesn't Live Here Anymore,* the female protagonists found themselves suddenly on their own (divorced and widowed, respectively) and discovered the inner resources they needed to succeed. In *Looking for Mr. Goodbar,* Diane Keaton played a schoolteacher who prowled the bars at night for sexual partners. Based loosely on a true story, it could be interpreted as either a cautionary tale for the sake of safety or a morality play that punished the sexually promiscuous protagonist. *Taxi Driver* introduced a very young Jodie Foster as a teenage prostitute that "You talkin' to me?" Travis Brickle (Robert DeNiro) tries to save. Some movies were like celebrations of strong women fighting for various causes, including *Julia, Norma Rae,* and *9 to 5.*

Other trends in the 1970s included hot pants (short-shorts), platform shoes, polyester suits, mood rings, skateboarding, and streaking. Self-help seminars, such as EST, and transcendental meditation became popular as the "me" generation looked inward.[9] While the use of illegal drugs, such as marijuana, continued from the 1960s, valium and alcohol became the leading causes of drug-related ailments, providing legal escapes from a tense world.[10] Of all the avenues of popular culture, television was the medium with which people spent most of their leisure time, and comedy was the most popular genre. Unlike other decades, however, the women in television sitcoms would begin to reflect the changing roles and concerns of real women.

THE TELEVISION INDUSTRY

Home Box Office (HBO) began its national coverage (via satellite) during the mid-1970s, convincing people to pay extra for this cable channel with its popular theatrical releases and original programming. Videocassette recorders, both Betamax and VHS, were introduced, with the VHS format eventually becoming the standard in most households for both recording television programs and viewing rented movies. ABC, NBC, and CBS still dominated what most people were watching on television, however.

While not in prime time, two significant series began in the 1970s. In daytime, Agnes Nixon's *All My Children* began in 1970 and introduced significant issues in its stories that were particularly important to women, including abortion and breast cancer. In late night, *Saturday Night Live* debuted in 1975, pushing the boundaries of social and political satire and introducing a cast that would also shine in other venues, including Gilda Radner, Jane Curtin, Chevy Chase, and Dan Aykroyd. In prime time, variety shows continued to be popular in the 1970s. Carol Burnett plus a host of singers, such as Sonny and Cher, had their own shows in the early part of the decade. While *Rowan & Martin's Laugh-In* continued to "sock it to us" at number one in the ratings at the end of the 1969–1970 season, two westerns from the 1950s, *Gunsmoke* and *Bonanza,* took the next two slots. Prime time during the 1970s also included the medical and detective genres. *Marcus Welby* made enough house calls to be the most popular program of the 1970–1971 season. Detectives in a variety of shapes and sizes were also popular, including those on *Cannon, Kojak, Baretta,* and *Barnaby Jones.* For the first time, women also got involved in the action, on *Police Woman* and *Charlie's Angels.* The latter show received mixed reviews from some who found the strength of the women exhilarating, but the emphasis on their looks and their orders from an unseen male boss annoying. Farrah Fawcett became a breakout star as women copied her hairstyle and men displayed her bathing suit poster. Nostalgia and traditional families were also popular, most notably on *The Waltons* and *Little House on the Prairie.* No matter what their race, many people began searching for their ancestry after the amazing success of the ABC miniseries, *Roots,* the multigenerational story of an African American family's rise from slavery. CBS's still popular news magazine, *60 Minutes,* broke through as a top-10 series in 1977, but audiences clearly preferred to watch comedy more than any other genre. A few sitcoms that had debuted in the 1960s continued to do well, including *Here's Lucy* and *Mayberry R.F.D.* However, a significant change was gonna come, and it would happen on CBS, willing to drop its popular older sitcoms for series that would attract a youthful audience more appealing to advertisers.

SIGNIFICANT COMEDY SERIES

Three CBS comedies that debuted in the early 1970s set the standard for quality series in the future. *The Mary Tyler Moore Show* was produced by

MTM Enterprises Inc., an independent production company, and first aired in September 1970. Grant Tinker was the head of MTM and built a reputation for protecting his creative staff from network interference. MTM became known specifically for its quality television series, including both comedy *(The Mary Tyler Moore Show, Rhoda,* and *WKRP in Cincinnati)* and drama *(Lou Grant* and *Hill Street Blues).*[11] *All in the Family,* produced by Norman Lear, debuted in January 1971 as a midseason replacement. Lear became famous for this and other "angry" comedies, such as its spin-offs, *Maude* and *The Jeffersons,* where characters always seemed to be irritated and insult humor was the norm.[12] Unlike the MTM comedies, which approached social problems almost casually as they touched the lives of characters, the Lear shows took social issues head-on, with plenty of loud arguments among family members. The third of the golden trilogy is *M*A*S*H,* which made its debut in 1972 after the success of the movie of the same name. Although set in the Korean War, this show's antiwar message was clearly aimed at U.S. involvement in Vietnam.

Besides introducing topical comedy, Norman Lear is also given credit for engineering "the renaissance of black situation comedy almost single-handedly" with *The Jeffersons, Good Times,* and *Sanford & Son.*[13] While MTM could not introduce a divorced woman on CBS in 1970, Lear did it in 1972 with *Maude,* married to her fourth husband after divorcing three, and in 1975 with *One Day at a Time.* In sharp contrast to Lear's style of testing boundaries of both the dominant culture and television, producer Garry Marshall created two very popular comedies in the mid-1970s, *Happy Days* and *Laverne & Shirley.* Both were set in the 1950s so he could remove the anxiety about sex and drugs from his shows about family values.[14]

The 1970s stand out in television history because of the number of comedies featuring women in primary roles. Certainly the consciousness of the television industry had been raised, not necessarily because of the women's movement, but because of the high ratings that several of these series garnered. Academic critic Ella Taylor said that out of a conjuncture of social and industrial changes emerged a "prime-time feminism."[15] The networks were suddenly interested in appealing to specific demographics rather than broadly based mass audiences. Taylor said the attention of advertisers and programmers on urban women between the ages of eighteen and thirty-five as a top spending group "served to legitimize 'women's issues' as a 'relevant' topic in television series."[16] This was true for many comedies in the early 1970s, but comedies later in the decade became more escapist. Based on popularity and their groundbreaking contributions with female characters or story lines, the following are of particular significance: *The Mary Tyler Moore Show, All in the Family, Maude, The Jeffersons, One Day at a Time,* and *Laverne & Shirley.*

The Mary Tyler Moore Show

The Mary Tyler Moore Show (CBS, 1970–1977) is credited by many for changing the image of single, working women in television comedy. To some, a new genre had been born. "Character comedy" and "warmedy" are two of the names used to describe the emphasis in this show on characters and relationships rather than situations. The humor is gentle and so is its main character, Mary Richards. While she speaks up for her rights at the office, a television newsroom, she is also often hesitant and insecure in her demands. Making her debut on CBS in 1970, Mary Richards found herself in the middle of a changing world, and, like many of us, she was feeling her way through it on a personal, rather than social, level.

The evolution of the Mary Richards character before the show was produced is indicative of how the images we see in television shows are influenced by personal prejudices and network guesses of what audiences will accept. In early 1970, Grant Tinker, then the president of the MTM production company, approached television writers James L. Brooks and Allan Burns about writing a new show for his wife, Mary Tyler Moore. Tinker said they did not want to put Moore in a domestic situation because she had already done that, but to be thirty and single seemed to need some explanation.[17] CBS refused to allow her character to be divorced because divorce was one of the things they claimed people did not want to see. One CBS executive was even concerned that people would think she had left Dick Van Dyke, who played her husband on his show.[18] It was finally decided to explain Mary's singleness by having her state in the first episode that she had just broken off a four-year relationship. Later there would be pressure from CBS programming executive Fred Silverman to get this "loser woman" married.[19] Fortunately, the producers were protected from such pressure by other CBS executives and Grant Tinker.

The setting for *The Mary Tyler Moore Show* was divided between the WJM newsroom where Mary worked and her home, at first a small flat in a house and later a one-bedroom high rise apartment. It was the first of many popular "workplace" comedies in the 1970s, where families at home were replaced by families at work. Mary could be seen as daughter to Lou Grant and sister to Murray and Ted. In "Party Is Such Sweet Sorrow" during the first season, she even turns down a better job to stay with her workplace family. In the last episode of the series, during their tearful good-byes, she calls her coworkers her family as they have a farewell group hug.

From the first episode where Mary applies for a secretarial job in the WJM television newsroom, it is evident that she is aware of her rights as a job applicant; she lets news producer Lou Grant know when he is asking inappropriate questions. His response is that she has spunk, but he hates spunk. Nevertheless, he offers her a job as associate producer of the news. In her stammering and gentle way, Mary had spoken up for her rights and been successful. Later in the series, Mary confronts Lou about her lower wages compared to the man who used to do her job. His first defense is that the man was married and had a family to support. Mary points out the unfairness and ridiculousness of basing pay on number of independents. Lou does not give her the raise she deserves because it is fair, however; he gives her the money later after she tells Ted to shut up while she is doing an editorial.[20] While Lou Grant's curmudgeonly acceptance of her could be misleading compared to the harder obstacles in many women's lives, it could also be encouraging to female viewers to see women starting to speak up for themselves. An important part of the women's movement in the early 1970s was "consciousness-raising"—making people aware of the unfair treatment (oppression) of women; in its gentle way, *The Mary Tyler Moore Show* was doing this. Many people also hoped, as Mary did, that if one were to explain reasonably to the perpetrator the inherent unfairness in a situation, of course the problem would be rectified. In her excellent analysis of feminism in several television series, Bonnie Dow called what we find on *The Mary Tyler Moore Show* "lifestyle" feminism, where the single women work in the public sphere and the married women work at home: "This means that although *Mary Tyler Moore* offers an alternative to traditional womanhood (at least in terms of location), it does so without an explicit critique of the problems of traditional womanhood. Feminism becomes a matter of lifestyle choice, not systemic oppression or social transformation."[21]

Through the seven years of the series, we see Mary start out as an applicant for a secretarial position and grow to be a producer of a news show, developing her own ideas and attending professional seminars and conventions around the country. Her progression does not come easily, however, as she frequently has to convince her boss, "Mr. Grant," that she should be given opportunities to advance. In "Mary Richards: Producer," for example, she finally convinces Lou to let her produce the news, a step up from being the associate producer. We see her struggle to put together a decent show with their inept anchor, Ted Baxter. After the broadcast, Lou pays her his highest compliment, "It didn't stink," and takes her out for a celebratory drink. In other episodes, Mary is completely discouraged by Lou, however. Occasionally a producer of documentaries, in "Mary the Writer," she wants to produce a feature about her grandfather. When Lou says her script is lousy, Mary is devastated. While one could argue that she should have been stronger and followed her own instincts, her response is perhaps typical of the millions of young women throughout the years who have been discouraged by the negative reactions of men they admired.

Mary also has been disappointed by other women. In "What Do You Do When the Boss Says, 'I Love You'?" Mary is thrilled about the new female station manager until the woman makes a play for Lou. In "What's Wrong with Swimming?" Mary hires a female sportscaster against the wishes of Lou and the other men at the station. When the woman refuses to cover violent sports, Mary is forced to fire her. In "A Girl Like Mary," she vies with Sue Ann for a female coanchor spot; both of them fail and the incompetent Ted remains sole anchor. Certainly these visions of women are unflattering. The female station manager abuses her position, as men have done in the past, by pressuring Lou; perhaps she had to become more "manlike" to succeed. The woman sportscaster is stereotypically squeamish about violence, and Mary is less competent than the incompetent Ted to anchor the news. The ditziness of regulars Sue Ann (the oversexed "Happy Homemaker"), Phyllis (the trend-conscious neighbor with no practical skills), and Georgette (the baby-voiced girlfriend, then wife, of Ted Baxter) all add to a potentially unflattering picture of women on this series. Its saving grace, however, is the occasionally strong portrayals of Mary and Rhoda, her best friend, along with two recurring guest roles of middle-aged women.

In its fourth season (1973–1974), *The Mary Tyler Moore Show* introduces the breakup of Lou Grant's marriage with Edie. Lou's daughters and his wife frequently come up in his conversations; it is evident that he loves his family very much. Edie's desire to leave him is something he cannot understand. In the Emmy Award–winning script by Treva Silverman, Edie explains to Lou that she wants to learn more about the rest of her, not just the part that is his wife.[22] Like thousands of middle-aged women in real life in the 1970s, Edie had gotten married very young (at nineteen) and, after twenty-six years of nurturing others, she feels it is time to live for herself. As Edie goes off on her own, she and Lou remain friends. Two years later, Edie is ready for marriage again, and Lou attends the wedding. Mary's Aunt Flo is an interesting contrast to her and perhaps an indication of how Mary would evolve as she gains confidence while aging. In the sixth season, Flo is introduced as a globe-hopping, award-winning journalist, who, coincidentally, inspires both a competitive spirit and romantic interest from Lou Grant. One cannot imagine Mary's aunt being afraid of going to jail on a First Amendment issue, as Mary does in "Will Mary Richards Go to Jail?"[23] On Flo's third visit, Lou proposes to her and she turns him down, respectfully, and continues her dazzling career.

Mary has her workplace family, but she also has other friends. A major difference between the single status of Ann Marie of *That Girl* and Mary Richards is that Ann always has her boyfriend/fiancé around while Mary dates different men throughout the series. Given the opportunity to get back together with her boyfriend of four years, Mary kicks him out, not willing to settle for a relationship based only on his terms. Other episodes make it clear she is taking the pill (in "Just around the Corner," Mary slips and answers "I will" when her mother tells her father to remember to take his pill) and that she is willing to have a relationship based simply on physical attraction (in "Not Just Another Pretty Face"). Mary also probably dates more frequently than most real women. In "Lou Dates Mary," as she is about to kick out an overly aggressive date, she complains that, out of the 2,000 dates in twenty years (averaging two per week), maybe 100 were good. One might ask why she felt compelled to go on so many dates if her experiences were so bad, particularly when she had so many friends at work and at home with whom she could spend time. In the 1973 episode, "Remembrance of Things Past," Mary goes out with an old boyfriend and they both profess their love for each other. As with her ex-boyfriend of four years from the beginning of the series, once again Mary is faced with a man who is not willing to consider her needs. Painfully, she breaks up with him again. Mary is heterosexual with an active sex life, and she would like to marry and have children, but she is not willing to settle.

While Mary Richards has good, platonic male friends in her boss, Lou Grant, and newswriter Murray Slaughter, what is most compelling about this show is her friendships with other women. In the women's movement, female friendships are seen as crucial in the promotion of gender equality. Such relationships are not only a positive assertion of the worth of girls and women, but they also serve as a supportive social structure in thinking through, and achieving, change.[24] Mary finds comfort and courage with her female friends. Rhoda, Phyllis, and later Georgette often stop by her apartment to talk out their problems. As critic Serafina Bathrick wrote, "All of these encounters, and the fluidity with which they occur, are associated with Mary's position as a single woman, and all of them serve to remind us that women's talk is neither trivial nor peripheral to women's lives."[25]

While they are initially antagonistic (in the first episode, they vie for the same apartment), Rhoda Morgenstern and Mary become best friends, despite their very different backgrounds. Their histories are stereotypes—Mary was the Protestant cheerleader in high school who got good grades and the football captain; Rhoda was the initially dumpy, insecure Jewish girl with the loud, overbearing mother. The two women, however, support and encourage each other to be their best. When Mary has to produce the election-returns show during a blizzard, Rhoda is there to help her. Rhoda, of course, also offers much moral support when Mary is fired over an obituary she helped her write late at night. Like most friendships, however, theirs is tested occasionally. Too much togetherness is the issue in "Where There's Smoke There's Rhoda." Rhoda stays with Mary for a few days while her apartment is repaired after a fire. Their contrasting personalities make them truly an odd couple as roommates. The closeness issue comes up again when Mary refuses to tell the unemployed Rhoda about a job opening at her TV station. Perhaps the most serious argument between the two happens in "Best of Enemies" when Rhoda reveals confidential information about Mary. The two miss each other terribly, despite their hurt feelings, however, and make up over garbage in the hallway. The two women also occasionally pursue men together, but they are never rivals. Interestingly enough, though, Rhoda is jealous of another woman friend of Mary's in "Some of My Best Friends Are Rhoda" because of the time it takes Mary away from her. When Mary's new friend refuses to let Rhoda attend her club because she is Jewish, Mary ends her relationship immediately and her friendship with Rhoda is reaffirmed.

While Mary Richards is more concerned about her career than finding a husband, Rhoda makes it immediately clear that marriage is very important to her. In the beginning of the *Mary Tyler Moore Show,* Rhoda is self-deprecating about her looks and her single status. Pressure from her mother undoubtedly is part of her impetus to marry, but she also grew up in a climate where society expected women in their thirties to have husbands. Mary constantly tries to build Rhoda's self-esteem, but, ironically, it is a beauty contest that helps boost her confidence. Rhoda is stunned in "Rhoda the Beautiful" when someone at work (she dresses windows at Hempel's Department Store) suggests she enter their beauty contest. Rhoda says the department store acknowledged some people's problems with the idea of judging women by their looks, so it is compromising by calling the winner "Ms." Hempel. Encouraged by Mary, Rhoda enters and wins, but at first she is reluctant to tell Mary and Phyllis—she claims she won third place. Alone with Mary, she admits she won first and begins to enjoy it, at least for a little while.

Rhoda seems insecure only when it comes to her looks and single status. She is confident as a window dresser, and her bond with Mary is strong.

The fact that neighbor Phyllis does not care for her seems mutual, and she makes light of it, even when Phyllis is relieved that her brother is gay so there is no chance that his dates with Rhoda will lead to marriage. It is her weight that seems to be the crux of Rhoda's self-esteem problem, an attribute tied in very much with the actress who played her, Valerie Harper. The media made much of Harper's plump figure, and yet she weighed no more than millions of women who were watching her on the series.[26] Even when Harper, and, consequently, Rhoda "dropped a ton," as Phyllis so indelicately put it, Rhoda is evidently scarred for life from the trauma of once being overweight. It is the slender Mary who is the model of what women should look like. While Mary is naturally slender, however, Rhoda, Valerie, and millions of other women have to work very hard to control their weight. Rhoda's lack of confidence is the result, at least in some part, of an unhealthy emphasis on looks by the culture she grew up in.

Rhoda (CBS, 1974–1978) was created as a spin-off for the 1974 season, and Rhoda moved back to New York City. She is married within weeks and her insecure feelings increased. Millions watched Rhoda and Joe's wedding, but the ratings soon fell. When she divorces and reestablishes herself as a career woman who can cope, the ratings rose again. It could be argued that this series indicated women were better off without men, that being married made one weak; indeed some feminists made that argument in real life. The lack of interest in Rhoda as a married woman, however, could also be that the writers did not know what to do with her character to continue to make the show appealing. Her insecurities over keeping her husband were certainly painful to watch. It was much more interesting to watch Rhoda deal with her insecurities with the help of her best friend, Mary, in Minneapolis or her sister, Brenda, in New York.

The Mary Tyler Moore Show went off the air in 1977 when Moore and others involved with the program decided they had run out of fresh ideas and they wanted to end while the quality of the program was still good. Mary Richards is thirty-seven years old by that time and still unmarried. In the last episode, she and everyone but Ted at the station lose their jobs when new owners take over. After seven years of hearing the theme song, however, audiences knew she was still "gonna make it after all."

All in the Family

Norman Lear was responsible for at least four of the most significant series in the 1970s with exceptional female characters; one was *All in the Family* and two others were spin-offs of this groundbreaking show. Debuting in January 1971, it dealt with major family discordance and social issues as never seen before in television comedy. Although *All in the Family* didn't become a hit until summer reruns, it was number one in the ratings for the next five years.[27] The series revolves around Archie Bunker; his wife, Edith; their daughter, Gloria; and their son-in-law, Michael Stivic. For the first few years of the series, the Stivics live with the Bunkers while Michael goes to college. For the most part, Archie is the center of this series; whatever happens, the camera looks to him for his reaction. He is a bigoted, uneducated, middle-aged working-class man who frequently gets into political and social debates with his liberal son-in-law. Facts just confuse Archie, who is desperately trying to hold onto the days "when girls were girls and men were men," as the series' theme song, "Those Were the Days," expressed. Controversial because of a fear by some critics that Archie's racial epithets would encourage racism and bigotry rather than expose such prejudice for its ignorance, the other three family members function to balance his negative diatribes.[28]

The most endearing character on the show is Edith, Archie's wife, whom he often refers to as "dingbat." Edith is the stereotypical housewife, running to the door when Archie returns from work to give him a kiss and a beer so he can sit in front of the television while she finishes preparing dinner. Her love and adoration for Archie are unmistakable; she sometimes breaks into singing "I Love You Truly," much to Archie's chagrin. Edith is a very loving, giving person who is trusting and tends to find good in everybody. In the beginning of the series, Archie is the autocratic head of the household and Edith willingly obeys. As the women's movement grew in real life, however, so did Edith. Norman Lear, who took an active role in the series, said that Edith's growth was a reflection of the growing awareness of women's issues by him and the other writers.[29] Jean Stapleton, who played Edith, said it was good that Edith was a housewife because the women's movement was not just about female nuclear physicists, but also about women running households. During the run of *All in the Family,* Stapleton felt that there was "a slow development going on with Edith and that's the way it's really going to happen in this country."[30]

One of the first signs of Edith's liberation is her reaction to Archie during a fight in "Prisoner in the House," originally broadcast in January 1974. Archie, who discovers that the plumber's assistant is a convict on work furlough, is determined to have the man fired. The audience on the laugh track claps when Edith finally speaks back to Archie and utters a rare "damn it!" when she insists he hang up the phone. In another episode, when Archie belittles Edith for volunteering at the Sunshine Home for senior citizens, claiming her work isn't worth money and insisting she quit, the proprietors decide to pay her because they value her so much. A few months later, Edith is validated again in "Edith's Night Out." After Archie refuses to take her out in her new red pantsuit, she goes to his favorite hangout, Kelsey's Bar, by herself. When Archie finally comes, he finds Edith at the piano, playing and singing with her many new friends. In a three-part episode ("Archie's Brief Encounter"), Archie feels Edith is neglecting him as she attends to the needs of the elderly residents; while she is gone, he goes to the apartment of an attentive waitress and kisses her. Edith finds out and moves into the Sunshine Home. When the two get back together, Archie tells Edith he really missed her. Edith confesses she only missed Archie when she thought about him, and that wasn't very often. With pride, she tells him that she used to think that she could count on only him; now she has learned that she can count on her, too.

Why did Edith stay with such a selfish, sexist man? Like many middle-aged women, she grew up in a generation where marriage was truly supposed to be "until death do us part." She also is living in a society that made it difficult, if not impossible, for an untrained woman to make a decent wage. In "Edith vs. the Bank," she finds out that there are different rules for men and women in applying for loans. More than anything, however, researcher Donna McCrohan's description of Edith probably offered the best explanation for her loyalty to Archie: "Instinctively drawn to the good in people, judging their intentions more than their actions—it's this attitude that enables Edith to adore Archie, which she does emphatically. Were she more critical, she'd have no use for him, which for Edith would be a tragedy."[31] Time and time again, Edith is proved to be morally superior to Archie, a characteristic that actually has been attributed to women in general and used against them (e.g., if women are morally superior, then they are more suited to staying home and raising children than working in a competitive marketplace). In "Edith's Accident," Archie gets mad because Edith left a note on an unoccupied car after she dented it with a can of peaches. When Edith finds a winning lottery ticket in her purse that belongs to Louise Jefferson, their next-door neighbor, Archie wants to keep it, but Edith insists on returning it. Despite her love of Archie, when Edith is asked to settle a dispute between a laundromat owner and Archie, she is too honest to lie in her husband's favor.

Notwithstanding her "dingbat" demeanor at times, Edith is instinctively wise and fair. In "Edith Has Jury Duty," she has the whole jury against her when she is the only one who votes not guilty; it turns out she is right. She takes a stand for the right to die with dignity when she honors the wishes of a resident of the Sunshine Home, and lets her quietly die as Edith holds her hand (an act for which she is fired). She is even able to help Mike understand his frustrating father-in-law by explaining how Archie never had the opportunities Mike had and that he is jealous. Edith also embraces people of all kinds. Louise Jefferson, her African American neighbor, is a good friend as is her feminist neighbor, Irene Lorenzo. Although surprised, Edith has no trouble accepting the feelings and rights of cousin Liz's female lover after her cousin died. Her most touching friendship, however, is with a female impersonator, Beverly LaSalle, whose life Archie had saved in his cab. When Beverly is killed by a street gang, Edith immediately loses her faith in God and refuses to go to church. She cannot believe in a god who would allow someone to be killed just because he is different. With Archie's help, she regains her faith, but she also learns a hard lesson in life. While Archie's prejudice is verbal and mostly ineffective, Edith is forced to recognize the lethal consequences of some people's hate.

All in the Family is known for its story lines that cover subjects never before seen in comedy, such as impotence and death. Often the stories would revolve around Archie or Mike, with Edith or Gloria reacting. Frequently Archie is put in situations where he has to interact with people of color or strong women, allowing audiences to laugh at his "dilemma." Even an episode on Edith going through menopause is more concerned about Archie's reaction. After Edith had been acting erratically, hysterical one minute and calm the next, Archie gives her thirty seconds to "change." When he goes to the doctor about Edith's problem, he comes back with pills to be taken three times a day—by him.

The most disturbing episode, however, deals with Edith and a rapist. "Edith's 50th Birthday" is a one-hour show where the rest of the family is planning a surprise birthday party next door at the Stivics, and Edith is by herself at home. She lets in an attractive, well-dressed man who claims to be a detective investigating rape in the area. When the door is closed, he makes his intentions known and begins to undo her clothes. She eventually saves herself by running to get a cake that had been burning in the oven and throwing it in the man's face; she then pushes him out the backdoor. True to form, Archie doesn't want her to report it, but Gloria convinces her to go to the police to stop the man from hurting others. According to McCrohan, "some critics complained that much of Edith's reaction merely strained the bounds of comedy: offering coffee to a rapist, worrying about kissing, and crying over a ruined cake."[32] Others found Edith's reactions to be true to her character. Lear reportedly spent more than a year preparing the episode, consulting with rape treatment experts and arranging private screenings for legal authorities and social workers.[33]

Edith was again set up to be a victim in "Edith's Christmas Story," only this time her body is the perpetrator. Afraid to tell Archie, she confesses to two women in her life—Gloria and friend Irene—that she has a lump in her breast. Irene comforts her by talking about her mastectomy years ago. When Archie finds out, of course, he assures Edith that he will still love her, no matter what. Although Edith's lump turns out to be only a cyst, the character did become the victim of a lethal stroke when actress Jean Stapleton decided to leave the series in 1980. In anticipation of feminist outrage for killing off Edith, Norman Lear reportedly donated $500,000 to promote the Equal Rights Amendment.[34] Archie could now continue in *Archie Bunker's Place,* in the bar he bought by forging Edith's signature years earlier to mortgage their house.

Was Edith a victim? Was she a lesson for other women who dared to show some independence? McCrohan said Edith was very saintlike in her behavior in the rape episode, divorcing flesh from spirit as she prepared for the inevitable and asked only that her rapist keep his clothes on and not kiss her.[35] Certainly she was a role model of unconditional love, fairness, and honesty in dozens of other episodes. And audiences cheered when she defied Archie, as they might when they saw their own mothers speak up for themselves. While her birthday and two Christmases were emotionally devastating to Edith, most of her life was pretty mundane. Edith was neither victim nor saint nor a lesson to keep in our places; she was a gentle awakening, a message that even housewives have rights and value far beyond what society has given them.

By comparison, Edith's daughter, Gloria, is an often strident, whiny "little girl" as Archie calls her. She serves, however, to present lessons about equal rights, usually via her relationship with her husband, Michael. Even though he is supposed to be a liberal, several episodes reveal Michael's attitudes to be quite sexist and Gloria has to set him straight. In an early episode, Gloria actually moves out of the house because she feels he isn't treating her like an equal. In "Mike and Gloria Mix It Up," Michael resents Gloria being the aggressor in their sexual relationship, and she gets angry. On several occasions, he makes decisions without considering Gloria, including that they would never have children because of the mess the world was in. When they do have a child and Gloria thinks she is pregnant again, Michael tells her that birth control is up to her. As in all the other "battle of the sexes" episodes, however, Gloria gets her way, this time by convincing Michael he should have a vasectomy. Gloria also fights to raise the consciousness of her mother and to force her father to treat her mother better, but that, of course, is harder. Her attempts are sometimes sabotaged by the stereotypes associated with her character. For example, on her twenty-third birthday, Gloria rants and raves at the family because it is also her "time of the month." She calls Archie stupid and accuses her mother of being a doormat, a nothing. Despite Gloria's unkind words, Edith comes through and repairs the damage Gloria also has done in her relationship with Michael.

While Michael is going to college, Gloria works as a salesperson in a department store to help support them. When she loses her job because she is pregnant, she fights back. She is able to comfort her mother over Edith's rape attempt because she, too, had experienced it, in a subway on the way home from work. Her heartfelt talks with Edith, particularly in the episode dealing with Edith's lump, depict her as a loving, intelligent young woman, yet her whiny arguments with her husband and father somehow lessen this image and make less significant her important statements about equality. Edith's gentle venture into equality and independence may have taken longer, but may have made her messages more easy to accept.

Two other female characters on *All in the Family* deserve mention, although they did not make regular appearances. Irene Lorenzo is a feminist who works on the dock with Archie (he helped her get a job, but was appalled when she was assigned to operate a forklift!). Irene and her husband have a comfortable relationship involving what many would consider role reversals, where he cooks and she fixes things. Naturally, she is a good friend of Edith's, but she grates against Archie and his sense of gender roles. She is neither strident in her feminism nor slow in discovering it; she just *is* a feminist. Louise Jefferson, an African American neighbor, is another friend of Edith's, who lives next door until she "moved on up" to her own series, *The Jeffersons,* discussed later. Like Edith, she is seen as morally superior to her husband, also a bigot.

Maude

A spin-off of *All in the Family, Maude* came shouting onto the television scene in 1972. Maude Findlay is a cousin of Edith Bunker who helped the household over a few days when the entire family was sick. As liberal as Archie is conservative, she soon is confronted with a number of personal and social issues on her own series. In her late forties, Maude is on her fourth husband, Walter, after divorcing the first three. Also part of her household at the beginning of the series is her divorced daughter, Carol; her nine-year-old grandson, Phillip; and her maid, Florida, an African American woman who is as witty as Maude, despite her subservient status. Maude's best friend is Vivian, a divorcee who later marries their widowed next-door neighbor, Arthur Harmon. Unlike the Bunkers and Mary Richards, Maude is comfortably nestled in her upper-middle-class household in suburban Tuckahoe, New York, but Maude is anything but comfortable.

Despite the supporting cast of characters, Maude is clearly the most important one, as indicated by both the series title and theme song. Comparing her to strong women in history, such as Joan of Arc and Betsy Ross, the lyrics quickly establish Maude as "enterprising, socializing, everything but compromising." While Mary Richards would timidly push for her rights, Maude's opinions are expressed adamantly and continually, whether they concern the political or the personal. Perhaps more significantly, the series often deals seriously with issues of concern to middle-aged women, a female demographic on television much outnumbered by the younger, perkier, and more svelte.

By far the most controversial episodes concern a two-part story line where the forty-seven-year-old Maude discovers she is pregnant and decides to have an abortion; Maude also pressures Walter to have a vasectomy. The episodes, "Maude's Dilemma" and "Walter's Dilemma," were broadcast only two months after the series made its debut in September 1972 and only two months before the 1973 *Roe* v. *Wade* decision made abortion legal around the country. Maude's financial status and the fact that she lives in a state where abortion is legal makes the termination of her pregnancy a clear option for her. Unhappy as Maude is about the pregnancy, however, she is resigned to her fate, as many women before her, until her twenty-seven-year-old daughter convinces her that she has the right to decide what to do with her own body. Although Carol's comparison of getting an abortion to being as simple as going to the dentist ignored the psychological aspects of such a decision, she makes her point about it being a viable option. Hundreds of viewers disagreed, however.

Both network and advocacy group pressure are constant influences on prime-time programming, and reliance on commercial support also gives advertisers some power over content. Like many special-interest groups, the Population Institute saw entertainment television as an ideal means of educating people about the perils of unchecked population growth. Producer Norman Lear was stimulated by its appeal to television executives to address population issues in programs; the institute even offered prestigious awards and cash prizes.[36] While Lear discussed the abortion episodes with CBS executives months before they were produced, CBS's standards and practices department (the censors) did not see the final scripts until just before production when it was too late to make changes. Although Lear enjoyed more freedom than most producers because of the popularity of his programs, CBS executives were still angry and nervous, but they succumbed to his threats to remove the show altogether if they did not allow the abortion episodes to be broadcast.[37]

Planned Parenthood in Los Angeles, serving as technical consultant on the script, readied itself for pressures from anti-abortion groups by preparing to put their own pressure on CBS and its affiliates.[38] As expected, the network received hundreds of calls and letters, many merely complaining justifiably about the inappropriate 8 P.M. time slot for presentation of such a serious issue. Organized protests from establishments affiliated with the Catholic Church, however, expressed outrage at the endorsement of abortion and attempted to prevent the second episode from airing. While some stations and advertisers succumbed and did not broadcast the episode, pro-choice groups convinced other stations to air it. When CBS quietly announced the repeat of these two episodes only two weeks ahead of their broadcast the following August, both pro-choice and anti-abortion groups rallied again; 39 out of the 198 affiliate stations refused to air the abortion episodes and no advertising was carried.[39] Although a pro-choice stance is important to most feminists, it is little wonder why few series address it, even more than thirty years later. Despite the fact that the majority of the population is pro-choice, television programmers and, more important, advertisers often succumb to vocal adversaries who threaten them with bad publicity and loss of revenue.

Of course, most episodes were not nearly as controversial as the abortion story line, but many were as compelling. For example, in a one-woman episode, "The Analyst," on her fiftieth birthday Maude is worried about aging and feels insignificant so she goes to a psychotherapist. Other episodes also deal with aging issues, such as menopause and facelifts. Although related to health, not age, a two-part episode depicts Maude as a manic depressive, and Lithium is prescribed to even out her moods. In an episode dealing with sexual harassment, Carol finds out she must go to bed with her boss to get a promotion.

Maude and Walter's relationship is tested in many multipart episodes, including a couple in which Walter has serious problems. The two-part "Life of the Party," aired early in the series' run, reveals that Walter is an alcoholic. After hitting Maude across the face during a fight, Walter realizes he needs professional help and seeks it. Later in the series, in the three-part "Walter's Crisis," he attempts suicide after he declares bankruptcy for his failed appliance store and can't find a job. Neither of these

major problems really threaten the marriage, however; we watch as
Maude learns to cope and stand by her man as he recovers. Ironically, it is
when Maude plans to run for the state senate that Walter decides to leave
her. By the fourth episode in this story line, Walter gives in and "allows"
her to run; in the fifth episode, she loses the election. Even liberated
Maude is expected to be nurturing and forgiving, but Walter, also in traditional fashion, finds her attempt at power outside the home threatening.
Did losing the election teach her to stay in her place? Yes and no. By the
series' end, Maude has become a congresswoman, but only by default. As
a congresswoman's assistant, she is appointed by the governor to replace
the congresswoman when she drops dead in office. It is interesting to consider why Maude stays with Walter after all their problems. Clearly after
three divorces, Maude isn't the type to stick with a marriage if it isn't
working. Perhaps she truly loves Walter and thinks their marriage is worth
saving, or maybe she is just tired of divorce. At any rate, their union illustrates that, although the adjustments are not easy, equality in marriage
takes a lot of hard work.

Many episodes of *Maude* depict the 1970s' television version of what it
is to be liberal and socially conscious. In one episode Maude gives a party
for a black militant leader and in another she invites an African American
girl to spend a vacation with a "white family." She also has her foster son
from Ethiopia come to visit. She helps a gay writer promote his book and
fights with Walter in another episode over a gay bar opening near them.
She more publicly fights other injustices, from what she considers harsh
marijuana laws (she and some friends protest by trying to get arrested) to
her own speeding ticket. In two episodes Maude and Walter are introduced
to wife swappers and decline to participate, yet both are tempted in other
episodes to have affairs.

While Maude could strongly argue against racism and defend the rights
of people to express their sexuality in their own way, she is also full of
contradictions. She has a black maid, even though she insists that Florida
use the front door. Florida isn't interested in assuaging Maude's guilt,
however, and uses the backdoor because it is more convenient when she
brings in groceries. Maude may be a feminist, but her white, upper-middle-
class background makes it difficult for her to understand that her needs and
concerns are not the same as women of color or other classes (a common
criticism of liberal feminism in the 1970s). Maude also gets upset when
her daughter, Carol, wants to sleep with her boyfriend in Maude's house.
When John Wayne is scheduled to visit her neighbor, Arthur, she promises
to give "Mr. Conservative" a piece of her mind. Instead, she melts over

him, even as he refers to her as the "little woman" and refuses to discuss politics with her because she is female. Of course, *Maude* is a comedy, so humor had to be mixed in with the personal crises and social diatribes. To have Maude lose her resolve and become star-struck with John Wayne instead of arguing with him is a situation many can laugh at because we recognize ourselves as potentially reacting the same way. Audiences also came to expect Maude's "God'll get you for that" when she was unhappy with someone. Some episodes also deal with silly situations, such as when Maude and Vivian attempt to retrieve Maude's brooch from a friend's body at a funeral home.

Maude's inconsistencies are understandable in the cultural context of her time, class, and age. Living in the midst of civil rights and the women's movement after being raised in more conservative times was difficult for many people. Though she slips at times, as is human to do, Maude is a feminist. At the Tuckahoe Bicentennial, she insists on featuring women. When her best friend, Vivian, joins a group of women who like catering to their men's every wish, she is appropriately appalled. She also certainly believes in a woman's right to succeed in both business and politics (she was nominated as businessperson of the year for her work as branch manager of a real estate agency and she ran for office), and she is pro-choice. Unlike her cousin Edith, whose consciousness is slowly awakened when it comes to her own rights, and unlike Mary Richards, who speaks up only for personal reasons, Maude asserts herself from the beginning and, more significant, she also asserts herself publicly for the rights of others. When the series ended in 1978 with Maude in Washington, D.C., as a congresswoman (regardless of how she got there), one could be sure she would pursue her liberal agenda with vigor, including women's rights.

The Jeffersons

Another spin-off of *All in the Family, The Jeffersons* also deals with an upper-middle-class family as did *Maude,* but there are significant differences from the other two Lear shows. First, the Jeffersons are an African American family who moved to the East Side of Manhattan from Queens (and their neighbors, the Bunkers) and, earlier, from Harlem. Second, the characters and story lines are very different. George Jefferson is described by many critics as a black Archie Bunker, bigoted and pigheaded, but he is also a social climber, often ashamed of his ghetto roots. His wife, Louise, has been a good friend to Edith Bunker. Unlike George, who is a separatist except for those many occasions where he thinks he could prosper by associating with white folks, Louise is an assimilationist; she cares about people and is not concerned about their color. She also is not a social climber and often reminds George of his roots. In *All in the Family,* their son Lionel is a good friend to Michael Stivic, Archie's son-in-law. Lionel, too, also serves as a model for integration. Unlike Maude, however, Louise is not the central focus of her series. Like Edith in *All in the Family,* Louise's role is primarily to humanize her bigoted husband. Although some episodes focus on her, most are concerned about George or the two as a couple. Story lines also generally do not address major social issues, although occasionally racial pride and prejudice are addressed.

What makes *The Jeffersons* an important series of the 1970s is that it was the most consistently popular of the several African American comedies introduced in that decade; it was a prime-time CBS show for ten years. Writer Rick Mitz said that more than any other program, it helped open the way to racial tolerance when it made its debut in 1975.[40] While George Jefferson is a bigot, his wife and son are not; the series also contains situation comedy's first interracial couple, neighbors Tom and Helen Willis. More significant for this book, the series also contains several interesting female characters.

While George Jefferson is often described as a black Archie Bunker, Louise is no Edith, even though the two were friends in Queens. Where Edith has "dingbat" tendencies and often defers to Archie, Louise is intelligent and always yells back at George if he gets testy. Louise is actually a civilizing force on her husband, a role that also is found in more recent sitcoms. In the stereotyped role of woman taming (domesticating) the wild beast, Louise is constantly chastising George for his behavior and arrogant attitude. He is particularly intolerant of their interracial neighbors, the Willises, and refers to their daughter, Jenny, as a zebra. Not only are Louise and Lionel friends of the family, but Lionel dates and later marries Jenny. On several occasions, George tries to impress people whom he thinks can help him get ahead, despite Louise's attempts to get him to be himself. Inevitably Louise is proved right; George does not get away with his uppity airs. Part of the humor is that he does not even understand some of the expressions used by the more well-to-do. For example, when a guest asks for a "Scotch—neat," he gets offended and snaps, "Don't worry, you'll get a clean glass."[41]

As in Edith's relationship to Archie, Louise is seen as morally superior to George. Louise is often the voice of George's conscience, not only when he forgets his roots and puts on airs, but also when his transgressions are more serious. George almost ruins Louise's foster home project when he teaches an orphan how to gamble. He tries to buy Louise an award at the Help Center where she works by donating a large sum of money. When he buys a term paper for Lionel and Lionel plans to use it, both father and son get into trouble; as Lionel's moral superior, Jenny breaks up with him over the incident. For each of George's misplaced attempts at helping, Louise must explain to him, often angrily, how what he did was wrong.

Louise is also morally superior in her work and better educated. While George operates a chain of dry cleaners and is constantly trying to increase his profits, Louise works at a Help Center in the community. She blames herself when a girl she tried to help attempts to kill herself. She also works for a time at a museum. While George is a high school dropout who decided to get his GED (a high school degree based on tests), Louise takes classes in French and art. Louise's activities, however, could also be seen as those of upper-class housewives; to help the less fortunate and take lessons in cultured subjects has been expected of careerless females in well-to-do families throughout history. Yet Louise is part of the nouveau upper-middle-class, and she has not forgotten her roots. She welcomes friends from her old neighborhood and helping others is a part of her nature, not her new social class.

In the series, George and Louise celebrate their thirtieth wedding anniversary, demonstrating a solid African American nuclear family. Some episodes in the ten-year run of the series revolve around one or the other being jealous of a member of the "opposite" sex they feel is getting too close to their spouse. These misunderstandings, however, lead to a strengthening of their relationship. The two actually fight often about many things, including George wanting Louise to stay home and celebrate their anniversary instead of going to a Help Center Convention, but the endings are always happy in typical sitcom fashion. George also is shown to have some redeeming qualities in some episodes. He is not only a doting grandfather, but Louise discovers that he has been sending $100 anonymously each month to the tenants in the Harlem apartment where he grew up, as a promise he had made to himself while still in poverty.

Louise's best friend is Helen, an African American woman married for more than twenty years to a white man and mother to Jenny, eventually Louise's daughter-in-law. The two normally get along well, but on at least one occasion jealousy rears its ugly head. In "Good News, Bad News," Louise is upset when Helen gets the job of editor of the Help Center newsletter and not she. In "Louise vs. Jenny," she and her daughter-in-law fight over who gets to take care of Lionel when he has a bad cold. In another "versus" episode ("Louise vs. Florence"), Louise fights with her maid during a party where George is trying to impress some rich people. Normally, however, Louise gets along very well with everyone—everyone but her mother-in-law, that is. Mother Olivia Jefferson is a cranky, nasty woman who dotes on her son and obviously is jealous of Louise being in his life. Although Louise initially puts up with her insults, she eventually begins retaliating with subtle but effective verbal slings.

Like Maude, Louise has an interesting African American maid. Florence is an attractive, sassy woman who often tells the Jeffersons to answer their own door. She is particularly acerbic to George, who often tries to exploit her, while she occasionally conspires with Louise. Eventually she becomes a live-in maid, but her laziness continues. When criticized for her depiction of a stereotype, actress Marla Gibbs said she saw her character as part of the black heritage of this country, that all African Americans came from a servant capacity.[42] Florence was more than a maid, however, and hardly a stereotype. Her refusal to wait on the Jeffersons hand and foot can be seen, not as lazy, but as a refusal to accept her subservient status. Her presence is a constant reminder to the Jeffersons of their roots, although George may refuse to recognize it, and she offers many opportunities to demonstrate class conflict.

Several episodes involve Florence dating. It is evident she would like a husband, and she even tries a video dating service to find one. In another episode, she plans on marrying a man she has known less than a month. Of course, her pursuits could be quite funny, such as when she pretends to be "many women" to a psychiatrist whom she is trying to attract at the Help Center. The man thinks she is schizophrenic and tries to have her committed.

Although the other women in *The Jeffersons* have lesser roles than Louise and Florence, they are interesting nevertheless. Helen demonstrates the ability of African American and Caucasian people to get along in her long-term mixed marriage. Unfortunately, Mother Jefferson represents the mother-in-law-from-hell stereotype. Jenny is perhaps the most interesting. As the offspring of a mixed marriage, she is very well-adjusted. As discussed earlier, she breaks up with Lionel when he is determined to do something morally wrong. She is also intelligent; she wins a scholarship to Oxford and works on a thesis on a ghetto gang. She and Lionel have a daughter in the spring of 1980, but they separate in 1981 and divorce in 1985. While the actor who played Lionel left the show in 1981, Jenny is shown periodically, raising her child as a single parent while she becomes a successful fashion designer. Even though the connection between a thesis on a gang and becoming a fashion designer is hard to fathom, Jenny can be seen as a positive role model. She also remains close with her in-laws, reinforcing the importance of family even when marriages break up.

Unlike in *Maude,* few "women's issues" became story lines in *The Jeffersons.* Both women went through midlife crises, questioning the value of their lives, but Louise did not go for psychotherapy as did Maude. The issue of Louise working comes up early in the series and the clash between her personal and social life is featured at least once, but George did not leave Louise over such clashes. Sexism on the job becomes an issue when George hesitates to promote a woman as manager of his dry-cleaning store, but this is treated as a personal flaw, not a systemic one. Of course, Louise is not the political activist that Maude is. As a matter of fact, in the 1970s many women of color considered women's liberation to be a movement for white, middle-class women and believed that most feminists did not address issues related to race and class (or, as in Maude's case, they just did not understand what the issues were). For example, middle-class white women were concerned about opportunities for careers; many lower-class African American women had been working for years—in dead-end, low-paying jobs.[43] Florence as a maid might scoff at "career opportunities" and, in her search for a husband, wonder why so many women found marriage confining. Certainly another income could have helped her get away from her servitude. While issues based on gender rarely appeared, issues of race came up fairly often in *The Jeffersons,* usually through George. In one episode he discovers he is the token black in a tennis club; in another, he and a young black employee are arrested as looters in one of his stores. Racism is clearly a more important concern in the black comedies of the 1970s than sexism.

One Day at a Time

Another groundbreaking comedy by Norman Lear (and not a spin-off) is *One Day at a Time,* making its debut in 1975. This series is significant, not only because it focuses on a divorced woman, but because it also features the trials and tribulations of her two teenage daughters. One was the classic "good girl" and the other was perhaps television comedy's most troubled adolescent, as a character and in real life, at that time. The series was not controversial as were some of Lear's other shows, but story lines, often told over several episodes, allowed the characters to be explored through situations previously not presented in series comedy.

Ann Romano married at the age of seventeen, and seventeen years later she is suddenly head of a single-parent household. Mitz called her "television's first feminist—not a liberated loudmouth like Maude, but a reasonable feminist."[44] Significantly, according to feminist critic Bonnie Dow, Ann "rejected her marriage because of its politics, under which she had no power."[45] The reigning feminist themes in the series' first four seasons, according to Dow, are self-actualization and achieving independence and fulfillment.[46] Unlike Mary Richards on *Mary Tyler Moore,* however, Ann is willing to fight more vocally for her rights, but her fight is on an individual level, not a political one.

Ann's new life as a liberated woman is sometimes incongruous. While she takes back her maiden name and insists that people address her as "Ms." Romano, she goes from a bad marriage to a relationship with her divorce lawyer, David, a man several years younger than she. As she begins a career in advertising and becomes more confident, she decides not to marry David and move to California with him. In a much later episode when she is in a position to have her own (male) secretary, she chases after him. It is human to be inconsistent at times, however, and the times themselves were confusing. A most disconcerting fact about Ann, however, is that she has no consistent women friends. During the second season, Ginny is a woman across the hall who becomes friendly, but she is written out after a year. Ann's female assistant at work, Francine, steals her accounts and later becomes an adversary at the same company. When the two become partners in their own company, Ann still has to be cautious. With many in the women's movement recognizing that "sisterhood is powerful," it would have been natural for Ann to bond, rather than compete, with other women. It certainly could have made her life easier.

While women friends were lacking in Ann's life, there were plenty of men. The superintendent of her apartment building, Dwayne Schneider, is her most constant friend. Frequently letting himself into her apartment with his own keys, Schneider initially is interested in Ann sexually, but he soon realizes she does not return his feelings. He becomes a sounding board for Ann's worries about her daughters, Barbara and Julie, and occasionally even helps all of them through some tough times. More significant, for the first time in television comedy, a lead character is shown in realistic situations that involve her ex-husband, Ed. In an early episode, Ann is jealous of her daughters' relationship to their dad's new girlfriend, Vicki. When Ed and Vicki decide to get married, Barbara and Julie are determined to get him back with their mom; later they try to break up the marriage so they can spend more time with their dad. As in real divorced families, gifts and money can also become issues. At one point Ann and Ed fight about his wish to buy his daughters a car. Worst of all, when he is having financial problems, he cannot pay Ann child support, a common situation for many divorced women. Ann threatens to take Ed to court for payment, even though she knows it will be a battle in an unfair system, but she softens her stance when he claims he is afraid of losing his wife because of money problems. While it would have been nice to see Ann take a strong stand and force Ed to meet his obligations, she is not the first woman to retreat at her expense for someone else's sake. While she and her daughters live in a small, simply furnished apartment and she struggles to work to support them, Ed and his new wife share a rather lavish home and lifestyle.

Ann is clearly sexual, and sometimes she finds herself in the awkward position of explaining to her daughters what she is doing. In one early episode, she needs to find a way to tell them she plans to have an affair with an airplane pilot in Chicago. She also has relationships over the years with a symphony conductor, a racecar driver, a comic, and an archeology professor (who asks her to go live with him in Greece). Perhaps the most interesting short-term affair Ann has is depicted over three episodes in "The Married Man." After Schneider informs Ann that the man she is dating is married, she intends on breaking up with him but decides they love each other too much. She explains to her daughters that it might not be proper, but she hopes they will understand how she feels about Neal (the girls had liked him). When Ann and Neal run into an old friend of his who assumes Ann is his wife, however, she tells Neal she felt like she had the starring role in a dirty joke. Although Neal leaves his wife by the third episode, the couple break up; Neal cannot make a commitment to Ann, so she tells him her self-respect is more important to her than he is. While Ann could be seen as a "home wrecker" and certainly a bad role model for her daughters, somehow her transgression is made understandable by her belief in love with a capital "L." The audience could also forgive her because she ultimately learns her lesson, even if it is about self-respect rather than the sanctity of marriage. In a decade of soaring divorce rates and wife-swapping, the sanctity and permanence of marriage was constantly tested.

Besides David in the first season, Ann had two other relationships that lasted more than three episodes. Nick became her partner doing freelance advertising in the fifth season. Initially hostile toward each other, the two become romantically involved. The next season begins, however, with Ann getting over the shock of Nick's death in an auto accident. Ann apparently ends her illustrious dating career when she meets Barbara's father-in-law in 1982. She and Sam Royer marry at the end of the series and are to move to England where Ann has been offered a job. Despite the fact that her only experience is as a housewife and mother at the beginning of the series, Ann, incredibly, is able to get a job in advertising within two years of her divorce. After five years, she starts her own advertising business with a partner, Nick, and continues with Francine after Nick's death. By the end of the series, she has a great job in England. Certainly one could make great strides in the advertising industry over several years, but to begin with only a high school education and no experience makes her truly an amazing woman. Coupled with her lusty personal life, Ann Romano could offer either hope or despair (in comparison) to the audience.

As the first popular sitcom to feature a divorced woman, *One Day at a Time* is also the first to feature children of divorce, and it is that aspect that is perhaps the most realistic of the series. As discussed earlier, Julie and Barbara's father is involved in several episodes dealing with such topics as jealousy and child support. Living with their mother, the girls also have to deal with Ann's sexuality and various boyfriends. More important, the two offer interesting, but very different, role models for girls who were watching.

Barbara is fifteen years old at the start of the series and is the classic "good girl." Valerie Bertinelli, who played Barbara, became a favorite with many teens and preteens because of the show. Barbara is cute, popular, sweet, and gets good grades. Tired of her nice and trustworthy reputation, however, Barbara and her good friend Bob (who had a crush on her for a long time) decide to spend a weekend in a motel. In a scene right out of *It Happened One Night,* the two have no intentions of having sex and so they hang a sheet between them. Although very angry when the two are found, Ann realizes she had been taking Barbara's good behavior for granted while she spent more time worried about her troubled daughter. Barbara also demonstrates many lessons about friendship as she is learning about it herself. In one episode, she refuses to tell on a guilty friend who vandalized a school office. In a more serious two-part episode, Barbara is accused by a new girlfriend of trying to steal her boyfriend; the girl threatens and subsequently attempts suicide, and her parents blame Barbara. In another episode, Barbara discovers that a boy she is dating is the father of a friend's baby. Once she graduates from high school, Barbara seems to be on her way to fulfill her potential. She attends a local college but eventually drops out and ends up working at a travel agency. Her near happy ending is that she marries a handsome, sweet dental student. Their tragedy is that Barbara learns she cannot have children. The classic "good girl" has problems like the rest of us.

Julie is seventeen when the series begins and very different from her sister. She is rebellious and troubled about what to do with her life; she is also clearly less innocent than Barbara, but her sexual activity usually is not openly discussed. Although each sister has her own episode where she is being pressured to have sex, Julie runs away with a boy she professes to love because she wants her freedom to do as she pleases. Over four episodes, Ann is sick with worry as many help in the search for the young couple. When they are found in a run-down motel room, however, Ann makes it clear that the rules will not change; Julie comes home anyhow, having discovered that freedom has a lot of costs. While Barbara later runs away with Bob, their relationship is not sexual; like many young girls who envy the evidently exciting life of "bad" girls, Barbara wants to lose her good-girl reputation. Julie is not pretending, however; she is almost as troubled as Mackenzie Phillips who played her.

Many plots deal with Julie trying to "find herself." In a two-part episode, she joins a religious cult. At various times she also works as a waitress in a run-down cafe, sings in a band, is a freelance fashion designer, and does counseling at a free clinic. In another two-part episode, she gets an apartment with a girlfriend—who dates men for a living. When she gets a job as an assistant to a middle-aged veterinarian, she falls in love with him but decides not to marry him, much to Ann's relief, when she discovers they have little in common. She dumps another fiancé, this time at the alter, when she realizes she loves the best man, Max. Max and Julie get married, but, as Phillips battled drug problems, the producers of *One Day at a Time* changed story lines to compensate for her absence. Julie and Max move to Texas during the 1979–1980 season after the actress was fired. Phillips returned the following year, only to be written out of the show again for health reasons during its last season. This time the audience learned that Julie had walked out on her husband and young daughter. Julie is a reflection of the troubled lives of the teenagers portrayed in *Dazed and Confused,* a 1993 movie about high school students in 1976. The character illustrates the restlessness, boredom, and lack of purpose of these late baby boomers while the actress lived their frequent use of drugs. Ann's approach in dealing with both her daughters is motivated by a feminist-inspired philosophy, according to Bonnie Dow.[47] Rather than dictate to her children, Ann wants her daughters to take responsibility and share in the decision making about their lives, an opportunity she had neither with her father nor her ex-husband.

Perhaps the most disturbing, and stereotypical, aspect of this series, however, is its portrayal of women as rivals over the affection of men. Ann does not know her rival when she dates a married man, but she and her daughters are involved in jealousy episodes on several occasions. In an early episode, Julie accuses Ann of trying to steal her college date. In at least two episodes, Barbara accuses Julie of stealing her boyfriend and, as discussed earlier, one girl attempts suicide at the thought of Barbara stealing her boyfriend. Add the rivalry between Ann and Francine over business and the picture of women together is quite unflattering.

In her book on prime-time families, Taylor refers to *One Day at a Time* as demonstrating "populist feminism."[48] She said Ann Romano was forced by circumstances to contemplate independence and she came to cherish it, as many women did who otherwise would have been untouched by feminism. Dow said, however, that *One Day,* "although addressing the politics between men and women fairly frequently and self-consciously...ultimately recasts material issues of power between the genders into therapeutic obstacles to be conquered through self-transformation."[49] Ann learns "one day at a time" how to survive in the world of work, develop her own social life, and handle the many crises associated with having a family. Despite her lack of female friends and somewhat unlikely rise in advertising, her problems with her daughters and her own personal crises ring true. Several episodes explore Ann's development as an individual. On her thirty-fifth birthday she has an identity crisis. Later on, Ann has a physical crisis, a heart attack—a warning perhaps of potential costs of economic independence. Regardless, Ann made single parenthood and being divorced seem okay—she was surviving, often thriving, in a way that could be encouraging to the many viewers in similar circumstances. Mitz said the politics of Bonnie Franklin who played Ann "permeated the script and the show."[50] Unlike Mary Richards who is uncomfortable when she asserts herself and Maude who thrives on it, both Bonnie and Ann have "a gentle, at-ease sense of feminism."[51]

Laverne & Shirley

A spin-off of *Happy Days, Laverne & Shirley* revolves around friends of the popular high school dropout, Fonzie, who all live in Milwaukee in the late 1950s. Laverne and Shirley got their own series in 1976 and soon rivaled their predecessor as the number one rated show. As producer Garry Marshall intended, the setting two decades earlier allowed the series to ignore current social issues and focus on laughs. Its humor was situational and largely physical—slapstick. What makes *Laverne & Shirley* an important series, however, is its emphasis on the friendship of the two lead characters.

Laverne and Shirley have a long history with each other. In their early twenties when the series begins, they graduated from high school together and even jointly got kicked out of Brownies years earlier. As working-class women, they share a basement apartment and work at the Shotz Brewery as bottle cappers early in the series. On several occasions the women take on other jobs, almost always together. When laid off, they become taxi drivers and later they work at a flower shop. In various other circumstances they sell children's shoes, work at a weight-loss camp, decide to become high fashion models, and become hospital volunteers. When Shirley wants to become a medical assistant, she convinces Laverne to take night courses with her. They also join the army together for a short, unhappy stint. What Laverne and Shirley are searching for in their lives is not quite clear, but they are doing it together. "Making Our Dreams Come True" was their popular theme song, in which "we'll do it our way" was emphasized. Sisterhood was powerful even then. The last two years of the series (it lasted until May 1983) take place in Burbank, California. Again, the women work together, this time in the gift wrap section of a department store, as they try to make it in the movies. Symbolically, the series went off the air as actress Cindy Williams (Shirley) refused to work so many hours while she was pregnant and Penny Marshall (Laverne) unsuccessfully carried on without her.

As with most female friends in prime time, Laverne and Shirley are very different. Laverne is brassy, loud, and adventurous, while Shirley is more cautious and thoughtful. In one episode where they fight over returning a wrongly issued check, the two dream of Shirley in heaven and Laverne in hell. While Shirley is determined to remain a virgin until she gets married, Laverne is much more wild. In one episode, Laverne has morning sickness after a party, making her wonder if she is pregnant. Although the series normally avoided serious issues, the women frequently help each other, often where it concerns dates. In an episode where Laverne asks Shirley to pretend she is dying so she can get to know a mortician, Shirley balks until Laverne sings to her "Friendship" ("If you're ever in a jam, here I am . . . "). Unlike Lucy and Ethel who sing this song to each other while they tear each other's matching dresses, Shirley is touched and, as usual, goes along with Laverne's scheme. They also occasionally sing "High Hopes" to each other when one of them is discouraged.

Laverne and Shirley date several men over 178 episodes, usually losers they dump or too-good-to-be-true guys who dump them. In one episode, Laverne is determined to marry a sailor she just met because she is afraid she won't get another chance to marry a great guy. Shirley convinces her, in her usual moralizing way, that she and her fiancé each deserve someone who loves them totally. In an unusually poignant episode, a firefighter

Laverne has been dating is killed in a fire, and Shirley helps her get over it. Although Lenny and Squiggy, their nerdy, annoying neighbors and coworkers, would have loved to date "the girls" as they are often called, Laverne and Shirley make it clear they are friends only. Carmine is Shirley's on-again, off-again boyfriend who moves to California to be near her in the series' last two years. It is interesting that the virginal Shirley eventually marries well (an army medic), but the more adventurous Laverne has not when the series ended in 1983. Could it be construed as a moral lesson for girls—the old virgin-whore dichotomy where men like to play with the bad girls but marry the good ones?

In addition to creating their own friends-as-family, Laverne and Shirley have other family members with whom to deal. Laverne's father, Frank, appears regularly, often trying to interfere in his daughter's life, but just as often being chastised by her. Three years into the series he marries his daughter's landlord, divorcee Edna Babish, a strong and loving stepmother figure to both Laverne and Shirley. In a touching episode, Laverne finally makes peace with her mother, who died when she was a child. At her mother's gravesite, Laverne lets go of her resentment for being left and introduces her mom to her best friend, Shirley. Shirley's mom, however, is very much alive and annoying, although she rarely appears. In another unusual, more serious episode, Shirley has to contend with the fact that her brother, a sailor visiting her, is an alcoholic. Laverne, of course, helps her deal with the situation.

Most of the time, however, the lives of Laverne and Shirley are filled with slapstick situations comparable to the antics of two other best friends in the 1950s, Lucy and Ethel. In dozens of episodes the laughs are based on physical humor. Over the seven and a half years of the series, Shirley rescues a horse from a glue factory and hides it in their bedroom, Laverne handcuffs herself to a homeless dog at a pound to protest its scheduled death, Shirley gets amnesia and thinks she is a stripper named Roxy, Laverne becomes a beer tester at work, and on and on. Despite the silly situations and occasional fights, however, there is always the dignity and durability of Laverne and Shirley's friendship.

WOMEN IN 1970s SERIES COMEDY

Approximately a hundred situation comedies debuted in the ten fall seasons from 1970 through 1979; of those, only sixty lasted more than one season. Dozens of female characters came and went in that decade, but others have lasted in both our cultural memory and syndication. While

Mary Richards, Edith Bunker, Maude Findlay, Louise Jefferson, Ann Romano, and Laverne and Shirley held particular significance, several others merit discussion.

The evolution of Major Margaret "Hot Lips" Houlihan on *M*A*S*H* (CBS, 1972–1983) over its eleven years on the air is interesting. Margaret has followed in her father's footsteps with a career in the army. As head nurse of the 4077th M*A*S*H unit during the Korean War, she is competent in her nursing skills, but interpersonally she has a difficult time. More a caricature, as is her character in the movie of the same name, "Hot Lips" has a long affair with married doctor Frank Burns, a wimpy, incompetent who is also regulation army. Over the years, "Hot Lips" evolves into Margaret, who dumps Frank and marries the man of her dreams (another career army person who seemed both heroic and handsome) only to be disappointed when he cheats on her. Margaret is occasionally bothered by her lack of closeness with other nurses, a concept that is explored in "Nurses." While in the end she is invited to coffee, her best friend throughout the series turns out to be Hawkeye. In the two-part "Comrades in Arms" episode, Hawkeye and Margaret make love when they are stuck in enemy territory and fear for their lives. Margaret assumes they will continue their affair back on the base; Hawkeye informs her otherwise. She is at first upset, but then she understands. It is to Hawkeye that Margaret talks about her feelings involving the other nurses, her demanding father, and her broken marriage.

Interestingly enough, it is through Hawkeye that issues of feminism are explored on *M*A*S*H*. Although he played Hawkeye, Alan Alda became creative consultant and part-time writer for the series. Alda's feminism occasionally is reflected in his scripts. In "Inga" particularly, Hawkeye is confronted with his mixed feelings for a woman doctor—although he is attracted to her, he is not willing to admit she could teach him new operating procedures. Hawkeye and Trapper John view the nurses mostly as sex objects to while away the time. Margaret, as a matter of fact, is the only nurse (and woman) with a major role on the series. Actresses who played the nurses would often be called by different names. An exception later in the series is Kellye, the only recurring nurse with a constant identity. Not considered as attractive as the other nurses, in one episode she tells Hawkeye how she feels neglected by him and he finally sees past her looks. In an episode called "Who Knew?" in the last season, Hawkeye questions his attitude toward all the nurses when he is asked to deliver the eulogy for a nurse with whom he went out. He begins to see the women as more than just sex objects, and he starts to question his resistance to becoming close to any of them.

While *M*A*S*H*'s rising consciousness was comfortably placed in the past, *The Partridge Family* (ABC, 1970–1974) was a very now, hip series about a musical family into whose lives feminism crept. Shirley Partridge, widowed mother of five, joins her children at their request in recording songs and performing around the country. Her two oldest children, Keith and Laurie, are attractive and appealing teenagers, inspiring many crushes from audience members. This TV family actually had hit records in real life, no doubt because of their appearance on the show. The series was in the top 25 its first three years then dwindled away over the final year. Meanwhile, it occasionally dealt with feminist issues in interesting ways. In one episode, the family performs to raise money for a feminist group, despite pressure from local people to not do it. Both Shirley and Laurie are for women's liberation, but their stance is very mild compared to Keith's girlfriend of the week (he had several over the run of the series). At first she is quite radical, becoming offended if Keith shows common courtesies, such as holding open doors. When he stops walking her to her door after a date, however, she misses it. It takes her tantrum over the family singing a love song at the rally and an argument with Keith to make her realize that she could like love songs and gentlemanly behavior, and still be for equal rights.

Laurie Partridge, although she is more often in the background to her heartthrob brother Keith and mischievous preadolescent brother Danny, is actually a good role model to young women. She gets good grades and is popular, but she also believes in women's rights and loyalty to friends. In one episode she campaigns for a less popular girl for president against Keith. She does not think it is fair that her brother will probably win based on his looks while her more homely friend is much more qualified. Despite Laurie's opposition, Keith does win as he probably would have in real life, yet there is still a happy ending. Laurie's friend becomes the presidential advisor. In another episode, Laurie again demonstrates strong loyalty to a friend when she takes the blame for cheating. Her friend is the principal's daughter who is scared that her dad will not understand the pressure she is under as his child. Another happy ending manifests itself when the girl finally confesses. Perhaps not exactly a model of how sisterhood is powerful, Laurie's strength of conviction was a nice change from the sitcom teen girls of the past.

Ethnic comedies made a comeback in the 1970s, but they were mostly dominated by men. In addition to *The Jeffersons,* Lear introduced *Sanford and Son* and *Good Times.* Although the latter (CBS, 1974–1979) was a spin-off from *Maude* concerning her maid, Florida, her oldest son J.J.

soon became the dominant character, a portrayal many thought to be a throwback to earlier stereotypes of African Americans, and Florida later became a widow. She is a strong, hard-working woman, but Esther Rolle who played her left the series because she was concerned about the role model that J.J. provided for young blacks.[52] She returned after a year when the producers promised that J.J. would be a more respectable character. Her good friend and neighbor, Willona, by the end of the series is promoted to head buyer at the clothing boutique where she works, and Florida is driving a bus to make ends meet.

Alice, loosely based on the movie, *Alice Doesn't Live Here Anymore,* debuted in 1976 on CBS and enjoyed a nine-year run. Alice is a widow with a preteen son, who has dreams of being a singer. Instead, she establishes yet another "workplace" family at Mel's Diner far away from home. Vera is the naive, childlike waitress who works nicely as a counterbalance to Flo, the oversexed and earthy ("kiss my grits") other waitress. Alice is the "normal" one, drawing support from her women friends and sometimes her grumpy boss, Mel, as she struggles to pay her bills and raise her son. Certainly her life fits the reality of many single moms. Alice sleeps on a sofa bed so her son can have the bedroom in their one-bedroom apartment, and her waitressing is typical of the service jobs available to women with few marketable skills and no job experience. *Alice* generally does not take on social issues, however; its realm is the silly situations involved in dating and dealing with characters that come into the diner.

Other workplace comedies in the 1970s included *Taxi, Barney Miller,* and *Welcome Back, Kotter,* but only in the former does a woman play a significant role. In *Taxi* (ABC, 1978–1982; NBC, 1982–1983), Elaine Nardo is a divorced mother of two working part-time at the Sunshine Cab Company in New York City. Like most other drivers, she has dreams of rising beyond her working-class job—she also has a part-time job at an art gallery with hopes of making it a full-time career someday. Elaine is a beautiful, intelligent, loving woman who is a good friend to the men with whom she works. Her best friend is everyone's sensible advisor, Alex, ironically the only cab driver who doesn't have dreams of something better. While both are shown to have relationships with others, none of them last as long as their friendship. Although Elaine and Alex most often do things together with other coworkers, *Taxi* chronicler Jeff Sorensen said it was their chemistry together that was central to the show.[53] Their friendship is often tested, however. In "Come as You Aren't," for example, Elaine convinces Alex to lie about being a cab driver so she can impress her art-world acquaintances in a cocktail party she has for them. When she gets disgusted at the charade and reveals that she and Alex are both cab drivers, Alex loses his opportunity to be with a beautiful woman and he is determined not to forgive Elaine. In desperation, Elaine yells to Alex as he leaves her apartment that he is probably her best friend, and he returns to her with a hug. In "Nardo Loses Her Marbles," Elaine offers to sleep with Alex, but he refuses to take advantage of her distraught state from overwork.

As in *Alice,* being a working mother is never made to look easy. Elaine's ability to balance her two jobs to pay bills and further her career in addition to being a good mother are made easier, however, with the emotional support of her cab-driving friends. When she complains about problems, as they all do, her friends listen and help when they can. Louie, the short, lustful dispatcher, constantly sexually harasses Elaine, however. Elaine threatens him, as do the other cabbies, when he actually drills a hole in the women's room so he can see her undress. Unfortunately, Elaine is used as a bargaining chip in one episode when the cabbies threaten to strike. Louie says he will agree to their demands if Elaine goes out with him. She reluctantly agrees, for the "good" of her friends, but Alex threatens Louie if he tries to touch her.

Elaine is a woman who handles her predicaments the old-fashioned way—she defends herself, but also looks to male friends for help. Perhaps she is too tired to get involved in the women's movement, but she certainly could have used some close female friends. Alex, however, is a good substitute—he is sensitive and Elaine can talk to him easily. One of the nice things about the series is that their friendship is clearly platonic; there is no "will they or won't they" question, which became popular in the 1980s in several series. Interestingly enough, however, Elaine again volunteers to use her body to help a friend in "Vienna Waits." On their last night of their trip to Europe together, Elaine realizes how miserable Alex has been watching her have a good time with other men who bought her things and took her to fancy places while he hasn't been able to find anyone. Elaine explains to Alex that they have been through so much together that she thinks their friendship can survive one night of love. It does. Elaine is certainly sexually liberated, although she insists on her own terms.

Another workplace comedy introduced in the late 1970s is *WKRP in Cincinnati,* on CBS from 1978–1982. Two females are part of the regular cast of characters at a struggling rock radio station. Jennifer Marlowe is the blonde and sexy receptionist. Contrary to the stereotyped dumb blonde, her boss relies on her to tell him what is going on. Men also fall all over her, giving her expensive gifts. She accepts them with good grace but is nobody's fool. Bailey Quarters is the smart, energetic assistant to the program manager, and she later works in news. A third woman plays a semiregular role: Mrs. Carlson is the owner of the station and mother of the station manager. She has little respect for her son and tends to intimidate everyone else except Jennifer. She is a rich woman who uses her power as she thinks fit.

Several comedies in the 1970s were named after the star female characters, besides those already mentioned. Like *Rhoda, Phyllis* is a spin-off of *The Mary Tyler Moore Show.* Generally the same know-it-all character in her own show, Phyllis became a widow and had to work to support herself and her daughter. Initially popular, the series dwindled off the air in 1977, only two years after its debut. *Flo* is a spin-off from the successful *Alice,* but the feisty waitress kept her own series only a little over a year. *Mork & Mindy* is a spin-off of the popular *Happy Days.* Mork is a space alien who is befriended by Mindy McConnell, a clerk at a music store run by her dad. Mindy eventually becomes a journalism student and works at a television station, while she still tries to help Mork adjust to earthling life. The series is basically slapstick, although Mork would explain to his "leader" at the end of each episode what lesson he recently had learned about human behavior. The silliness of the show continued when Mork and Mindy married, with Mork becoming pregnant and giving birth to an egg with a fully grown man. It went off the air after three years. *Angie* is the Cinderella story of a waitress who married a doctor. Angie's mother keeps a place at the kitchen table for her husband who had walked out on them nineteen years earlier. Progressive the show was not. It lasted less than two years. *Fay,* the story of an attractive, forty-something divorcee, debuted about the same time as *One Day at a Time.* Described by Brooks and Marsh as a "somewhat risque comedy," it lasted only one season.[54] Fay had divorced her cheating husband of twenty-five years, found a job as a secretary to two lawyers, and moved into her own apartment. She dates frequently while her ex-husband keeps trying to get her back and her unhappily married friend lives vicariously through her active sex life. It is interesting to anticipate why Ann Romano was acceptable to viewers and Fay wasn't. Both actively dated, yet Ann also had her two daughters to attract a younger audience as well.

While comedies in the first half of the 1970s tended to focus on issues and character development, the second half of the decade is a bit schizophrenic. Two of the most popular shows are anchored in the 1950s, *Laverne & Shirley,* discussed earlier, and its parent show, *Happy Days.* Based on the movie, *American Graffiti,* the latter centers around three teenage boys, the family of one of them, and their hoody friend, Fonzie, the breakout star of the show, a high school dropout who makes girls swoon and can have them come to him at the snap of his fingers. Two "cool" female characters appear on the show a few times, however. Pinky Tuscadero is a friend of Fonzie, and rides a motorcycle. Her sister, Leather, has her own rock group.

Two series are standouts in the late 1970s for their focus on sex. *Soap* is a satire of daytime drama with plenty of sex and even a homosexual. It focuses on two sisters, one who married rich and the other solidly middle class. Lasting four years on ABC, *Soap* deals with not only the usual adultery of soap operas, but also possession by the devil, kidnapping by aliens, and changing sexual preferences. *Three's Company* is full of sexual innuendoes and double entendres. Sharing its popularity with *Happy Days* and *Laverne & Shirley* on Tuesday nights, this series involves two women sharing an apartment with a man, who has to pretend he is homosexual so the landlord will let him stay. The humor is anything but cerebral, depending on pratfalls and wordplay for its laughs. Janet is the sensible brunette who works in a flower shop. Chrissy is the stereotypical dumb blonde who works as a typist. Their roommate, Jack, would be delighted to sleep with either, or both, of them.

After Vietnam and Watergate, the nation evidently needed a break. Comedy in the 1970s went from socially conscious, such as *All in the Family* and *Maude,* to the mild and mindless *Happy Days* and *Three's Company.* The image of single, working women had gone from Mary Richards to Chrissy Snow. As the 1980s came on the horizon, the continued success of the situation comedy was in jeopardy, and so were the rights of women.

NOTES

1. Gorton Carruth, *What Happened When: A Chronology of Life & Events in America* (New York: Harper & Row, 1989), 1026.

2. Susan Faludi, *Backlash: The Undeclared War against American Women* (New York: Crown, 1991).

3. Flora Davis, *Moving the Mountain: The Women's Movement in America Since 1960* (New York: Simon & Schuster, 1991), 388.

4. Toni Carabillo, Judith Meuli, and June Bundy Csida, *Feminist Chronicles: 1953–1993* (Los Angeles: Women's Graphics, 1993), 183.

5. Carruth, 1026.

6. Carruth, 1082.

7. Gillian G. Gaar, *She's a Rebel: The History of Women in Rock & Roll* (Seattle, WA: Seal Press, 1992), 115.

8. Joplin's death on October 3, 1970, occurred about two weeks after another rock legend's drug-related death, Jimi Hendrix. The following summer, the death of Jim Morrison in Paris also was related to drugs.

9. Writer Thomas Wolfe is credited with labeling the 1970s as "The Me Generation." For more trends in this and other decades, see Julian Biddle, *What Was Hot! A Rollcoaster Ride through Six Decades of Pop Culture in America* (New York: Citadel, 1994, 2001).

10. Carruth, 1090.

11. Jane Feuer, Paul Kerr, and Tise Vahimagi, eds., *MTM 'Quality Television'* (London: British Film Institute, 1984).

12. Michael Arlen, "The Media Dramas of Norman Lear," *All in the Family: A Critical Appraisal,* ed. Richard Adler (New York: Praeger, 1979), 187–95.

13. David Marc and Robert J. Thompson, *Prime Time, Prime Movers* (Boston: Little, Brown, 1992), 54.

14. Horace Newcomb and Robert Alley, *The Producer's Medium: Conversations with Creators of American TV* (New York: Oxford University Press, 1983), 235–36.

15. Ella Taylor, *Prime-Time Families: Television Culture in Postwar America* (Berkeley, CA: University of California Press, 1989), 85.

16. Taylor, 85.

17. Robert S. Alley and Irby B. Brown, *Love Is All Around: The Making of The Mary Tyler Moore Show* (New York: Dell Publishing, 1989), 3.

18. Alley and Brown, 4.

19. Alley and Brown, 30.

20. Serafina Bathrick, "*The Mary Tyler Moore Show:* Women at Home and at Work," *MTM 'Quality Television',* ed. J. Feuer, P. Kerr, and T. Vahimagi (London: British Film Institute, 1984), 127.

21. Bonnie J. Dow, *Prime Time Feminism: Television, Media Culture, and the Women's Movement Since 1970* (Philadelphia: University of Pennsylvania Press, 1996), 52.

22. Alley and Brown, 104.

23. While Mary refuses to reveal her source for a news story, she makes it clear she is more concerned about her own freedom than any higher purpose involving freedom of the press. She does go to jail, however, encouraged by her boss.

24. See Patricia M. Lengermann and Ruth A. Wallace, *Gender in America: Social Control and Social Change* (Englewood Cliffs, NJ: Prentice-Hall, 1985), 82.

25. Bathrick, 119.

26. Alley and Brown, 96.

27. Tim Brooks and Earle Marsh, *The Complete Directory to Prime Time Network TV Shows: 1946–Present,* 7th ed. (New York: Ballantine, 1999).

28. See Richard Adler, ed., *All in the Family: A Critical Appraisal* (New York: Praeger, 1979) for a variety of critical reactions to *All in the Family* during its first two seasons.

29. Donna McCrohan, *Archie & Edith, Mike & Gloria* (New York: Workman, 1987), 67.

30. McCrohan, 67.

31. McCrohan, 64.

32. McCrohan, 75.

33. McCrohan, 75.

34. Rick Mitz, *The Great TV Sitcom Book* (New York: Richard Marek, 1980), 259.

35. McCrohan, 75.

36. Kathryn C. Montgomery, *Target: Prime Time—Advocacy Groups and the Struggle over Entertainment Television* (New York: Oxford University Press, 1989), 30–31.

37. Montgomery, 33.

38. Montgomery, 33.

39. Montgomery, 47.

40. Mitz, 347.

41. Mitz, 343.

42. Mitz, 346.

43. Davis, 365.

44. Mitz, 365.

45. Dow, 72.

46. Dow, 73.

47. Dow, 71.

48. Taylor, 89.

49. Dow, 74.

50. Mitz, 368.

51. Mitz, 368.

52. Brooks and Marsh, 354.

53. Jeff Sorensen, *The Taxi Book* (New York: St. Martin's Press, 1987).

54. Brooks and Marsh, 299.

Ricky spanks Lucy. *I Love Lucy.* Courtesy of Photofest.

Family caucus: Aunt Trina (left), Mama (middle), Aunt Jenny (right), Papa (left), and Uncle Chris (right). *Mama.* Courtesy of Photofest.

Beulah (Hattie McDaniel) at work. *Beulah.* Courtesy of Photofest.

Connie practices first aid with Mr. Boynton. *Our Miss Brooks*. Courtesy of Photofest.

Susie at work with Mr. Sands. *Private Secretary.* Courtesy of Photofest.

Donna and daughter Mary shoe shopping. *The Donna Reed Show.* Courtesy of Photofest.

Laura, Rob, Sally, and new date. *The Dick Van Dyke Show.* Courtesy of Photofest.

Jed, Granny, Jethro, and Elly May. *The Beverly Hillbillies.* Courtesy of Photofest.

Samantha, Endora, and Darrin mix magic. *Bewitched.* Courtesy of Photofest.

Jeannie gets Tony into trouble. *I Dream of Jeannie.* Courtesy of Photofest.

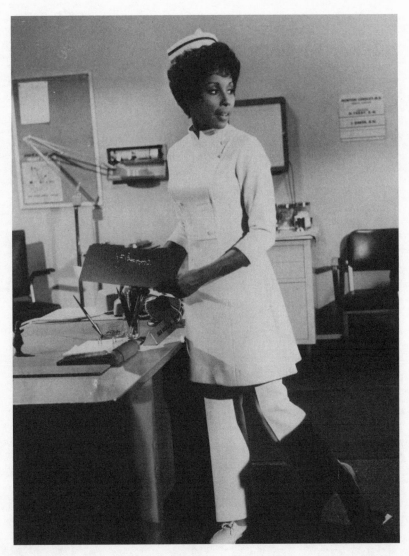

Julia at work. *Julia.* Courtesy of Photofest.

Ann Marie in New York City. *That Girl.* Courtesy of Photofest.

Mary and Rhoda in the talk that binds. *The Mary Tyler Moore Show.* Courtesy of Photofest.

Louise and George Jefferson, Irene, and Edith. *All in the Family*. Courtesy of Photofest.

Carol, Maude, and Vivian. *Maude.* Courtesy of Photofest.

Julie, Barbara, and Ann. *One Day at a Time.* Courtesy of Photofest.

Laverne and Shirley. *Laverne & Shirley*. Courtesy of Photofest.

Allie and Kate. *Kate & Allie*. Courtesy of Photofest.

The singing Huxtables: Sondra, Theo, Denise, Cliff, Clair, Vanessa, and Rudy. *The Cosby Show.* Courtesy of Photofest.

Blanche, Dorothy, and Rose. *The Golden Girls*. Courtesy of Photofest.

Mary Jo, Suzanne, Julia, and Charlene. *Designing Women*. Courtesy of Photofest.

Nancy tells Jackie and Roseanne she's gay. *Roseanne*. Courtesy of Photofest.

Murphy's pregnancy test. *Murphy Brown.* Courtesy of Photofest.

Jill tells Tim she wants a baby. *Home Improvement.* Courtesy of Photofest.

Grace, Russell, and Quentin: Russell explains how to wear a jockstrap. *Grace Under Fire.* Courtesy of Photofes

Maxine, Khadijah, Regine, and Synclaire singing "My Girl." *Living Single*. Courtesy of Photofest.

Who's pregnant? Phoebe, Monica, Chandler, and Rachel. *Friends*. Courtesy of Photofest.

Will's mom, Karen, and Grace. *Will & Grace*. Courtesy of Photofest.

Ellen tells Susan she's gay. *Ellen*. Courtesy of Photofest.

Chapter 5

1980s: WORKING MOMS AND GOLDEN WOMEN

The 1980s began with many problems left over from the 1970s, including the push for ratification of the Equal Rights Amendment in three more states and the hostage crisis in Iran. The backlash against feminist issues also continued, only more intensely, with the election of a conservative Republican president.

The television industry was having its own crisis with ownership changes and new competition from both cable and a fourth commercial broadcast network. While many during the first half of the 1980s were concerned about the future of series comedy, by the end of the decade there was another golden age of sorts, with women taking a more prominent role. The struggle of women in real life occasionally became the focus on some serious prime-time comedy.

CULTURAL/HISTORICAL CONTEXT

The 1980s was marked by the struggle of feminists to hold on to gains made in the 1970s. Unfortunately, on June 30, 1982, time ran out for ratification of the Equal Rights Amendment and it was defeated. From the local to national level, abortion rights also were hampered. More frightening, however, were the illegal and violent attempts to close clinics and intimidate patients and health care providers. The political climate was also not good for basic civil rights. One federal statute under reinterpretation was Title IX, which prohibited sex discrimination in federally funded educational institutions. In a 1984 decision, the Supreme Court accepted the Reagan administration's position that it ban discrimination only in specific programs within an institution that received federal funds, rather than throughout the institution. In 1986, a federal district judge in Chicago dismissed a $20 million sex discrimination case against Sears, a national department store. The Equal Employment Opportunity Commission (EEOC) had filed the suit in the mid-1970s because so few of the female employees at Sears held high-paying commission sales jobs or management positions.[1] Sears reportedly claimed that women didn't want demanding jobs. In 1988, daycare promised to become a more pressing issue as the birthrate rose to its highest level in almost a quarter of a century, and, according to the Census Bureau, more than half of new mothers stayed in the job market.[2]

While some of the news for women was bad in the 1980s, several positive steps were also taken. Wage discrimination cases were boosted by a 1981 Supreme Court decision, which ruled that women could sue for equal pay even if the work was not identical with that of male employees. In 1983, the Supreme Court stood firmly behind the *Roe* v. *Wade* decision and ruled that government could not interfere with the fundamental right of abortion unless it was clearly justified by accepted medical practice. In 1988, over President Reagan's veto, Congress passed the Civil Rights Restoration Act, restoring full coverage of Title IX provisions prohibiting sex discrimination in education by recipients of federal funds. Landmarks for women in the 1980s included the first female astronaut (Sally Ride) and the first president of a national veterans' association (Mary Stout of the Vietnam Veterans of America). Although President Reagan appointed the first woman, Sandra Day O'Connor, to the Supreme Court in 1981, it was the Democratic party that nominated the first woman, Geraldine Ferraro, as a vice presidential candidate, running with Walter Mondale in 1984. Reagan was reelected, however, in the biggest Republican landslide in history. In 1987, with congressional approval, March became "Women's History Month."

While the first and last parts of the 1980s were marked by high inflation and rising unemployment, the middle of the decade saw an economic boom. Several major events shook up the business world, however, including AT&T's forced divestiture from its regional operating companies, the near collapse of the savings and loans industry because of mismanagement and corruption, and the biggest stock market crash in the history of the United States. Federal studies connected the use of tampons made by Procter & Gamble to the deaths of at least twenty-five women from "toxic shock

syndrome," leading to its recall. In 1987, a federal judge ordered the producers of a birth control device, the IUD, to establish a fund to compensate
women who had been harmed by the device.[3]

The *Challenger* disaster is probably a vivid memory of most Americans
from the 1980s. Thousands of schoolchildren watched in 1986 as the first
"teacher in space," Christa McAuliffe, died upon takeoff, along with six
astronauts. Acquired immune deficiency syndrome (AIDS) also became a
larger part of the national consciousness as popular film and television
actor Rock Hudson succumbed to it in 1985. As people scrambled for jobs
and complained about the rising crime rate and the falling quality of education, the federal deficit was also increasing. Terrorism increased in the
Middle East throughout the decade, perhaps most notably in Beirut where
241 were killed after the bombing of U.S. Marine headquarters. On a positive note, communism ended in several countries, including Poland and
East Germany.

A growing mania for physical fitness and appearance inspired the purchase of home exercise equipment in the United States, which exceeded
$1 billion in 1984, and cosmetics, which exceeded $10 billion in sales.[4]
Colorful leg warmers became popular, and business suits in a variety of
colors became part of the practical wardrobe of many women. Businesses,
and later the home market, became revolutionized by personal computers
and fax machines.

The world of popular culture experienced several revolutionary
changes. A part of the generation that grew up with the Beatles in the
1960s died when John Lennon was murdered in December 1980 in New
York City. While people mourned his loss, a new generation of music was
on the horizon, assisted by Music Television (MTV), a cable channel that
debuted in 1981 with music videos of popular artists. MTV is probably
responsible to a great extent for the phenomenal success of Michael Jackson, particularly with his *Thriller* album, and Madonna, with popular sin-
gles such as "Like a Virgin" and "Material Girl." The middle-aged but
gorgeous Tina Turner made a major comeback with her *Private Dancer*
album, containing the hit "What's Love Got to Do with It?" On the radio,
"shock jocks" such as Howard Stern were beginning to garner criticism
and stiff fines for "indecency" as defined by the Federal Communications
Commission. "Rap" music was becoming more mainstream, although
many objected to lyrics that were derogatory toward women. On a positive
note, musical artists were recording songs and doing concerts to raise
money for various important causes. For example, "We Are the World"
had dozens of popular artists harmonizing to make money for African

famine relief. The decade also saw the skyrocketing success of compact discs and CD players.

In print, Danielle Steele continued to write popular romance novels, with many also enjoying success as made-for-television movies. Tom Clancy's "technothrillers," such as *Red Storm Rising,* and legal thrillers, such as Scott Turow's *Presumed Innocent,* also enjoyed bestseller-status. Toni Morrison published *Beloved,* a bestseller, later to become a movie starring media mogul Oprah Winfrey. The western, the most popular genre on television in the late 1950s, made a comeback with Larry McMurtry's Pulitzer Prize–winning *Lonesome Dove,* also made into a well-liked mini-series on television. Newspaper readership did not keep up with population increases, and many evening newspapers changed to morning editions, in recognition of competition from television news. *Ms* magazine grappled for economic survival during the decade in its attempt to keep editorial content free from advertiser input. As many women struggled to raise families and maintain jobs outside the home, a controversial 1989 article by Felice Schwartz published in the *Harvard Business Review* proposed that employers should separate women into "career—primary" and "career and family" categories and treat them accordingly. The latter became known as the "mommy track," which feminists said violated antidiscrimination laws and ghettoized women.[5]

The movie industry enjoyed several major hits, many which were sequels to popular series, including *Return of the Jedi* from the *Star Wars* trilogy, *Raiders of the Lost Ark* and its sequel *Indiana Jones and the Temple of Doom* with megastar Harrison Ford, and the Rambo series, based on Sylvester Stallone's revengeful Vietnam veteran. The biggest box office hit of the decade was *E.T.: The Extraterrestrial,* a movie about a young boy and an alien he helps to get home, produced by Steven Spielberg. In 1986, Randa Haines became the first American woman ever to be nominated by the Directors Guild of America as best director of a motion picture for the critically acclaimed *Children of a Lesser God.* Steven Spielberg produced Alice Walker's Pulitzer Prize–winning book *The Color Purple* about the life of a Southern woman, starring Whoopi Goldberg. Katherine Hepburn won an unprecedented fourth Oscar for her role as half of an aging couple in *On Golden Pond.* In *The Accused,* Jody Foster, in an Oscar-winning performance, portrays a real rape victim who faces prejudice as she seeks justice. In her book on the backlash against women, Susan Faludi described at length "how Hollywood restated and reinforced the backlash thesis: American women were unhappy because they were too free; their liberation had denied them marriage and motherhood."[6] A good example of this perspective is *Fatal Attraction,* released in 1987. In this popular film, Glenn Close portrays a single career woman who becomes obsessed with a married man, portrayed by Michael Douglas. After a one-night stand, she stalks him, visits his wife on false pretenses, and ultimately tries to kill them, only to end up dead herself.

THE TELEVISION INDUSTRY

The 1980s began with the rise of hour-long drama, particularly of the serial variety. Many claimed that the comedy genre was dying, and might virtually disappear, as had two other formerly popular genres, the variety show and western.[7] Despite the death knells, the final two-and-a-half hour episode of the popular 1970s comedy, *M*A*S*H,* in March 1983, garnered the largest television audience up to that time for a nonsports program.[8] In 1984, *The Cosby Show* revitalized series comedy and led the ratings for the rest of the decade.

While the content of the medium experienced some changes, the decade also was filled with major transformations in the business of television. In 1985, ABC became the first television network ever to be sold, with Capital Cities Communications Inc. the new owner. NBC was later sold to General Electric, while CBS was warding off several threatened corporate takeovers. While the networks were adapting to new administrations, their competition increased tremendously. Cable television penetration grew from just under 22 percent in 1980 to over 56 percent in 1989.[9] Along with the growth in cable came many new networks to compete with the big three, including the Cable News Network (CNN); ESPN with sports; and Lifetime, promoted as a network for women. In 1987, a new broadcast network, Fox Broadcasting Company (FOX), began aggressively competing for young adult viewers. After decades of dominating the television industry, the viewership shared by ABC, CBS, and NBC had dropped from 85 percent to 67 percent by the end of the decade.[10] Video games and prerecorded videocassettes also took away from traditional television viewing. The percentage of homes with videocassette recorders grew from less than 5 percent early in the decade to almost 66 percent in 1989.[11] Video store rentals began to exceed box office receipts.

The Reagan years seemed to inspire a fascination with the rich, corporate world in fictional television. Prime-time soap *Dallas* (CBS, 1978–1991), about an oil-rich family, finished the 1980–1981 season in the number one slot in the ratings. Its success was followed by other popular prime-time soaps, including *Dynasty, Falcon Crest,* and *Knots Landing.*

Action was plentiful in shows such as *The A-Team,* about a group of rene-gade Vietnam veterans, and *Magnum, P.I.,* about a private detective who was also a Vietnam veteran. The bright spot among all the testosterone was Angela Lansbury as Jessica Fletcher on *Murder, She Wrote.* Debuting in 1984 on CBS, the series revolved around the great skills of a middle-aged female murder mystery novelist who was always helping the police to solve crimes. A few dramas in the 1980s were dominated by couples professionally involved together in government or detective work. Audi-ences watched to see if their sexual tension would evolve into romance, such as in *Scarecrow & Mrs. King, Remington Steele,* and *Moonlighting.* A few critically acclaimed dramas debuting in the 1980s were ensembles of characters involved in various situations. *Hill Street Blues* and *St. Else-where* revolved around a police station and hospital, respectively. *L.A. Law* involved a law firm in Los Angeles, and *China Beach* centered on a combination hospital and entertainment center in Vietnam during the war. The lives of seven "yuppie" friends in Philadelphia was the subject of *thirtysomething.*

Cagney & Lacey offered women a female version of the "buddy film" that had been popular in the movie industry for years.[12] The pleasure view-ers took in the individual strength of these female New York City detec-tives was intensified by the depiction of their strong friendship. Mary Beth Lacey (Daly) was married with two children and a loving husband who was often unemployed. Christine Cagney was single, the daughter of a cop, and determined to become chief of detectives some day. Many episodes focused on social issues particularly important to women, includ-ing rape, wife beating, and breast cancer. One episode on the bombing of an abortion clinic presented various positions on abortion, with Mary Beth Lacey revealing that she had an abortion before she met her husband.[13] Before *Cagney & Lacey* first aired as a made-for-television movie on CBS in 1981 and until the series was canceled in the spring of 1988, the National Organization for Women and particularly Gloria Steinem were strong supporters of this series, endorsing it as feminist and important to keep on the air.[14]

Made-for-television movies in the 1980s often addressed issues vital to the women's movement. In 1980, for example, chapters of the National Organization for Women in several cities helped promote *The $5.20 an Hour Dream,* a movie about a divorced mother and factory worker trying to get a higher-paying job on the assembly line.[15] In 1989, despite threat-ened boycotts by advertisers, NBC aired *Roe v. Wade,* the story of the abortions rights case that led to the 1973 Supreme Court decision.

SIGNIFICANT COMEDY SERIES

Many of the strong images of females in prime-time series comedy in the 1980s were the products of women. *Kate & Allie* was created by Sherry Koben, and *The Golden Girls* was created by Susan Harris. The latter half of the decade would find two very powerful women who not only wrote for prime-time television, but were producers as well. Linda Bloodworth-Thomason's *Designing Women* debuted in 1986 on CBS. Creator, co-executive producer, and headwriter of the series, Bloodworth-Thomason's half-hour comedy starred four women who often got involved with social issues, earning her the title of "advocacy producer."[16] Diane English was creator, co-executive producer, and head writer of *Murphy Brown,* a half-hour CBS comedy about a hard-edged, successful network news magazine reporter, which debuted in 1989. Although initially not a producer, Roseanne (previously Roseanne Barr, then Arnold) eventually took creative control of her own show, the popular *Roseanne.*

Despite predictions of its demise, comedy made a comeback as the most popular genre in the latter half of the 1980s, spurred on by the success of *The Cosby Show* and reinforced by the series of several creative women. Based on popularity and their groundbreaking contributions with female characters or story lines, the following are of particular significance: *Kate & Allie, The Cosby Show, The Golden Girls, Designing Women, Roseanne,* and *Murphy Brown.*[18]

Kate & Allie

Kate & Allie (CBS, 1984–1989) depicts two best friends since childhood who are divorced and decide to share a Greenwich Village apartment in New York City for mutual financial and emotional support. The series focuses on their trials and tribulations as they attempt to raise their children, deal with ex-husbands, establish and maintain careers, and engage in the world of dating in their thirties. Although whether the series was feminist is open to debate, many delighted in the fact that it featured two women who were undoubtedly supportive friends.[17] The series offered reassurance for the millions of separated or divorced women with children in the early 1980s.[18]

Although Kate and Allie have many shared experiences and obviously are loving friends, their personalities are quite different. As Brooks and Marsh described them, "Kate was glamorous, contemporary, and a bit frivolous while Allie was old-fashioned, proper, and industrious to a fault."[19]

Kate McArdle is in her thirties and the mother of a teenage girl, Emma. By her own account, Kate and her frequently unemployed actor-husband, Max, lived like gypsies until she got tired of it. Still somewhat adventurous and liberal, Kate got a divorce and took on the sole responsibility of supporting her and her daughter. In the beginning of the series she is working in a travel agency, and later she and Allie establish a catering business together. Allie Lowell is also in her thirties and has two children, Chip (eight years old at the beginning of the series) and teenaged Jennie. Married to a doctor for sixteen years while living in Connecticut, Allie's husband dumped her for a younger woman. A housewife all those years, it is natural for Allie to become the homemaker in her combined household with Kate. Although she initially plays the self-sacrificing "wife" role as chief cook and cleaner, Allie is encouraged by Kate to go back to college (she had dropped out her senior year to get married) and, after she graduates and has gone through a series of menial jobs, the two start their own business.

Indicative of the show's focus, the *Kate & Allie* theme song is "Friends," written by John Leffler and Ralph Schuckett. Before the opening credits to each episode, however, is a "teaser" that usually places Kate and Allie on location somewhere in Manhattan, shopping, skating, or doing any of a variety of activities available in this big city. The teasers emphasize their friendship but heighten the contrast in their personalities. Kate is usually shown as the stronger and braver one—she is the one who rows the boat in Central Park and roller skates around Allie while the latter is afraid to move. In their casual discussions as they roam about the city, Allie usually espouses a conservative view while Kate takes a more liberal position. For example, as Kate is rowing on the lake, she talks about how she thinks a woman should be as strong as a man "in a feminine way," while Allie opts for the old-fashioned notion of women being weak and having men do things for them. Kate's idea of being strong yet feminine begs the question of what is feminine, however, and sometimes the women act in contradictory ways. While Kate usually takes a liberal feminist position, she enjoys men whistling at her at construction sites and shows Allie how it can feel good to be "ogled." Despite Allie's claims that she likes the old-fashioned traditional roles of men and women, we see her take great pride in finishing her college degree and running her own business. One could argue that Kate and Allie's occasionally contradictory behavior is realistic, however. Gender roles can be confusing and confining to all concerned; like many women, Kate and Allie are often seen struggling to define their own terms, in the teasers as well as in the main story lines.

While other sitcom women had friends, *Kate & Allie* was celebrated by many as the first major comedy "that really shows what women are like when we are alone together."[20] In an early episode where Kate's boyfriend gives her an engagement ring, she later wakes up Allie to talk about it. Kate tells Allie she is glad that she was there when Ted proposed because she has been there for all her big events; Allie concurs that Kate has been there for all her major events too. The two women are frequently waking each other up or finding each other during the day (at school or work) to exchange news, as if things have little meaning until their friend knows. At the end of each episode (in the "tag"), we see the two women, usually in their living room with soda or beer, discussing earlier events. Like real friends, they validate each other's experiences, give each other advice, and share their joys and sorrows. As in real life, however, friendships do not always go smoothly. In one episode, for example, Kate defends Allie to her boss after Allie has made a major mistake while working at the travel agency. Allie soon gets tired of hearing Kate's story about how she defended her, and refuses to speak to Kate. After three days of the silent treatment, the children decide to handcuff the women together until they make up. When Allie explains to Kate how she is humiliated by Kate always rescuing her and that she is tired of "always being the weak one," Kate immediately apologizes and promises to try not to make her feel that way again.

Throughout the series, there are several men in Kate and Allie's lives. Most consistent is the presence of their ex-husbands as they visit the children. On at least one occasion, each has an affair with her ex, but only Allie misses her old life. Dumped by Charles for a younger woman, Allie must deal with her jealousy as she sees her children spending time with the "other woman" when they visit their dad. In the last season, Allie marries a sports announcer, Bob, who frequently travels, allowing the series to continue its focus on her and Kate. When Kate first meets her most significant boyfriend, Ted, a plumber, their class differences initially get in the way, but it is clear the two have an intense physical relationship. After her engagement to Ted, she learns that he is looking forward to having a family. Kate doesn't want to have any more children and breaks up with Ted so he can find someone who shares his dreams. Ted, of course, is upset because all he wants is a marriage like his mom and dad's. In a thinly disguised reference to women's liberation, he says he "doesn't like what's going on out there." Kate's response is that he should give it some time— "it just got started." Ted and Kate remain good friends, but she never remarries during the series.

While Kate does not relish the traditional wife and mother role, she does come across as conservative when it comes to having children. In an earlier episode, she wants to have a baby, after helping a friend at work deliver hers. Her friend, however, is single and has not told the father about the child. Although Kate is not judgmental about her friend having a baby out of wedlock, she does encourage her to tell the father. At the end of the episode, she tells Allie it wouldn't be fair for her to have a child without the father. Kate is much more liberal about her sexuality, however. She is not at all upset at having a purely physical relationship with Ted in the episode that introduced him. Allie also learns to loosen up, and has affairs both with a college professor and with Bob before she has known either very long.

One of the best aspects about the relationships that Kate and Allie have with men is that they are not jealous of each other. Unlike the frequent portrayal of women in the media as rivals for the affection of men, each of these women is happy for the other when she has a love interest. In one episode, the two read a novel by a former college professor of theirs that revolves around the professor's passionate love for a student who was inseparable from her best friend. Each one fantasizes that she is the love interest, but encourages the other that she must be the one. When Allie gets the professor's autograph and it seems to indicate that she is the heroine, Kate lets her believe it to boost her confidence, even though she knows the professor wrote the same thing in everyone's book. It is only when Allie is on her way to meet the professor for a drink that Kate lets her know so he can't take advantage of her.

Despite the emphasis on Kate and Allie's friendship, we never lose sight of the fact that they are mothers. Their daughters, Jennie and Emma, are the same age; through them we see the development of another close friendship. Both girls are attractive and bright, but they go through the normal traumas of teenagers. When Emma's dad moves to California for his acting career, we see the heartbreak of yet another child of divorce separated from a parent. We also see Jennie trying to fit in with a girl she thinks is cool, and later deciding to have sex with her boyfriend. Throughout all their traumas, Kate and Allie are there to support them in their own ways. Kate, as the "cool" parent, fancies herself a buddy to Emma until Emma accuses her of acting cute and "bopping around." A rude awakening to Kate, who still thinks of herself as young, she promises to stop. Despite Allie's more conservative demeanor, she unflinchingly supports Jennie when she is arrested for shoplifting because she believes in her daughter's honesty. When Allie sees she is losing the battle to talk Jennie out of having sex with her boyfriend, she relents, saying "if you think you are mature enough to make love, I want you to make love maturely," and tells her to go to the doctor for birth control. Six years younger than his sister, Chip's problems, of course, are quite different. The entire household, for example, is pressed to explain death to him when his new kitten dies.

The relationships that Kate and Allie have with their parents are also explored in a few episodes. When Kate's dad comes to town to introduce her to his fiancée, Kate takes an immediate dislike to the woman, who is quite pushy. Kate's dad breaks up with his fiancée because of Kate, and becomes despondent. Interestingly enough, when Allie is not around to discuss the matter with Kate, it is Allie's daughter, Jennie, who helps Kate solve the problem. Allie's relationship with her mother is not so easily resolved. Several episodes indicate that Allie's mother has always been critical of her. In one episode, Allie complains to Kate that her mom makes her feel ten years old. She recites to her friend, "A daughter may forget the mistakes in her life, so she needs a mother to twist the knife." In comparing their mothers in terms of advice about sex, Allie says that her mom told her it was something she had to do to keep a man, while Kate's mom said it was something she should do well. In looking at their relationships with their parents (and their ex-husbands), it is easy to see why Kate has more confidence than Allie.

How realistic *Kate & Allie* was in depicting the lives of divorced mothers during the 1980s, of course, depends on the episode as well as the life circumstances of viewers. Certainly the two women are better off financially than the thousands of their real-life counterparts whose incomes and social class often plummet after separation or divorce. Allie's struggle to develop the skills and the confidence to support herself is, however, one in which many displaced housewives have found themselves. Perhaps the most realistic aspect of this series is the enduring, loving friendship of the two women. In the tag of one episode, Kate asks Allie that if she had a man, would she be sitting there with her eating chocolate cake? Although Allie replies that she wouldn't be sitting there with her at all, we know better. When Allie came home from her date, we know she would wake Kate up to talk about it.

The Cosby Show

Created by Ed Weinberger, Michael Leeson, and Bill Cosby, Ed.D., *The Cosby Show* (NBC, 1984–1992) depicts an African American family with two professional parents and five children. Credited with reviving the sitcom genre, it enjoyed immense popularity and critical acclaim. Without a doubt, Bill Cosby is the star of his show. A successful standup comedian whose material often involved his family, Cosby based the Huxtable family in the series on his own life. When NBC ordered the series, he insisted on total creative control, "which he used to shape the series into a showcase for the educational and child-rearing theories he had developed."[21] Cosby also hired Dr. Alvin Poussaint, a Harvard psychiatrist, as a script consultant to make sure there were no stereotypes about sex, race, age, or religion. The humor was to be gentle and inoffensive, making us laugh from recognition rather than at the expense of others.

In the series, Cosby portrays Heathcliff Huxtable, an obstetrician in his forties who works out of an office in his New York City brownstone home. Clair is his beautiful wife and an attorney working full time. They have four daughters and one son, ranging in age at the beginning of the series from five to twenty years old. The fact that they are African American is always present in subtle ways, as they surround themselves with the paintings, books, and music of black artists. A Huxtable tradition is continued when daughter Denise attends Hillman College, a mostly black school in the South. The family watches a broadcast of Martin Luther King Jr.'s "I Have a Dream Speech" in one episode, and the elder Huxtables tell of their fight for civil rights in the 1960s. While most television critics were charmed with the portrayal of the Huxtables as a family, not just a black family, coping with life's everyday problems, others were not so kind.[22] Complaints included that *The Cosby Show* avoided the important issue of racism and that the Huxtables, as a two-career, upper-middle-class family, did not reflect the reality of the lives of most African Americans.[23]

According to critic Mark Crispin Miller, consumption is a way of life on *The Cosby Show,* with the designer clothes and purchases of the family often a subject of discussion.[24] Miller said Cliff Huxtable is a "willing advertisement for the system that pays him well" and an indication to whites that blacks can and do have material equality so there is no need for black lawlessness.[25] A study years later involving fifty-two small focus groups in the Springfield, Massachusetts, area to determine the effects of *Cosby* on racial attitudes seemed to confirm Miller's concerns.[26] Sut Jhally and Justin Lewis found that, because of the success of the Huxtable family, white viewers thought that if blacks fail, they have only themselves to blame, and that there is no need for affirmative action because racism is no longer a problem. Jhally and Lewis see class as the underlying problem in poverty, not race, but class barriers are generally not acknowledged nor recognized by either *Cosby* or its viewers. According to these researchers,

the potential impact on black audiences is self-blame for their circumstances and not the invisible structures of class. The Huxtables are black,
but they have obtained the American dream through hard work.

The series undoubtedly was successful at "recoding ethnicity," however, breaking the racial stereotypes of earlier comedies with African
Americans portrayed as a loving, intact, and financially secure family.[27]
Clair Huxtable, an example of the "superwoman" heralded by advertisers
in response to the women's movement, is a difficult role to emulate in real
life.[28] The mother of five children, Clair works full time as an attorney, yet
she seems to spend hours with her husband and children and is available
at a moment's notice for even the most minor crisis. Both parents share in
cooking and child care duties, but nobody seems to clean the immacu-
lately kept household. Several studies have shown that most husbands
don't help with household duties and child care; it is even less likely that
an obstetrician like Cliff would have the time. Over the eight years of the
series, only a handful of episodes deal with Clair as an attorney; the
emphasis is usually on her role as wife and mother. On the rare occasions
she is shown working on a brief, she does not yell at Cliff for disturbing
her—she exchanges light-hearted banter or joins him for some cuddling
time. In one episode she does show signs of burnout and the family rallies
around her. While she is successfully raising a nice family and having a
brilliant career, Clair also looks gorgeous. When the already svelte Clair
hires an aerobics instructor to help her get into a new dress, we don't see
the overweight Cliff concerned about his protruding gut.

Without a doubt, however, Clair espouses feminist rhetoric. While Cliff
rarely needs to be reprimanded about equal rights, her son, Theo, and various male friends of the children frequently need reminding. When her
oldest daughter, Sondra, brings home Elvin, the man she will eventually
marry, he has many old-fashioned notions of male-female relationships,
and Clair proceeds to set him straight. She explains, for example, that she
does not mind doing things for people (in this context, her husband) as
long as the gesture is reciprocal and the respect mutual. Clair's daughters
also frequently find themselves in the role of teaching nonsexist behavior.
In an early episode, the second oldest daughter, Denise, lectures her
brother on how degrading it is to refer to women as "burgers," simultaneously teaching younger sister Vanessa that such terminology is not "cute"
as Vanessa first thought it, but insulting. In his analysis of the discourses in
The Cosby Show, John Downing pointed out, however, that sexism on the
show is "basically exemplified by callow youths," drawing attention to
the problem, but not really getting into the heart of it.[29] Nevertheless,

Downing also noted that Cliff's condemnation of everyday sexism may communicate powerfully to the male audience because he does not come across as a "henpecked wimp."[30]

With Cosby as the star of the show, the role of his wife is secondary, despite the surface equality in their relationship. Ella Taylor, in her study of families on prime-time television over a forty-year time span, calls the Huxtable household a patriarchy, "set by Cosby himself, whose prodigious charm overlays a subtle message: Father knows best, or else."[31] Despite the fact that he has four daughters, Cliff Huxtable obviously favors his son, Theo. He is shown on several occasions putting his arm around his son, and proudly stating, "my boy." Although Theo is depicted early in the show as not being a good student, the series ends with his graduation from New York University with a bachelor of science degree and daughter Denise phoning home that she and her husband are expecting a baby, traditional roles for both.

Sondra, the oldest of the Huxtable children, is in her last year at Princeton University at the start of the series. After graduation she marries former sexist Elvin Tibideaux and puts off going to law school while she and her husband start their own business, the Wilderness Store. By the end of the series, she and Elvin have duplicated the lifestyle of her parents: she is a lawyer, he is a doctor, and their family life has started with twins. Sondra has become the second-generation superwoman. Denise, on the other hand, is the family's problem child. Although she has carried on the primarily male family tradition of attending Hillman College, Denise receives bad grades and drops out, only to drift from job to job. When she returns after a year of being a photographer's assistant in Africa, she brings home a husband and a stepdaughter. She eventually takes education courses with the hope of becoming a teacher for disabled children, and she ends the series pregnant with the Huxtables' third grandchild. When third daughter Vanessa goes off to college, she returns with a fiancé who is considerably older than she. The introduction of Dabnus, a maintenance man, also raises the issue of class differences, though the Huxtable parents express more concern over the age difference and Vanessa finishing school. Eventually, sensible and smart Vanessa realizes her mistake, and she breaks off the relationship amiably. In her high school years, Vanessa is used to illustrate the ills of alcohol consumption after she and her girlfriends play a drinking game. As she would learn later with her fiancé, mom and dad know best, and the issue is solved in twenty-three minutes. Rudy is the youngest child, a very cute, sweet little girl who interacts charmingly with Cosby as her dad. She is not all sugar and spice, however; in one episode she joins the Pee Wee League football team. While we see all the younger Huxtable children going through the growing pains of school and dating, it is with Rudy that the change is most dramatic. Barely in school when the series starts, we see her embarrassed to start junior high because her "bust is a bust." Another episode involves her adjusting to the start of her period. Clair is eager to celebrate "woman's day" with her, a female family tradition marking the beginning of menstruation, but Rudy, like many girls, is upset and embarrassed.

Another female was added to the household in the 1990–1991 season, Clair's 17-year-old distant cousin Pam. With her mother in California to care for her ailing grandmother, the Huxtables take Pam in, allowing her to continue school with her friends. Coming from a much poorer background, Pam is impressed with her new environment, and all family members have to do some adjusting. Cosby, determined to take on women's issues more wholeheartedly, also hired four women writers for that season, with the assumption that they would add a sensibility the male writers did not have.[32] With Rudy it was the beginning of her period, with Pam the sensitive issue of teenage sexuality is explored. When Pam's boyfriend pressures her to have sex, she approaches Cliff and asks him for birth control. While he makes it clear to Pam that he would prefer she not have sex, he agrees to give her birth control if her mother consents. The mother agrees, but Pam ends up telling her boyfriend she is not ready, a decision that the Huxtables wholeheartedly endorse, and that is typical for situation comedy but not particularly realistic.

After five straight years in the 1980s as the country's most popular program, *The Cosby Show* found itself with tough competition in the 1990s. *Roseanne,* depicting a much more strident and working-class family, became the most popular show, indicating a desire by audience members to see families struggle with the economy and each other, as they were doing. Cosby himself blamed some of the audience erosion on critical attacks in the press, but also said some of the stories about women's issues may have offended viewers, despite the importance of breaking down "some of the foolishness that goes with stereotypes of the female in the country."[33] Regardless of the criticisms of *The Cosby Show* and the unfairness of expecting it to represent all African Americans, the series is enjoyable for what it is—a comedy about ideal family life. In a tribute to the series as it came to its final network broadcast in 1992, Coretta Scott King (widow of Martin Luther King Jr.) praised it for teaching viewers "so much about the importance of strong, caring parents, about the values of honesty and openness in family communication that seem to be lacking in many homes today."[34] Perhaps more significantly, the audience didn't seem to mind identifying Clair and Cliff with gender equality. Although the word "feminist" was not used, lessons of feminism were frequent.

The Golden Girls

Susan Harris's *The Golden Girls* broke new ground by starring four women, three in their fifties or sixties and one octogenarian. The series is a celebration of female friendship and sexuality in the "golden years" of life. Broadcast on NBC (1985–1992), it was an immediate hit and stayed in the top 10 for most of its run. Critically acclaimed, each of its four lead actresses won the best actress or supporting actress Emmy at least once, and the series won as best comedy twice. As with most television series, the lead characters are a study in contrasts, with their conflicting personalities comprising an interesting household they share in Miami, Florida.

Blanche Devereaux is a sexy widow whose home the women share. Reminiscent of her namesake, Blanche DuBois in *A Streetcar Named Desire,* this Blanche is also a southern belle who refuses to admit she is aging. Although she works in a museum, Blanche lives and breathes men, priding herself on her very active sex life. Rose Nyland, a naive widow from Minnesota, is a scatterbrain, constantly telling stories from her beloved little town, St. Olaf, and always not quite connecting with what the others are discussing. Dorothy Zbornak is a substitute English teacher in the local public school system. A divorcee, her husband, Stan, left her for a much younger woman after thirty-eight years of marriage. Dorothy is a strong, intelligent woman and the most outspoken of the group. Her mother, Sophia Petrillo, is the feisty octogenarian who also lives with them. With a sharp tongue and quick wit, Sophia also remains active with part-time jobs and volunteer work.

The opening theme song, "Thank You for Being a Friend," establishes perhaps the most important message of the show. While family members have died or moved away, these women have formed their own family and stick by each other through illnesses, disappointments, and heartache. Although they met each other through Blanche's notice for roommates on a supermarket bulletin board, the three women became fast friends. In the first episode Sophia joins them when her senior citizens' home burns down. The debut episode also immediately sets the tone for the joy of their friendship. When Blanche discovers that the man she was to marry is a bigamist, she hides in her room for days. After the other women have tried unsuccessfully to console her, Blanche suddenly appears on the patio where they are gathered and tells them she found herself humming in the shower that day. She says she is feeling good because of them, that they are her family and she is glad to be alive.

Like most friendships, the golden girls' relationship does not always go smoothly. In one episode, they vie for the attention of a debonair TV actor performing locally. In yet another episode, Dorothy is consumed with guilt when she kisses Rose's estranged boyfriend, but she has no intentions of stealing him away from her. For the most part, fortunately, the women are not presented as rivals for the affection of men. A more serious rivalry occurs when Blanche gets Dorothy a job at the museum where she works and accuses Dorothy of backstabbing when she gets a great assignment. The other women frequently put down Rose for her lack of intelligence, Blanche often indicates to Rose and Dorothy that she thinks she is far prettier than they are, and Sophia's constant putdowns of her daughter Dorothy can really get annoying, yet it is usually more like the banter of close friends or siblings who accept each other as they are.

Despite their conflicting personalities (they even once consult a psychiatrist about their incompatibility), the women always manage to work out their problems and are there for each other in crises. In one episode, Dorothy and Blanche stay up all night with Rose to help her get over her dependency on pain pills. When Rose has to deliver a eulogy in the Bahamas, the other women fly with her, dealing with Rose's fear of public speaking and Dorothy's fear of flying. Rose flies to New York City with Dorothy to be with her when she sees a medical specialist. The golden girls are shown at least once in each episode around their kitchen table, usually eating cheesecake and having their all-important (even when seemingly unimportant) talks.

While the friendship of the golden girls is true to the lives of many women, their sex lives are incredible. Blanche is notorious for the countless men in and out of her bedroom, but the other women also have dating lives that could have sent thousands of lonely senior citizens to Miami. Proud that her initials stand for BED (Blanche Elizabeth Devereaux), Blanche's men tend to be faceless; we usually hear about them rather than see them. There are some interesting exceptions, sometimes teaching the vain Blanche a lesson. In an episode where she is stood up at a bar, she talks to the handsome stranger next to her and they make a date. When she finally realizes he is blind, it confuses her—she has attracted a man not by her looks but by her personality. On the other hand, Rose most often is shown dating Miles, an attractive older man who turns out to be a former accountant for the mob and in the witness protection program. Several episodes deal with the problems in their relationship, including one where Rose thinks Miles is just plain dull and another where she thinks he is cheap. When she and Miles agree to go on a cruise together, she runs to Blanche for advice—Rose is afraid of having sex with him. With another steady boyfriend the problem is quite different—Rose is upset over his impotence.

As the only divorcee, Dorothy's life is frequently complicated in her relationship with her ex-husband, Stan. Naturally angry with him for his betrayal after so many years of marriage, Dorothy eventually forgives him. As they are about to remarry, however, she is brought to her senses when he asks for a prenuptial agreement, and she calls off the wedding. Like many divorced couples, however, their lives are entangled because of their long, shared history. When Stan faces heart surgery, for example, Dorothy takes him in during his convalescence, but she is very glad when she can kick him out. Dick Van Dyke plays a lawyer who Dorothy is crazy about until she realizes that she cannot accept his new lifestyle—as a clown. In an episode that can appeal to the "groupie" in many women, she has a passionate affair with the musician who plays George in a "Beatle-mania" group; for her it is a fantasy come true. As the series ends, however, Dorothy remarries—a man she knows for two episodes, Blanche's handsome uncle, played by Leslie Nielsen. Her mother, Sophia, has the most fantastic love life of all. She sometimes has a date when the other women do not, and she offers proof that people in their eighties are still interested in sex. In one episode, she goes to Blanche for advice on how to seduce her new boyfriend. Sophia is not bothered by the fact that elderly women far outnumber elderly men; several of her dates are considerably younger than she. In a two-part episode, she has a short-lived marriage with her late husband's former business partner and they run a pizza stand together.

Although it is most often filled with verbal humor, *The Golden Girls* occasionally deals with more serious issues. In a two-part episode, Dorothy goes to several doctors who cannot tell her why she feels so ill and tired all the time. Finally, a New York City doctor identifies her problem as chronic fatigue syndrome, but her condition does not recur in subsequent episodes. Other episodes also deal with health issues, including Rose having heart surgery. Blanche must face changes in her life when she thinks she is pregnant and discovers she is starting menopause. A visit from Rose's sister illustrates the difficulty of adjusting to change in one's life—having been independent all her life, her sister is now blind and has trouble accepting the fact she needs help. The right to die is explored when a seriously ill friend wants Sophia to be there when she takes her own life. Addictions are also addressed—Rose's with pills and Dorothy's with gambling.

Several episodes explore family issues, such as when Blanche's daughter tells her mother she wants to be artificially inseminated and raise a child on her own, and when Dorothy's daughter leaves her husband after he cheats on her. Grandchildren and nieces also make appearances. A few episodes address homosexuality, most notably when Blanche's brother tells her he is gay and when a lesbian friend of Dorothy falls for Rose.

Although all four women have jobs or do volunteer work, the focus is usually on their social lives and their friendship. Occasionally, however, issues based on their outside activities are raised. Blanche faces sexual harassment when her psychology professor makes a pass and makes it clear she will fail unless she obliges. In another episode, Rose is fondled by her dentist and does not know what to do. When Rose loses her job as a grief counselor, she is faced with being fifty-five years old and having no other outside work experience. After she gets another job, she loses her pension and looks for better-paying work, but is faced with age discrimination. Dorothy's job as a substitute teacher forces her to face important issues, including the illegal alien status of one of her star pupils. In another episode, she is pressured to pass a failing football student so he can continue playing. The importance of work and feeling needed is demonstrated in an episode where Sophia is rejuvenated by a job at a retirement home—until she discovers Dorothy had the job created for her.

The popularity of *The Golden Girls* perhaps may have indicated a desire for audiences to see older, successful women on television, a demographic that had been virtually ignored in the past. These women are not feminists, and feminist issues are rarely addressed. In an episode where Rose helps to produce a show on "women's issues," the focus is on women living together. It turns into a tabloid circus when it is discovered the host is concerned with lesbianism and assumes housemates Dorothy and Blanche are lovers. Despite the lack of overt feminism, these women are certainly liberated—independent and sexually free. In many instances they are forced to face issues important to feminists, such as sexual harassment, but they address their problems on a personal basis in their struggle to cope with a changing world.

Designing Women

The first hit series of creator, head writer, and co-executive producer Linda Bloodworth-Thomason, *Designing Women* revolves around four women coworkers in Atlanta. Much of the action takes place at Sugar-bakers, the interior design business owned by sisters Julia and Suzanne Sugarbaker and operated out of the former's stately home. Julia is a widow in her early forties with a grown son. A very intelligent and attractive woman, she could be described as a liberal feminist, often speaking passionately against sexism and other wrongs she observes. Suzanne is her younger sister, a shallow, self-centered ex-beauty queen who prefers to live off alimony from her several ex-husbands rather than contribute very much to the business. Mary Jo is a divorced mother of two, who is also bright, attractive, and passionate about many issues, usually in agreement with Julia. Finally, of the original four women, Charlene is the sweet, somewhat naive, romantic who is also intelligent and the business manager of Sugarbakers. Later in the series, her equally naive cousin Carlene joins them and eventually replaces Charlene. When Suzanne moves away in 1991, she is replaced first by obnoxious and ambitious cousin Allison Sugarbaker and then, for the final season, the rich, savvy former court reporter and recovering alcoholic Bonnie Jean (B.J.) Poteet. While several men also appear occasionally as boyfriends or ex-husbands, Anthony is the constant male presence, often finding himself caught up in both the professional and personal lives of the women. An intelligent and wrongly accused African American ex-convict, Anthony rises from being the delivery person for Sugarbakers to becoming a partner.

When Bloodworth-Thomason created *Designing Women,* her idea was to "get four women together and listen to them talk."[35] Talk, of course, is a very important part of women's friendship, but the talk on this series isn't always supportive. Suzanne in particular is often the instigator and recipient of verbal barbs. With her emphasis on her appearance and her general lack of interest in social issues, she often finds herself at odds with the other women, including her sister. When attacks come from outsiders, however, the others are quick to defend her. In a particularly compelling story line, Suzanne is voted "most changed" at her high school reunion because of her weight gain. Knowing that Suzanne is self-conscious and hurt, the other women show up for support as she accepts the award and explains how she has indeed changed—inside—in recognition of more important things than looks. In an episode where Suzanne is about to lose a beauty queen title she won years ago, Julia delivers a passionate speech in defense of her sister, bragging how she enthralled an entire crowd during the talent segment of the competition. Suzanne is used to competing with other women in beauty contests, and that mentality also carries over into her personal life. In at least two episodes she rivals Mary Jo, once for the affection of a good-looking stranger on a cruise ship and also when Suzanne is dating Mary Jo's ex-husband. The other three women are generally quite sympathetic with each other, endlessly discussing their problems and being mutually supportive during times of crisis. For example, they help Charlene when she finds a lump on her breast and must have surgery. Julia finds much support when her steady boyfriend suddenly dies, and Mary Jo consistently finds comfort from her friends as she struggles being a working mom. While the conversations may get intense as they debate issues, all four of the women are there to help each other cope with life's problems.

In the seven years of the series, the relationships of the designing women with men varied from romantic to contentious. Suzanne has been divorced three times and seems to see men as meal tickets. When her baseball player ex-husband publishes a book that indicates he had cheated on her when they were married, she swears to get revenge. Another ex-husband, a novelist, however, writes a beautiful tribute to her and other women of the South, including her friends. Julia evidently had a happy marriage until her husband died. Through a couple seasons she has a steady boyfriend, Reese, but when the actor moved on to another series, his character dies of a heart attack, leaving Julia to grieve.

Mary Jo has had perhaps the most complex relationships with men, including her ex-husband, Ted. Since the two must occasionally see each other because of their two children, they also witness each other's new love interests and adjustments are not always easy. When Mary Jo starts dating J.D., Ted's best friend, Ted finds excuses to constantly interrupt them. In another episode, Mary Jo is reunited with an old friend whom she had promised to marry if they found themselves without partners by a certain time. She is not willing to settle, however, and continues to search for a soul mate. In an episode based on a real (but flawed) study, Mary Jo is upset by a report that predicts her marriage chances are very slim. Somewhat distraught, she turns to Suzanne to help her learn how to meet guys. Several later episodes depict an anxious Mary Jo determined to get artificially inseminated because she wants to have another baby but has no one in her life with whom to do it. Another episode finds her determined to have her breasts enlarged, claiming that men will find her more attractive and treat her differently. She even "stuffs" her bra and proceeds to prove her point to Julia at a local bar. Although Mary Jo often expresses envy of Suzanne's breast size, she eventually decides against changing herself.

At the beginning of the series, Charlene is the only one of the women who has never been married, but she dreams of having a family some day.

One episode indulges her fantasy of being a war bride during World War II. As the romantic of the group, it is fitting that she does meet her ideal man—the strong, loving Bill Stillfield, an Air Force colonel—and they marry in 1989. After she has their daughter, she worries about still being attractive to him and becomes jealous of a female copilot. She is also flattered by the attentions of another man as her husband must frequently be away. Charlene is off the series and to England with her family in 1991.

Frequently *Designing Women* takes on a "battle of the sexes" tone, and CBS was reportedly initially nervous that people would interpret the show as antimale.[36] Beyond the usual complaints about men that women may have when they sit around and talk, gender lines sometimes are drawn in the presence of lovers. On a ski trip with their boyfriends, the four women find themselves trading insults with their dates. Accused of being either "wimps or jackasses," one of the men complains that when dealing with the women, they can't tell "a real compliment from a tactical maneuver."[37] On a more serious level, sexual harassment and inequality are addressed in an episode dealing with the Clarence Thomas/Anita Hill hearings.[38] Julia and Mary Jo are outraged at the treatment of Hill; Mary Jo even wears a T-shirt claiming, "He did it." Toward the end of the episode, when the hearings are over and Hill has been discredited, Mary Jo flips out in front of a television camera. After saying that all that women want is to be treated with equality and respect, she threatens to take her car to a central point in the United States and shout from the tallest tower, "Hey, don't get me wrong, we love you, but who the hell do you men think you are?!"

Linda Bloodworth-Thomason has said that she sees her series as her own personal column on television, and she takes it seriously.[39] She said the episode she wrote on the Thomas/Hill hearings was "a valentine to all the women who felt Anita Hill was treated unfairly."[40] To illustrate her points, Bloodworth-Thomason used several clips of actual footage from the hearings, a highly unusual technique for comedy, as her characters watch and debate. Television critic Kathryn Baker has described the Bloodworth-Thomason scripts on *Designing Women* as "not formula sitcom fare, but rather thoughtful essays on such subjects as AIDS or the ordination of women as priests."[41] In the episode addressing AIDS, Mary Jo delivers an impassioned speech at a Parent-Teacher Association debate over sex education in her daughter's school. As a young, AIDS-infected friend of hers watches, she explains how condoms can save their children's lives. In the previously discussed show where Suzanne goes to her high school reunion, Julia and Mary Jo are fasting for Operation World Hunger, making it one of six series episodes across the three major networks making up "Prime Time to End Hunger," an unprecedented cooperative effort among the three to increase volunteerism in the fight against hunger, poverty, and homelessness.[42] The show addresses the problem of wife abuse when Charlene discovers her cousin is being abused by her husband. Charlene convinces her to take the children and go to a women's shelter. Interracial dating, pornography, animal rights, homosexuality, the problems of working mothers, juvenile delinquency, racism, dealing with grief, and the judicial system are examples of other issues addressed in this series. In the infrequent times that the program actually addresses the designing business, it often involves the women debating ethical issues, such as whether they should redecorate the home of a married man's lover or should they accept materials from a company whose workers are on strike.

As discussed earlier, much of *Designing Women* focuses on talk among the main characters, an important aspect of female friendship. In Bonnie Dow's analysis of the feminine discourse in the series, she pointed out that distinctions are often blurred between public discourse, so long identified with men, and the private talk of women.[43] Julia's role can be seen as that of consciousness-raiser, so important in the feminist movement in the late 1960s and early 1970s. Dow said that Julia "takes the personal and makes it political, validating the feelings and experiences of the other women by placing them in a larger cultural context. Julia rarely disagrees with the impressions of the others; she simply expresses them in larger terms, and her opinions are undeniably feminist in orientation.[44] Dow cited incidences of all four original female characters resisting patriarchy and the dominant culture, even Suzanne who made a career of objectifying herself. Dow also wrote that *Designing Women* rejects "monolithic definitions of femininity or feminism, allowing multiple opportunities for female identification."[45] Lauren Rabinovitz wrote about the use of feminine excess in feminist sitcoms as a source of humor with the two seen as binary opposites.[46] Claiming the majority of *Designing Women*'s narratives are about the ways in which the site of feminine excess may be displaced from Suzanne onto the other characters, she gave as an example the time when Julia performs as a sexy lounge singer. With Julia showing how femininity is an assumed masquerade of sexualized behavior, costuming, and performance, Rabinovitz said "what is most striking, however, is the program's repetitive argument that such a political, albeit sexualized, displacement is itself a product of feminist desire, since this is a world where feminism signifies women's individual choices, and Julia may just as easily choose to be coy and feminine as assertive and independent."[47] One could argue, then, that femininity and feminism are not opposite; they coexist in Julia and other women.

Much was reported in the press of actress Delta Burke's (and Suzanne's) weight gain a year or so after the series started. However, Jeremy Butler said it made Suzanne an icon of the "unruly woman."[48] Basing his ideas on Kathleen Rowe's discussion of Roseanne (of the popular sitcom, addressed next), Butler explained how the unruly woman, by creating herself as spectacle to suit her own needs and desires, establishes her own subjectivity, and is seen by patriarchy as a threat.[49] Butler also remarked that the title, *Designing Women,* connotes women with designs. He said designing women "are preeminently powerful and a constant danger to men. They author their own plans and are thus *subjects* rather than *objects* of narratives."[50] Butler saw all four of the original designing women as part of an unruly sisterhood. He analyzed the language used in the series as evidence of the disruption of patriarchy, particularly the seemingly confused language of Bernice, an older character introduced in the second season who constantly twists language for her own needs.

Butler pointed out that the narratives on *Designing Women* are polysemic, offering a range of interpretations as feminist and patriarchal discourses grate against each other in the episodes. In the one involving the Thomas/Hill hearings, for example, a secondary plot involves Mary Jo and Julia spouting feminist support for Anita Hill while in costumes from *Whatever Happened to Baby Jane?* and taking on the personas of two strong, but eccentric and bitchy actresses, Joan Crawford and Bette Davis. Their unruliness, particularly Mary Jo's in her speech before the television camera, allows viewers who accept patriarchy to dismiss them as strident and crazy. The dominant feminist discourse has been "clawed back," to use John Fiske and John Hartley's terms, to that of the dominant, patriarchal ideology.[51] It is interesting to note that very few women in television comedy have labeled themselves feminists. In the Thomas/Hill episode, Mary Jo blames people like George Bush and Phyllis Schlafly who "want to make people believe that feminists are all these big-mouthed, bleeding-heart, man-hating women who don't shave their legs."[52] She goes on to say that if believing in equal pay and mandated child care makes her a feminist, then she is proud to be one. While Mary Jo blames particular individuals for the derogatory stereotypes of feminists, she has left out perhaps the biggest culprit—the media—which, ironically, will soon portray her as a big-mouthed, crazy feminist on the news. Significantly, episodes of *Designing Women* often have what Bonnie Dow has called "open endings" that "imply that the problem has *not* been completely resolved, or that if the problem has been resolved on an individual level, it still remains on a larger level."[53]

Roseanne

Known initially as Roseanne Barr, then Roseanne Arnold, now just her first name suffices to identify both the star and her popular series. Debuting in October 1988, *Roseanne* finished its first season second in the Nielsen ratings only to *The Cosby Show* and tied it for first the following year. Despite Roseanne's propensity to outrage people with her rude behavior and to live her life as tabloid headlines, *Roseanne* remained in the top 10 well into the 1990s. She deserves much of the credit for the chances her series took with characters and story lines, although the fight for creative control was long. Roseanne complained that the writers were a major problem from the beginning: "They'd attack me, then ignore me, treat me like I was stupid. It was all a class thing and a women's thing. I wanted them to write more from the woman's point of view and they thought it meant putting in tampon jokes and castration jokes."[54] She eventually became executive producer with end credits indicating that the series is based on a character she created.

Roseanne is one of the several family situation comedies that debuted during the 1980s, but this family was quite different from the others. The series takes place in Lanford, Illinois, and focuses on Dan and Roseanne Conner, in their middle thirties at the beginning of the series; their three children, thirteen-year-old Becky, eleven-year-old Darlene, and six-year-old son D.J. (they later have another son); Roseanne's younger sister, Jackie; and a variety of other family members and friends. The Conner family is lower middle or working class, constantly struggling to make ends meet. Both Roseanne and Dan suffer periods of unemployment, and at one time have to borrow money from Roseanne's sister, Jackie, so they can get the electricity turned back on. Often contrasted to *The Cosby Show,* where *Roseanne* differs the most, according to television critic David Bianculli, is that it is less concerned with proper behavior, language, and role models.[55] Although the Huxtables gently tease their children, the Conners, particularly Roseanne, can sound somewhat cruel. In an oft-quoted line from the first season, when one of her children asks Roseanne why she is so mean, she responds by saying that she hates kids and she is not really their mom. Another child, who is looking for a school book, is told by Roseanne that she sold it. Despite the more frequent barbs, story lines clearly indicate the Conners love their children every bit as much as the Huxtables love theirs. The most visible difference between the two households, however, is the Conners' shabbier, messier home and the obesity of the two parents.

Many television critics discussed the series and title character as an extension of the standup comedy of Roseanne, who touted herself as a "domestic goddess" as she made housewife jokes about her husband and children.[56] Certainly one of the outstanding features of this family sitcom is that the mother character is central. Roseanne is a high school graduate who met her husband in school and soon settled down to raise a family in their home town. Work is not an option; she has had a variety of jobs to help support her family, including assembly-line worker in a factory, telephone solicitor, order taker at a fast food restaurant, bartender, cleanup lady, and waitress. Finally, in 1992, Roseanne becomes her own boss when she, her sister, and a friend open up their own restaurant. Although her husband, Dan, is often the recipient of her sarcastic remarks, they clearly love each other and are sexually active, making it evident that sexiness is not the sole domain of the slender. Her sometimes nasty comments to her children also do not mask the love she has for them. She not only gets involved in their lives, but also shows concern over their friends. For example, when she learns that Darlene's friend, David, has a drunken, negligent mother, Roseanne has David move in with them and he becomes part of the family.

Several other women play important roles on *Roseanne.* Jackie is Roseanne's younger sister, an insecure, single woman at the beginning of the series who has a string of failed relationships. After she loses her factory job (she worked with Roseanne), she attempts careers as a truck driver and a police officer, but fails at both. Jackie spends a lot of time at the Conners and is an important presence in the lives of her nephew and especially her nieces. Becky, the oldest Conner daughter, loves boys and shopping at the mall with her friends. Darlene, two years younger, is more interested in sports at first and goes through a very moody, dark period. Although she has more interests in common with her dad, she is a wisecracker like her mom. Crystal went to high school with Roseanne and is her best friend. A divorcee and mother of a young son, she becomes Roseanne's mother-in-law when she marries Dan's father. Nancy is the friend with whom Roseanne and Jackie run their restaurant (The Lunchbox). Although Nancy dates men throughout several episodes, she reveals herself to be a lesbian in 1992.

Gender relations on *Roseanne* are sometimes mixed, both in their presentation and their interpretation. For example, critic Lawrence Christon wrote that male-bashing, which he thought was epidemic on television, was "nowhere more acute" than in this series with even the young son the target of ridicule.[57] In one scene, which Christon labeled a form of "reverse sexism," Roseanne says that a guy is like a lump—first you take off what his mom did to him, then what the beer commercials show him, then his ego.

Television critic Marvin Kitman, on the other hand, found the "vicious, anti-male stuff in it" to make a lot of sense and thought the show funny and refreshing.[58] While Dan and Roseanne frequently have loud disagreements (which she often seems to win), they also emotionally support each other throughout all their financial crises and problems with the kids. They are also physically attracted to each other, and their lovemaking is alluded to in several episodes. In one episode, however, there is a disturbing connection between sex and violence. When Dan gets mad at Roseanne for throwing out some of his belongings ("junk" to her), he threatens to throw out something of hers. The two begin an angry contest of tossing each other's stuff out the front door. After Dan has attempted to throw out the sofa, the two look at each other with sudden passion and rush off to the bedroom. Physical violence, however, is not part of their relationship and, when Jackie gets involved with an abusive boyfriend (Fisher), Roseanne makes sure her sister leaves him, while Dan gets thrown in jail for beating him up.

Jackie has had a number of interesting relationships with men. Having a man is important to her, even if it means going to bars and having one-night stands. Besides the abusive relationship with Fisher, whom she almost married, Jackie dates a younger man for awhile, but most of her relationships are not long lasting. When she has a one-night stand with Fred (who works with Dan), she becomes pregnant and is determined to raise the baby on her own. Fred, who wants to marry her, threatens to sue for custody of the baby in an episode that pits the women against the men, mothers against fathers. The two do get married, but eventually divorce.

Dating and sex are also important issues for the two teenage daughters on *Roseanne*. When Becky begins dating Mark, her parents disapprove. In one episode, Jackie helps Becky talk to Roseanne about getting birth control pills. Unlike other sitcoms, however, this teenager does not decide to wait after her little talk with Mom. When Roseanne agrees to take her to the doctor but tells Becky she shouldn't feel pressured, Becky lets her know she and Mark have already been having sex and use condoms—they just want to be extra careful. At seventeen years old, Becky runs away with Mark and gets married. Dan is so angry that he doesn't speak to her on the phone for quite awhile, making Roseanne the intermediary, although she is upset too. Eventually Becky and Mark end up moving in with the Conners, with Becky delaying her college education, much to the disappointment of her parents, while Mark goes to school. When Mark quits (he is not doing well) and gets a full-time job, Becky fulfills her dream of going to college.

At the beginning of the series, Darlene is not at all interested in boys. Her first love, however, turns out to be living in her own house—David (who happens to be Mark's brother). David is a sensitive young man who lets Darlene boss him around. He is devastated when Darlene goes away to an art school while he remains at her parents' house. Later Dan gets mad when he finds out they've been sleeping together at her school, but he takes it out on David, not Darlene. After Darlene and David break up, Darlene is candid about her sexual relationship with a new guy at school. Eventually Darlene and David do get married, producing Roseanne and Dan's first grandchild in the series' finale.

The sexuality of both teenage daughters is presented as a fact of life that their parents cannot control; the best Roseanne and Dan can hope for is that their daughters practice safe sex and they don't have to hear it. Sex and sexuality are actually topics that frequently come up in the lives of the Conner household. When D.J. starts spending a lot of time in the bathroom, it becomes clear that he is masturbating. Treated as a natural, although embarrassing, phenomenon, many jokes are made about him and his "little buddy." In a 1994 episode that deals with both sex and sex roles, Becky complains to Jackie that Mark is no longer interested in sex. Roseanne finds out and encourages Dan to talk to Mark about it. At the city garage (where Dan, Fred, and Mark are all now working), Fred tries to get the men to open up, obviously encouraged by Roseanne earlier. In stereotypical fashion, the men are terribly embarrassed and have trouble discussing their personal problems. The women on this show seem quite comfortable talking about sex, but the men tend to get reticent and even angry; they particularly don't want to know intimate details about each other. The episode ends with a sex-role-reversal parody, evidently to reinforce how ridiculous it is for men to act like women and women to act like men.

Roseanne also deals with homosexuality with two gay characters. When Roseanne discovers that her boss at the lunch counter, Leon, is gay, she immediately accepts it and even attempts to help him resolve a fight with his lover. Later Leon becomes a partner in her restaurant, The Lunch Box. When her friend Nancy announces she is a lesbian, Roseanne also accepts it, although Dan often feels uncomfortable in Nancy's presence. In a particularly interesting episode from the 1993–1994 season, Roseanne and Jackie accompany Nancy to a gay bar. Roseanne gets quite upset after Nancy's latest lover (guest star Mariel Hemingway) kisses Roseanne lovingly on the lips. She is afraid that she might have latent homosexual tendencies, but her fears are not presented as a homophobic reaction; rather, her response is a healthy questioning of sexuality.

Family is very important on *Roseanne,* but the series makes it clear, unlike any popular comedy before it, that family can cause us many psychological problems. Jackie and Roseanne have a lot of anger toward their father, who mistreated them when they were young and cheated on their mom. An episode that deals with his death shows Roseanne working hard to let go of her anger so she can go on with her life. Jackie and Roseanne's mom, Bev, is the kind of mom who constantly nags her daughters and finds fault. Jackie has not been able to deal with her problems and she is in therapy. At one point, Roseanne goes to therapy with Jackie, and the episode demonstrates that Roseanne is part of her trouble because she is always trying to run Jackie's life.

Destructive family relationships, teenage sex, homosexuality, financial problems, and class conflict are all issues that are regularly addressed on *Roseanne*. Subconscious racism is addressed in one episode when Roseanne refuses to open her restaurant to an African American man who turns out to be the father of the girl in D.J.'s school play. When he asks if she would have kept him out if he were white, she immediately says yes, but after he leaves, she starts to wonder if that is true. Most of the other problems/issues addressed on *Roseanne* are handled in this same open fashion. Answers are often not given, and problems do not easily go away. When the formerly active Darlene suddenly starts wearing black and mopes around the house, her teenage depression is not solved by a shopping trip—it lasts over many episodes. The Conners' economic problems are an ongoing concern until a bizarre twist in the last season of the series—the Conners become millionaires through the Illinois State lottery, although they remain in their house. In the last episode after her grandson is born, Roseanne is shown reminiscing. She ends the series in May 1997 in a flash-forward where she is a writer and a widow.

Kathleen Rowe discussed how Roseanne represents the historical unruly woman who creates a spectacle of herself, for herself, building "her act and her success on an exposure of the 'tropes of femininity' (the ideology of 'womanhood,' the perfect wife and mother) by cultivating the opposite (an image of the unruly woman)."[59] Much has been made of Roseanne's obesity as part of her making a spectacle of herself and defying patriarchal standards of beauty. While there was turmoil on the set of *Roseanne,* its star was busy "mooning" people off the set and causing an uproar when she screeched through the National Anthem at a baseball game, then grabbed her crotch.[60] Interestingly enough, despite the love/hate relationship the public had with Roseanne, her series remained a solid top-10 hit into the 1990s. Roseanne Conner is definitely not the role model found in so many other television moms, but she certainly struck a nerve of truth for many people.

Murphy Brown

Debuting in November of 1988 on CBS, *Murphy Brown* was created, written, and produced by Diane English, joining Linda Bloodworth-Thomason and Susan Harris as a major female force in 1980s' television comedy. The series finished only thirty-sixth in the Nielsen ratings its first season, but it received high praise from most critics and was nominated for several Emmys during its run.[61] By the beginning of the 1990s it was a solid top-10 hit, and it remained on the air until May 1998. Often compared to *The Mary Tyler Moore Show* from the 1970s, *Murphy Brown* is about the staff of a network television news magazine, *F.Y.I.*, produced in Washington, D.C. The center of this ensemble cast is a single woman (played by Candice Bergen), but the one key difference, as television critic Kay Gardella put it, "is that Bergen isn't playing Mary Richards, but Lou Grant," a gruff, no-nonsense professional.[62] Murphy is known for her tough interviews and has been banned at the White House. In the debut episode, viewers learn that Murphy, in her early forties and on the staff of *F.Y.I.* for many years, is returning from a month at the Betty Ford Clinic, where she battled a drinking and smoking problem. Her new boss is the neurotic twenty-something producer, Miles Silverberg, who hired former beauty queen, Corky Sherwood, to be part of the on-air team. Murphy is not happy with either. Her other colleagues are longtime friends and professionals—Jim Dial, her stuffy coanchor, and Frank Fontana, a competitive but somewhat insecure (especially with women) investigative reporter. Eldin is the painter of her townhouse, who never finishes and creates murals that we never see. Another recurring gag in the series is Murphy's string of secretaries.

Diane English said *Murphy Brown* is autobiographical. She explained that she "wanted to write a woman who is no longer scrambling to get to the top but who got everything she ever wished for and now is just a little sorry for it. She loves what she is doing but is paying a big price."[63] The price Murphy is paying, at least in the first few seasons, is that she has no friends nor social life outside of work. Her closest friends are the two men with whom she has been working for years, Jim and Frank, and her house painter. Platonic male-female relations on television are rare, but Murphy manages to remain friends with all three. In the first season, Murphy is concerned about her biological clock and wants to have a baby. Frank is flattered when she asks him to be the father, but the two cannot bring themselves to make love. Murphy and Jim share a special moment in another episode where she is pregnant, and he, much to his embarrassment, must take her for a sonogram. When she asks him to look at the baby inside of her while she is hooked up to the machine, he is in awe. Despite Murphy's long friendship with both newsmen, however, there are no holds barred when it comes to getting stories. In "Buddies Schmuddies," for example, Murphy and Frank fight over an investigative story and refuse to cooperate, misleading each other and eventually both losing. Jim's nickname for Murphy is "slugger," like she is one of the guys, and he competes mightily with her for a part-time anchor spot in one episode. Eldin, originally just the house painter who never finishes, becomes a good friend to Murphy and, in the 1992 season, the "nanny" to her son. Always around when she comes home from work, Eldin is there to listen to her rantings and ravings, bringing her down to earth with his unflappable, commonsense reactions. When he becomes a millionaire after selling one of his paintings, he still doesn't leave Murphy. The two are moved to tears when he does finally leave in 1994. Eldin is willing to turn down his life's dream—to study with a great painter in Europe—to remain with Murphy and her son, but she, in turn, sacrifices their comfortable relationship and insists he go. In the series' finale, however, he returns out of concern for her and remains to "touch up" her townhouse.

Unfortunately, Murphy has no female friends. She resents Corky, the only other regular female character, who was obviously hired for her looks and perkiness to cover soft features. Murphy also becomes jealous of her when it becomes clear that Corky isn't the bimbo Murphy thought she was. When the two must do a morning show together, Corky's skills at cooking and being a gracious host make her look good while Murphy's aggressiveness and lack of domesticity look foolish in this context. Corky tells Murphy from the very beginning that she admires her and hopes to someday be as good a reporter as Murphy. In another episode, Corky and Murphy are assigned to do a hard news story together, but Murphy sends her on menial tasks. When Corky comes up with important information, Murphy uses it but doesn't plan on giving her credit. Corky gets even, however, when she reads the entire story on the air, instead of just introducing it.

While Corky is learning to be a competitor in the field of hard news, she also makes it clear that she wants a husband and family. In a two-part episode at the end of the first season, she marries an old school friend, Will Forrest, an author. Murphy is shocked when asked to be Corky's maid of honor, but ends up getting very involved in the process. At one point, Corky must read her diary in court to save Will from a plagiarism lawsuit, an episode that indicates just how far she will go for love. Corky's dreams are broken, however, when the marriage ends in divorce. Murphy actually ends up being supportive of her, along with the rest of her coworkers. The 1994–1995 season has Corky striking up an office romance with Miles. Both are obviously attracted to each other, but reluctant to get involved since they work together. They do eventually elope, but Corky stays at her job in Washington, D.C., when Miles takes a job in New York City. Interestingly enough, Miles is replaced with a female producer, Kay Carter-Shepley (played by Lily Tomlin), a woman who is as tough, and sometimes tougher, than Murphy.

Murphy has not had good romantic relationships with men, always putting her career first. She was married for five days to a man (Jake Lowenstein) with whom she was arrested at the Democratic National Convention in 1968. When Murphy must interview him after all those years, it becomes known that the key to their sexual passion is confrontation and she has a hard time resisting him (another prime-time lesson connecting sex with violence, however nonphysical). He asks her to marry him while on the air and she accepts. When they are alone in the studio and fighting about when to get married, they call it off and make love on the desk. For several episodes, Murphy has an on-again, off-again romance with Jerry Gold, an obnoxious talk show host with whom she also fights and makes love. When the two try to have a relationship while doing a series together on political issues, however, Murphy becomes supportive and polite instead of her usual combative self, and the show becomes boring. Scholarly critic Bonnie Dow is convinced that this "reiterates that personal happiness and professional success are incompatible for Murphy, implicitly arguing that, for women, the qualities the public world requires are radically different from those necessary for success in the private world of relationships. Murphy simply cannot win."[64] While Murphy is struggling with her relationship with Jerry, Jack reenters her life and, once again, she cannot resist him.

At the beginning of the 1991–1992 season, Murphy is pregnant and does not know who the father is. Although the father turns out to be Jack and he offers to marry her, Jake also volunteers to help her. She rejects both, and thus began a national debate in real life. In May 1992, Vice President Dan Quayle, delivering a speech in San Francisco, blamed the Los Angeles riots partially on the breakdown of the family structure and said Murphy Brown wasn't helping by "mocking the importance of fathers by bearing a child alone and calling it just another lifestyle choice."[65] His attack became front-page news in dozens of magazines and newspapers as well as on television news and talk shows. The season premiere of *Murphy*

Brown in fall 1992 was an hour-long episode that indicated what a hard time Murphy was having adjusting to being a single, working parent. At the end of the hour, Murphy is on her show with several kinds of real family groups and says, "Perhaps it's time for the Vice President to expand his definition and recognize that whether by choice or circumstances families come in all shapes and sizes. And ultimately, what really defines a family is commitment, caring and love."[66] In a bizarre public-relations move, Vice President Quayle sent the fictional Brown baby a stuffed elephant and a note saying he helped to start "an important discussion on ways to strengthen our family values."[67]

After the birth of her baby, Murphy is introduced to a new potential love interest, Peter, who is a professional international journalist. He and Murphy are tremendously attracted to each other, but their competitive instincts and failed previous relationships make them a bit wary. When Peter returns and they decide to go ahead with their affair, they do so with the assumption that it will "crash and burn" eventually. Once again Murphy is depicted as allowing her career to interfere with her love life, but it works both ways. Supposedly on a romantic island holiday, Murphy and Peter sneak behind each other's backs to break a story. The 1994–1995 season explores the relationship of the two as they try to figure out what they mean to each other, realizing that they may not want to "crash and burn." They get engaged, but it does not last long.

Although no other topic on *Murphy Brown* has gathered as much attention as her decision to be a single mother, the last season of the series deals with Murphy's diagnosis of breast cancer, her subsequent surgery, treatment, and exploratory surgery when it is suspected the cancer has returned. This story arc, of course, had the ability to raise awareness of the detection and treatment of a life-threatening disease to millions of women, as well as the emotional and physical toll it has on people's lives. *Murphy Brown* is also rich in intertextuality, regularly exploring current issues, many based on news events and the business of news. The use of image consultants and other attempts to raise ratings, such as a tabloid-like episode that deals with hookers, are parodies of the news business as is the extreme competitiveness of the characters themselves. Murphy goes to jail for a time for not revealing her sources and she also must face a Senate Ethics Committee, English's parody of the Thomas/Hill hearings.[68] After O.J. Simpson was chased on Los Angeles freeways in his Ford Bronco, a similar incident occurs on *Murphy Brown*. In a mix of fiction with reality, several real news people are frequently mentioned in the story lines and have cameos, including Linda Ellerbee, Mike Wallace, Charles Kuralt, Lesley Stahl, Joan Lunden, and Katie Couric.

According to Diane English, CBS News personnel are also often consulted on story lines about Murphy's life.[69]

English has said that "we want to show all points of view, but ultimately a point will be made at the end—and it will be whatever I decide it will be."[70] She has admitted that, although her primary purpose is to entertain, Murphy is a liberal democrat because English is and, of course, the character is modeled after her.[71] Feminists have debated, however, over the reality of Murphy and whether or not the show is pro-feminist. Journalist Linda Ellerbee quipped that "half the time I think the show is a documentary. For the first time, it is an accurate portrayal of women journalists."[72] According to English, Murphy's concentration on her career is also an accurate picture of English's life as a comedy writer and producer, spending most of her waking hours on work with little attention to a social life and having a family. In an early episode where Murphy is working with a Russian woman journalist, the two commiserate on their lonely lives as newspeople. When asked if she ever thinks of having children, Murphy says, "All the time." Bonnie Dow, however, saw Murphy Brown as a "comic scapegoat ritually punished for inappropriate manifestations of patriarchal traits such as competitiveness, ambition, egoism, and interpersonal insensitivity."[73] Dow saw Corky as a feminine foil for Murphy's feminist character, who has been masculinized in order to make it in a patriarchal world. Much of the humor comes from Murphy's inability to handle interpersonal situations and be nurturing. Frank, interestingly enough, is the one who must show her how to hold her baby next to her instead of at arm's length. Stories after the first year of her son's birth, however, downplayed Murphy's role as a mother and focused on work, with romance coming into and out of her life.

Two episodes stand out in dealing with gender issues. During the first season, Murphy insists on joining the Dunfries Club, the last all-male club in Washington, D.C. Although he is initially against it, Jim ends up supporting her presence in the club, telling the others that Murphy is a good reporter and a good friend and that they "tick him off." Earlier, on the news set, the regulars are discussing gender relationships, with Frank concerned about whether to open doors and cry openly at movies while Corky is worried about whether to wear a bra. In an episode parodying the *Iron John* book on the men's movement in the early 1990s, the *F.Y.I.* men go to a drumming session to find their true selves and open up. Since Murphy is to write a story on it, she is a witness. At first ridiculing the raw emotions of the men, she grabs the "talking stick" and ends up describing the pain of being a daughter when her dad wanted a son.

A few episodes offer more incite into Murphy through her parents. Divorced from Murphy's dad, her mother is a tough woman who has trouble expressing her emotions. In an episode during the first season, Murphy resents her mother's interference at work, and a confrontation results in the two finally seeing each other as human beings. In another episode, Murphy wants her parents to come see her receive a prestigious award, but she is afraid they won't be able to stop arguing long enough to attend. We see that her childhood was full of contention and competition, so it is not surprising Murphy has trouble relating to others.

Diane English said she doesn't get involved in the politics of feminism, but, in a statement reminiscent of Mary Jo's speech on being feminist in the Thomas/Hill episode of *Designing Women,* she said that "if feminism means that my female characters or my friends or myself are respected, in all walks of life, then I'm a feminist."[74] Candice Bergen has said she didn't approach her part of Murphy from a feminist point of view. She does, however, think the simple existence of Murphy is a case in point for feminism even though feminist rhetoric doesn't "make for the stuff of a great sitcom."[75] Dow interpreted *Murphy Brown* as postfeminist with Murphy's "surrender to women's supposed biological imperative [to have a child]...the ultimate postfeminist moment."[76] Murphy has made it in a "man's world" by sacrificing her personal life and her femininity, and yet she still feels compelled to have a baby in her forties. When she is holding her baby for the first time, for example, she sings to him one of her favorite Motown songs, "(You Make Me Feel Like a) Natural Woman." Does this mean that not having a baby is unnatural for a woman? Are childless women somehow unfulfilled? Or is this merely showing a softer side to Murphy, the side that Dow complained had been eradicated in order for Murphy to succeed in a patriarchal society?

WOMEN IN 1980s SERIES COMEDY

Despite the claims of the death of the sitcom in the early 1980s and the failure of many introduced during that time, more than fifty new sitcoms lasted more than a year, with several enduring considerably longer. Although *The Cosby Show* was undoubtedly the most popular traditional family comedy during the 1980s, several others also enjoyed success. *Family Ties* (NBC, 1982–1989) debuted as a generation-gap comedy, with liberal parents from the 1960s raising conservative children, but it soon became the showcase for teenage son, Alex Keaton, played by Michael J. Fox. The mother on the show, an architect, is actually a strong character, but viewers were more interested in the cute antics of Alex. Mallory is the teenage daughter who does poorly in school and seems to lack common sense, although she evidently has talent in fashion design. Jennifer, on the other hand, is a smart nine-year old in the beginning of the series, who gets involved in a rock band and eventually attends college. *Growing Pains* is another series that had a teenage heartthrob, Kirk Cameron, as Mike Seaver. On ABC from 1985 until 1992, the show revolved around Jason Seaver, a psychologist; Maggie, his wife and a journalist; and their children. Interestingly enough, for the first several years of the series Jason works at home so Maggie can pursue her career again. We occasionally actually see her work, particularly once she gets a job at a local television station. In 1989, after having a fourth child, she wins a "Working Mother of the Year Award." Carol is the Stevens' teenage daughter, a bright, pretty young woman whom we see grow from the bespectacled nerd her brother deems her to a competent young woman attending law school at Columbia.

Other comedies during the 1980s also looked at family life. *The Wonder Years* is a nostalgic visit to the late 1960s and early 1970s, focusing on a teenage boy, his family, and friends. On ABC from 1988 until 1993, Kevin Arnold's mom, Norma, is the traditional housewife who cooks and soothes over feelings as her grumpy husband supports the family. Norma's consciousness is slowly raised as she takes a pottery class and discovers her joy in it is not shared by her resentful husband. She eventually enrolls in a community college to improve her secretarial skills. When the series ends, the older Kevin, in voiceover, talks about how his dad died a few years later and his mom supported herself working full time. Winnie Cooper is the pretty girl next door who seems to be Kevin's true love, although their relationship is on-again, off-again. She is smart, popular, and sensible, and we see her struggle, with Kevin, over typical teenage issues, such as peer pressure and whether to make out with her boyfriend.

A most insulting family comedy began on FOX in 1987. Targeting its programming toward a young audience, the network attempted to attract them by trying to shock and titillate. *Married...with Children* succeeds in its outrageous portrayal of a hateful, nuclear family. Al Bundy sells shoes and is shown in the opening credits handing out money to his family, even the dog. Peg, who dresses in tight outfits and walks in high heels like her feet are bound, is the ultimate in laziness. She is a housewife who neither cooks nor cleans and nags her husband for sex and money. Their teenage daughter, Kelly, is portrayed as a bimbo slut; Peg even encourages Kelly to use her body to get what she wants. Bud is the smart but nerdy, sex-obsessed son. None of the Bundys seem to like each other. Next-door neighbor and feminist Marcy is a loan officer at a local bank. She and her first husband seem the perfect couple and are often the butt of Bundy jokes. After her first husband leaves her, Marcy finds herself in bed with another man after a wild banking seminar and marries him. *Married... with Children* was an instant hit with FOX and remained on the air for ten years with its demeaning portrayals of everyone.[77]

Who's the Boss?, beginning in 1984 on ABC, offered the interesting premise of a man working as a housekeeper in suburban Connecticut for a divorced career woman with a child. Angela Bower is in advertising, president of an ad agency in New York City in the beginning of the series, then president of her own company. While she is very competent in her business (she went to Harvard Business School) and a loving mother, she is inept in the kitchen. Angela was also an insecure, overweight child, not popular with boys. Mona is her sexy mother, who seems to feed on Angela's insecurities as an attractive woman. It is Mona who convinced Angela to hire Tony because "a man can do meaningless, unproductive work as well as a woman."[78] Tony Micelli, a widowed former ball player, has moved from Brooklyn to Connecticut in an attempt to give his daughter, Samantha, a better life. As Tony becomes a father figure to Angela's son, both Angela and Mona become important influences in Samantha's life. A smart, pretty preadolescent, when she wants to play on a boy's baseball team, the adults in her life make it so, as the episode explores prejudice against girl athletes. Throughout the series, Angela and Tony are involved in a "will they or won't they" sexual attraction that was popular during that time. The two go through a number of other relationships, but they finally marry at the end of the series run when the children are grown.

Several sitcoms of the 1980s depict the growth of young girls, including *Full House* and *Punky Brewster.* Of particular note is *The Facts of Life,* which began in late 1979 on NBC and ran throughout most of 1988. The series follows the lives of four girls who attend a private school. Each has a distinctive personality, but they remain fast friends throughout their school years. Blair Warner is the beautiful, rich snob; Jo is the athletic one from the Bronx who likes to work on cars; Natalie is the budding, overweight journalist; and Tootie, the youngest, is the first African American girl who plays Juliet at Eastland. While issues involving class differences, honesty, and sexuality would occasionally come up, the strength of this show is its focus on the friendship of the girls. For several years Mrs. Garrett is their surrogate mother, first as the school dietician and later as their employer in a gourmet food shop. When she gets married and moves away she is replaced by her sister, who becomes equally loyal to the girls.

Another celebration of female friendship, this time with African American adults, is found in *227*, on NBC from 1985 until 1990. Mary Jenkins is a no-nonsense married woman who lives in Washington, D.C., with her husband and daughter. She and her best friend Rose sit on the stoop of their apartment building and, in a celebration of women's talk, endlessly discuss what is going on around them. A frequent topic of their conversation is Sandra, the local sex-pot who sees men as her life's work. Pearl, an older woman raising her teenage grandson, would often poke her nose out her window and join the conversation. Brenda is the attractive, smart daughter, and Lester is the sensitive, supportive husband. Next to *The Cosby Show*, however, *A Different World* was the most popular comedy starring people of color. A 1987 spin-off of *Cosby* based on the character Denise, it was scheduled immediately after *Cosby* on Thursday nights and undoubtedly enjoyed the audience flow. The different world is Hillman College, a mostly black school, where Denise initially shares a room with Jaleesa, a twenty-six-year-old divorcee, and Maggie, a white chatterbox. Denise drops out of school after three semesters and Maggie leaves about the same time, but the series went on until 1993. Several other females are regulars on the show, such as Freddie, who is studying to be an archeologist, and Kim, who is a premed student. The character of Whitley Gilbert, however, is a standout because of her character growth and the development of her involvement with Dwayne, a once nerdy student turned college professor. Whitley is a rich, snobby, attractive young woman who takes pleasure in stealing other women's boyfriends. She starts the series as an art major and later becomes an art buyer. Her courtship by Dwayne and their eventual marriage soften her character, making her less snobbish and more understanding. While the other women at the school are good friends to each other, Whitley's misfortune has been her competitiveness with other women, no longer necessary once she is married. Sociologist Herman Gray claims that this series "was one of the few shows about blacks that consistently staged serious explorations of contemporary social issues from the perspectives of its leading female characters."[79] Undoubtedly the series' success had much to do with actress Debbie Allen, who took over the series in its second year as its producer-director.

Several series in the 1980s featured single people, with perhaps the most legendary being *Cheers*. A workplace comedy set in a Boston bar, *Cheers* debuted to very low ratings on NBC (1982–1993), but critical acclaim kept it alive until it became a top-10 hit as part of the *Cosby* lineup on Thursday nights. In the debut episode, Diane Chambers is the snobby and intellectual graduate student who is abandoned by her fiancé (her professor) in the Cheers bar. Sam Malone, former baseball pitcher, alcoholic, and owner of the bar, offers her a waitressing job, which she accepts since all her education has trained her for little else. Thus begins a love/hate relationship between Sam and Diane that lasts for five years. On their wedding day, Diane leaves Sam (and the series) to finish a book for publication, as if marriage and writing are incompatible. Diane is replaced by Rebecca Howe, who is presented as an ambitious flake. At the end of the series in 1993, after years of chasing after men with money, Rebecca, ironically, marries a plumber and looks blissfully happy. Carla is the feisty divorced waitress who starts out with four children, has another by her ex-husband, then one by a college professor, and finally she has twins by her philandering second husband. Despite Carla's complaints about her kids and lack of money, birth control doesn't seem to be part of her repertoire. Lilith, who joins the Cheers gang when she gets involved with bar regular Frasier, is yet another educated woman who, like Diane, becomes the butt of jokes but also manages to put people in their place.

Yet another workplace comedy, *Anything but Love* (ABC, 1989–1992), started with the interesting premise of a man and woman who work together being platonic best friends. Hannah Miller meets Marty Gold on an airplane in the debut episode. He is a successful writer whom she admires, and that is what she wants to be. He suggests she apply for the job of researcher at the magazine where he works, and she gets it. With ratings problems and creative differences, however, the series begins to focus more and more on the sexual attraction between the two until they finally make love in an episode spent in bed discussing orgasms.[80] An important force in Hannah's life is her best friend since kindergarten, Robin, who lives in her building. While *Anything but Love* doesn't hold much promise for platonic male-female friendships, it does portray strong female friends who talk over all their problems and dreams with each other.

Coach, about the head coach of Minnesota State University's football team, offers a modern look at "Beauty taming the Beast," but the subtext occasionally seems quite hostile. Hayden Fox is the beast, the basically sexist dull lug in love with a beautiful, intelligent television journalist, Christine Armstrong. Christine is frequently correcting Hayden for his lack of social graces, and he often finds himself in the position of having to apologize to her. Sometimes, however, situations become dangerous for Christine, thanks to Hayden. For example, when they become engaged, he accidentally gives her a ring he can't afford, but he is too embarrassed to ask for it back. Instead, he and his coaching assistants, Luther and Dauber, drug Christine and try to saw the ring off her finger. In another episode where they are to get married, she falls off a balcony. Why Christine loves Hayden is a mystery, but certainly this program shows a backlash against strong women.

While the 1980s were more conservative than the 1970s in many ways, television comedy again occasionally broke new ground in terms of family lifestyles and issues incorporated into story lines. Female voices were being heard more through an increase in women producers and writers with network clout, as exemplified by Linda Bloodworth-Thomason and Diane English. Sitcoms in the 1990s would continue to break new ground in terms of lifestyles and subject matter, but they would also bring back some tired images for the twenty-first century.

NOTES

1. Flora Davis, *Moving the Mountain: The Women's Movement in America Since 1960* (New York: Simon & Schuster, 1991), 339.

2. Gorton Carruth, *What Happened When: A Chronology of Life & Events in America* (New York: Harper & Row, 1989), 1259.

3. Carruth, 1227.

4. Carruth, 1175.

5. Toni Carabillo, Judith Meuli, and June Bundy Csida, *Feminist Chronicles: 1953–1993* (Los Angeles: Women's Graphics, 1993), 129.

6. Susan Faludi, *Backlash: The Undeclared War against American Women* (New York: Crown, 1991), 113.

7. Richard Turner, "The Grave Condition of TV Comedy," *TV Guide,* 21 July 1984: 4–8.

8. Carruth, 1160. This series-ending episode was watched by 125 million people.

9. Neil Hickey, "Decade of Change, Decade of Choice," *TV Guide,* 9 December 1989: 33.

10. Hickey, 29.

11. Hickey, 34.

12. See Julie D'Acci, *Defining Women: Television and the Case of Cagney & Lacey* (Chapel Hill, NC: Universityof North Carolina Press, 1994) for an excellent description about how this particular television series contributed to the social construction of gender. D'Acci had access to the set of *Cagney & Lacey,* producer Barney Rosenzweig's personal files, extensive interviews with the principals involved in the creation of the series, and viewer letters, which all offer a unique look at the negotiations involved in creating a television series and how the audience interprets its meaning and impact on their lives.

13. For an excellent description of how the producers of *Cagney & Lacey* created controversy over this episode in hopes of attracting a large audience, see

Kathryn C. Montgomery, "Packaging Controversy," in *Target: Prime Time— Advocacy Groups and the Struggle over Entertainment Television* (New York: Oxford University Press, 1989), 194–215. The exploitation of women's issues and the portrayal of women as victims to increase ratings, of course, are themselves controversial, despite the potential social good such story lines can accomplish.

14. See, for example, Gloria Steinem, "Why I Consider *Cagney & Lacey* the Best Show on TV," *TV Guide,* 16 January 1988: 4–6.

15. Carabillo, Meuli, and Csida, 93.

16. Richard Zoglin, "Sitcom Politics," *Time,* 21 September 1991: 44–47.

17. For a discussion of alternative feminist readings of the series, see Robert H. Deming, *"Kate and Allie:* 'New Women' and the Audience's Television Archive," *Private Screenings: Television and the Female Consumer,* ed. Lynn Spigel and Denise Mann (Minneapolis, MN: University of Minnesota Press, 1992), 202–14. Whether a series espouses feminist ideology or not depends on the interpretation of the viewer. Deming says *Kate and Allie* "reproduces hegemonic definitions of gender, sexuality, and the gendered patterns of its own consumption, but it also provides for opportunities to resist and subvert these constraints" (206).

18. Carabillo, Meuli, and Csida, 102. According to the authors, the number of one-parent families headed by divorced women grew 181 percent between 1970 and 1981, from 956,000 to 2,700,000. In the same time period, one-parent families headed by women separated from their husbands grew from 1.1 million to 1.6 million.

19. Tim Brooks and Earle Marsh, *The Complete Directory to Prime Time Network and Cable TV Shows 1946–Present,* 7th ed. (New York: Ballantine, 1999), 471.

20. Barbara Ehrenreich and Jane O'Reilly, "No Jiggles. No Scheming. Just Real Women as Friends," *TV Guide,* 24 November 1984: 10.

21. Brooks and Marsh, 188.

22. Television critic Lee Winfrey called *The Cosby Show* "a beautiful thing" and said the critics of the series were "a handful of two-bit sociologists and self-appointed experts on racial affairs" who were scrutinizing the show with "myopic malice" ("Black-&-White Response to 'Cosby Show' Critics," *New York Daily News,* 27 August 1985: 77). In his description of his role in the production process, script consultant Dr. Alvin Poussaint said the public's expectations of the Cosby series was similar to its demands of black professionals and the black middle class, putting pressure on them to represent the full range of the black experience ("Prof keeps 'Cosby Show' on Track," *Star-Ledger,* 23 September 1990: TV-23). For a good explanation of the entire production process of the show, see Sally Bedell Smith, "Cosby Puts His Stamp on a TV Hit," *New York Times,* 18 November 1984: section 2, page 1+; and Ronald L. Smith, *The Cosby Book* (New York: S.P.I. 1993), 175–99.

23. For example, William Sampson (in "Typical Black Family? C'mon!," *Chicago Sun-Times,* 23 August 1986: 17) faulted the show for showing parents tak-

ing the time to talk to their children when they have been disobedient instead of physically punishing them. He also complains about the easy compromises made between husband and wife when there are disagreements. Issues facing black families especially, such as money problems and incidents with law enforcement, are ignored in the series. He sees the Huxtables as an ideal and an escape from real family life (a complaint made with hindsight about family comedies in the fifties with their all white casts, such as *Ozzie and Harriet* and *Father Knows Best*). While generally enthusiastic about the series, Mary Helen Washington wished it would deal more realistically with not only issues relating to race and gender, but also class privilege ("Please, Mr. Cosby, Build on Your Success," *TV Guide,* 22 March 1986: 4+).

24. Mark Crispin Miller, "Cosby Knows Best," *Village Voice,* 2 December 1986: 53–54.

25. Miller, 54.

26. Sut Jhally and Justin Lewis, *Enlightened Racism: The Cosby Show, Audiences, and the Myths of the American Dream* (Boulder, CO: Westview, 1992).

27. See Michael R. Real, "Bill Cosby and Recoding Ethnicity," *Television Criticism: Approaches and Applications,* ed. Leah R. Vande Berg and Lawrence A. Wenner (New York: Longman, 1991), 58–84.

28. An example of such a commercial was for Enjoli perfume, which had a woman proclaim in song that "I can bring home the bacon, fry it up in a pan, and never let you forget you're a man."

29. John D.H. Downing, "'The Cosby Show' and American Racial Discourse," *Discourse and Discrimination,* ed. Geneva Smitherman-Donaldson and Teun A. van Dijk (Detroit, MI: Wayne State University Press, 1988), 59.

30. Downing, 60.

31. Ella Taylor, *Prime-Time Families: Television Culture in Postwar America* (Berkeley, CA: University of California Press, 1989), 162.

32. Smith, 214.

33. Bill Carter, "Cosby Ready to Go on Despite the Inroads by Fox's 'Simpsons,' " *New York Times* 22 February 1991: C13, C18.

34. Coretta Scott King, "Goodbye, Bill," *TV Guide,* 25 April 1992: 19–20.

35. Mark Gunther, "CBS and the Steel Magnolia," *New York Times,* 3 March 1991: H30.

36. Robert DiMatteo, "New Series," *Video Review* September 1986: 114. Television critic Clifford Terry described the pilot as mostly a "full-press, anti-male barrage as they [the four women], curiously, come in contact with men who are all dolts and drips, philistines and philanderers" ("Pattern Dulls 'Designing Women,' " *Chicago Tribune,* 29 September 1986, sec. 2: 5).

37. John J. O'Connor, "2 Views of Relations between the Sexes: Cynical and Wary," *New York Times,* 28 March 1988: C20.

38. Held in 1991, the hearings were to confirm Clarence Thomas as a Supreme Court judge. Anita Hill, a university law professor, accused him of sexually harassing her years earlier when they had worked together. For an analysis

of Linda Bloodworth-Thomason's creation of her *Designing Women* script on this issue as well as other influences on her series, see Lynn C. Spangler, "Designing the Hearings on *Designing Women:* Creative and Business Influences on Content," *Outsiders Looking In: A Communication Perspective on the Hill/Thomas Hearings,* ed. Paul Siegel (Cresskill, NJ: Hampton, 1996), 205–27.

39. Richard Zoglin, "Sitcom Politics," *Time,* 21 September 1992: 47.

40. Bill Carter, "Television Gets on the Bandwagon of the Thomas-Hill Contretemps," *New York Times,* 4 November 1991: C15.

41. Kathryn Baker, "Prodigious Writer by Design," *New York Post* 25 March 1988: 94.

42. Rick Kogan, "'Fat Episode' Expands Delta's Appeal," *Chicago Tribune,* 11 December 1989, sec.2: 2.

43. Bonnie J. Dow, "Performance of Feminine Discourse in *Designing Women,*" *Text and Performance Quarterly* 12 (1992): 125–45.

44. Dow, 135.

45. Bonnie J. Dow, *Prime-Time Feminism: Television, Media Culture, and the Women's Movement Since 1970* (Philadelphia: University of Pennsylvania Press, 1996), 119.

46. Lauren Rabinovitz, "Ms-Representation: The Politics of Feminist Sitcoms," *Television, History, and American Culture,* ed. Mary Beth Haralovich and Lauren Rabinovitz (Durham, NC: Duke University Press, 1999), 149.

47. Rabinovitz, 150.

48. Jeremy G. Butler, "Redesigning Discourse: Feminism, the Sitcom, and *Designing Women,*" *Journal of Film and Video* 45 (1993): 15.

49. Butler, 14. See also Kathleen Rowe, "Roseanne: Unruly Woman as Domestic Goddess," *Television: The Critical View,* 5th ed., ed. Horace Newcomb (New York: Oxford University Press, 1994), 202–11.

50. Butler, 17.

51. John Fiske and John Hartley, *Reading Television* (London: Methuen, 1978).

52. Butler 20, from the episode written by Linda Bloodworth-Thomason, "The Strange Case of Clarence and Anita."

53. Dow, *Prime-Time Feminism,* 119.

54. Mary Murphy, "Roseanne Bites Back!," *TV Guide,* 23 February 1991: 3. For a good description of the production process and the creative differences on *Roseanne,* see Judine Mayerle, "Roseanne—How Did You Get Inside of My House? A Case Study of a Hit Blue-Collar Situation Comedy," *Television: The Critical View,* 5th ed., ed. Horace Newcomb (New York: Oxford, 1994), 101–16.

55. David Bianculli, "The Real Thing," *New York Post,* 18 October 1988: 77.

56. See, for example, John J. O'Connor, "Roseanne Smirks through the Trials of Life," *New York Times,* 18 October 1988: C22; and Daniel Ruth, "A New Hit? Fat Chance," *Chicago Sun-Times,* 18 October 1988: 45.

57. Lawrence Christon, "Does 'Roseanne' Rise above It All?," *Los Angeles Times,* 11 December 1988, Calendar section: 8+. When Darlene accuses D.J. of being stupid after he knocks over her school project, Roseanne consoles him by telling him he's not stupid—he's just clumsy, like his daddy.

58. Marvin Kitman, "'Roseanne': Blue-Collar Zingers Right on Target," *New York Post,* 18 October 1988: 12+.

59. Kathleen K. Rowe, "Roseanne: Unruly Woman as Domestic Goddess," *Television: The Critical View,* 5th ed., ed. Horace Newcomb (New York: Oxford, 1994), 206. For more on the concept of unruly women, see Kathleen Rowe, *The Unruly Woman: Gender and the Genres of Laughter* (Austin: University of Texas Press, 1995).

60. "Mooning" consists of bending over and exposing one's buttocks. President Bush publicly condemned Roseanne for her apparent disrespect of the National Anthem at the San Diego Padres game in the summer of 1990.

61. Hilary de Vries, "Laughing off the Recession," *New York Times Magazine,* 3 January 1993: 24.

62. Kay Gardella, "'Murphy': Making It after All," *Daily News,* 14 November 1988: 70.

63. "Inside Hollywood! Women, Sex & Power," *People Extra,* Spring 1991: 63.

64. Bonnie J. Dow, "Femininity and Feminism in *Murphy Brown,*" *Southern Communication Journal* 57 (Winter 1992): 150.

65. Rich Brown, "Murphy Brown Gives Birth to Controversy," *Broadcasting,* 25 May 1992: 3.

66. Richard Zoglin, "Sitcom Politics," *Time,* 21 September 1992: 44.

67. Associated Press, "Quayle Offers Peace," *Times Herald Record,* 22 September 1991: 6.

68. Diane English on Prodigy Interactive Personal Service, 28 September 1993.

69. Jill Brooke, "On 'Murphy,' Sources Are Everything," *New York Post,* 27 March 1989: 62.

70. Jeremy Gerard, "'Murphy Brown' Stays on Top of the News," *New York Times,* 16 October 1989: C20.

71. Zoglin, 47.

72. Brooke, 62.

73. Dow, "Femininity and Feminism," 146.

74. Robert S. Alley and Irby B. Brown, *Murphy Brown: Anatomy of a Sitcom* (New York: Dell, 1990), 22.

75. Alley and Brown, 100.

76. Dow, *Prime-Time Feminism,* 151.

77. For an interesting analysis of the series and why it was so popular with African Americans, see Clarence Lusane, "Assessing the Disconnect between Black & White Television Audiences: The Race, Class, and Gender Politics of *Married...with Children,*" *Journal of Popular Film and Television* 27.1 (1999): 12–20.

78. Quoted from the series in Brooks and Marsh, 1116.

79. Herman Gray, *Watching Race: Television and the Struggle for "Blackness"* (Minneapolis, MN: University of Minnesota Press, 1995), 104.

80. Peter Noah, personal interview, 17 April 1991. Wendy Kout, who created the series, wanted Hannah and Marty to remain friends, but she left after the first six episodes over creative differences. When Peter Noah took over the series as producer and head writer, he also was determined to keep them friends, but told ABC, when the series renewal was in jeopardy, he would do anything they wanted to keep the series on the air.

Chapter 6

1990s AND BEYOND: POST-FEMINISM AND BEST FRIENDS

The 1990s saw the continued erosion of women's rights, particularly concerning reproduction, until, ironically, the election of a president who cheated on his wife and was accused of sexual harassment. Great strides were made in technology, including faster, cheaper, smaller, and more powerful computers used for shopping, research, and e-mail. But for all our achievements, both the 1990s and the beginning of the twenty-first century were marked by violence.

Despite more fragmented audiences, the nation came together to watch many news events. Television played a particularly crucial role in calming and uniting us after the terrorist attacks on September 11, 2001. Socially conscious comedies with Caucasian stars continued from the 1980s, while the new television networks targeted a young, primarily black audience with sitcoms starring African Americans.

CULTURAL/HISTORICAL CONTEXT

When Bill Clinton became president in 1993, he repealed the "gag rule" that prohibited doctors in federally funded clinics from providing abortion information and encouraged the research and development of RU-486, a drug used in other countries that allowed women to abort fetuses in the privacy of their own homes. Unfortunately, several people connected with abortions were killed by terrorists in the 1990s, including doctors. The U.S. Senate's confirmation of Clarence Thomas as a Supreme Court judge in 1991, despite allegations from Anita Hill that he sexually harassed her years earlier, angered many women. Also unsettling were several accusations against President Clinton, including that he had illicit sex with young White House intern Monica Lewinsky. In 1999, he was acquitted by the Senate in his impeachment trial on charges of perjury and obstruction of justice in his effort to hide his sexual indiscretions.

In the beginning of the 1990s the country was in a recession, with thousands of people being laid off from large corporations as companies merged and restructured. As the decade progressed, however, the economy began to recover, with interest rates down, spending up, and jobs on the rise. Growth was especially big in the area of technology, with computer and Internet-related companies spurring the stock market. "Dot-com" companies, so-named because of their Internet addresses, would inspire consumers to spend billions of dollars for goods and services sold via the Internet. By the end of the decade, 80 million Americans used personal computers to pay bills and send or receive e-mail from family and friends.[1] Cell phones also became ubiquitous as did DVD players for movies. The economy took a turn for the worse, however, and at the turn of the century, dot-com companies and many others saw their stocks plummet and unemployment rise.

Denial of job opportunities based on gender continued to be a problem, but there was some progress. In 1992, for example, the State Farm Insurance Company agreed to pay millions of dollars to more than 800 women who were denied jobs as agents, in what was the biggest sex discrimination settlement in U.S. history under the Civil Rights Act of 1964. However, in 2001, the National Organization for Women cited the National Committee on Pay Equity, which says a woman takes home 72 cents for every dollar a man does.[2] That figure is even less when divided by race, with African American women taking home 65 cents and Latinas 52 cents to each dollar a man takes home in wages.

One way to make legislators more sensitive to women is to increase the number of women in government. In 1992, the Feminist Majority began its Feminization of Power Campaign, noting that women were only 5 percent of the members of Congress and only 18.4 percent of all state legislative seats. They were successful: that November the percentage of women in Congress doubled to 10 percent, and the number of women in the Senate increased from two to six seats. Carol Moseley Braun of Illinois became the first elected African American woman senator, and California made history by being the first state to elect two women to the Senate. By 1998, women were 13 percent of the House of Representatives and 9 percent of the Senate. President Clinton named Madeline Albright secretary of state, making her the first woman to hold that position. Former First Lady Hillary Clinton was elected in 2000 to represent New York as a senator. There were many other "firsts" for women in the 1990s, including the first woman ever to command a military base and the first war memorial dedicated to women—the Vietnam Women's Memorial. In 1993, Toni Morrison, author of six novels including *Beloved,* became the first African American woman to receive the Nobel Prize in literature. Meg Whitman, CEO of eBay, an online auction house, became the first female Internet billionaire.

Violence was rampant around the world in the 1990s and early twenty-first century. Operation Desert Storm in 1991 was a combined air and ground assault on Iraq and Iraqi forces in Kuwait. Millions of people in the United States watched the war live on television as journalists from the Cable News Network (CNN) reported from Baghdad while it was bombed. In this Gulf War, women comprised 35,000 of the 540,000 U.S. troops, and eleven of these wonen died. On a more positive note, the Soviet Union collapsed after President Gorbachev suspended the Communist Party, and several states declared independence. Apartheid ended in South Africa when blacks won the right to vote in 1994. In Europe, East and West Germany united into one country after the fall of the Berlin Wall.

In the United States, riots broke out in South Central Los Angeles in 1992 after a jury acquitted the police officers involved in the 1991 beating of black motorist Rodney King. More than fifty people died in the riots, and there was more than 1 billion dollars worth of property damage. The nation was further racially divided as millions watched the televised trial of former football hero O.J. Simpson for the murder of his ex-wife, Nicole Brown Simpson, and her friend Ronald Goldman. While overall crime was down, people were increasingly afraid of violence in public places. In 1993, terrorists exploded a bomb in the parking garage under New York City's World Trade Center, killing six people and injuring more than a thousand. In 1995, a bomb exploded in the Federal Building in Oklahoma City, Oklahoma, killing 169 people, including children in a day care center. But all-out war seemed to come to our shores six years later as terrorists flew planes into the twin towers of the World Trade Center and the Pentagon, leaving more than 3,000 dead. A fourth plane crashed into the ground near Pittsburgh, Pennsylvania, as American heroes/passengers evidently fought the hijackers to prevent them from reaching their expected target, the White House. A war on terrorism was declared, promising to last for years. In incidents at various businesses, disgruntled employees went on shooting sprees throughout the decade, killing supervisors and others nearby for real or imagined slights. Perhaps most frightening in the 1990s were the shootings in at least eight schools throughout the country where assassins as young as eleven years old gunned down classmates. The most deadly was at Columbine High School in Littleton, Colorado, in 1999 where two students randomly killed twelve classmates and one teacher, wounding twenty-three others.

Violence also was more prevalent in music lyrics, particularly "gangsta rap" that spoke of killing cops and hitting women. As Time-Life editors described it, "with new trends emerging almost yearly, pop music in the '90s was–depending on your point of view–dynamic and diverse or diffuse and fragmented."[3] Both hip-hop and country music skyrocketed in popularity. Garth Brooks' *Ropin' the Wind* in 1991 was the first album to debut on the top of both the country and popular music charts. Hip-hop group the Fugees sold 18 million copies worldwide of their 1996 album *The Score*. With its roots in heavy metal and punk rock, the "grunge" sound from Seattle became popular, typified by the group Nirvana. In addition to the antiestablishment mentality that grunge encouraged, it also influenced a kind of antifashion fashion, with torn jeans, flannel shirts, and body piercing. A gentler kind of pop music was to be found in groups such as Hootie & the Blowfish in their album *Cracked Rear View,* and the sweet harmonies of the Backstreet Boys. Women were a strong force on the music scene, including Alanis Morrisette and her *Jagged Little Pill,* the best-selling pop album of the decade. Mariah Carey and Boyz II Men had the top single of the decade, "One Sweet Day." The Spice Girls, with a lot of makeup, few clothes, and sugary lyrics, inspired wannabes among preteen girls. From 1997 to 1999, the groundbreaking Lilith Fair, an all-women music tour, made the rock-festival circuit with a decidedly feminist flair.

The romantic and tragic love story in *Titanic* made it by far the highest-grossing film of the 1990s, with a box office of more than $600 million and an Academy Award for Best Picture. The long-awaited " prequel" to the popular *Star War* series, *Episode I*: *The Phantom Menace,* was second and the dinosaur thriller, *Jurassic Park,* was third. Julia Roberts became a major star with *Pretty Woman,* playing a hooker transformed by a millionaire businessman, in a modern Cinderella story not particularly liberating. In 2000, she won the Oscar for best actress for her role in *Erin Brockovich,* the real-life story about a woman who takes on a large corporation responsible for polluting water that is killing people. Sandra Bullock also became a major star, starting with her heroic role in the major action film, *Speed,* with Keanu Reeves. Women flocked to theaters to see *Thelma & Louise* about two women who end up on the run after one kills a man attempting to rape the other. Tom Hanks won an Academy Award for best actor two years in a row, first for *Forrest Gump,* where he portrayed a slow-witted man with a heart, and then for *Philadelphia,* where he played a lawyer stricken with the AIDS virus. Many popular books of the 1990s were made into successful movies, including *The Bridges of Madison County* by Robert James Waller, which was on the hardcover best-seller fiction list the longest, at 160 weeks.[4] About a married woman in the Midwest who has a brief affair with a photographer, the movie starred the versatile Meryl Streep and Clint Eastwood. The early part of the twenty-first century saw the phenomenal success of two movies based on books of fantasy. Academy Award–nominated *Lord of the Rings: The Fellowship of the Ring* was the first of the trilogy to be released, written by J.R.R. Tolkien decades earlier. *Harry Potter and the Sorcerer's Stone,* based on the first in a series of children's books about a boy who goes to sorcerer school, appealed to both children and adults. Written by J.K. Rowling, the series includes a strong, smart girl, Hermione, one of Harry Potter's two best friends.

The nonfiction book on the best-seller list the longest was John Gray's *Men Are from Mars, Women Are from Venus,* a tome that emphasized the two genders as truly opposite sexes. A men's movement was spurred by *Iron John,* a book by Robert Bly that urged men to get in touch with their "inner warrior" and "wild man." Susan Faludi's *Backlash: The Undeclared War against American Women* gave dozens of examples of collective retribution against women for the gains they had made, particularly in the 1970s. Oprah Winfrey, long a star of her own talk show and an acclaimed movie actor, began making a major impact on the book industry in 1996 with the introduction of her "book club" as a monthly segment on her show. More than twenty-eight novels quickly became best-sellers after her recommendation. Martha Stewart also became a media mogul with twenty-seven how-to books on domestic skills selling more than 9 million copies, two big-selling magazines, a popular Internet site, and a television show.

THE TELEVISION INDUSTRY

While two more broadcast networks began (UPN and WB) and dozens more cable networks, huge conglomerates were being created by mergers, putting television programming decisions in the hands of fewer and fewer people. In 2001, film and television company Walt Disney owned ABC, General Electric owned NBC, and Viacom owned CBS, purchasing UPN in 2002. The broadcast networks also had their own production companies, syndication outlets, and ownership of several cable networks.

Despite the narrowing of program sources, several quality prime-time television shows got their start in the 1990s, particularly in the genre of drama. *ER,* a medical drama created by popular novelist Michael Crichton, usually dominated the ratings and contains several strong female roles. *Dr. Quinn, Medicine Woman* follows the struggles of a female doctor in the Old West.[5] History also made its way into the critically acclaimed *I'll Fly Away* about race relations in the South in the late 1950s and *Homefront* about life in a small town just after World War II. *Northern Exposure* is about a quirky group of characters living in Alaska, including air taxi pilot Maggie O'Connell. Cops and courtrooms are combined in the long-running and critically acclaimed *Law & Order* on NBC. *NYPD Blue* on ABC broke new ground in its nude "butt shots" in competition with the more liberal cable channels. Prime-time soaps aimed at teenagers became popular, starting with *Beverly Hills, 90210* on FOX, followed by *Melrose Place, Felicity,* and *Dawson's Creek.* The FOX network created a cult following with *The X-Files* about two FBI agents assigned to unsolved cases often dealing with bizarre phenomena, including alien abductions. Interestingly, the female agent, Dana Scully, is the scientist and skeptic. Aliens are part of the regular cast in such *Star Trek* spin-offs as *Star Trek: Voyager,* with the first female captain of the *Star Trek* series. In *Buffy, the Vampire Slayer,* it is up to a teenage girl to save people from the walking dead. In a nation reeling from presidential scandal, in 1999 NBC began its popular and critically acclaimed *The West Wing,* a fictional account of the president of the United States and his advisors. Although on pay cable channel HBO, *The Sopranos,* debuting in 1999, became both a critical and popular hit into the twenty-first century, winning Emmys for best drama as well as for several of its actors. About a mob family in New Jersey, this very violent and sexy show features two interesting women, Carmela Soprano, the mob boss's wife, and Dr. Jennifer Melfi, mob boss Tony Soprano's therapist.

Daytime talk shows proliferated, with hosts such as Jerry Springer encouraging participants to reveal intimate secrets and fight about them in front of millions. Their popularity, led by Oprah Winfrey with her more uplifting format, peeked in the 1990s and real court room dramas, led by *Judge Judy,* began to gain large audiences. Reality in prime time became extremely popular with the success of CBS's *Survivor,* which puts people in an isolated location and encourages them to backstab each other for the million-dollar prize. Big-money game shows made a comeback in a big way with *Who Wants to Be a Millionaire?*, hosted initially by daytime talk show host Regis Philbin.

Toward the end of the decade, narrative comedy shows were vying with sitcoms for critical acclaim. Winner of an Emmy for Outstanding Comedy against four sitcoms, *Ally McBeal* (FOX, 1997–2002) is about an insecure woman looking for true love while she works in a law firm in Boston.[6] Feminist critic Brenda Cooper claimed that producer/writer David E. Kelly constructed in this series a "preferred feminine spectator position that appropriates dominant male gazes" and presents the male characters as comic as women invade male space and return their gaze.[7] *Sex and the City,* which debuted on HBO in 1998, is another Emmy-winning comedy that is not a sitcom. Focusing on four women who are best friends and live in New York City, the series is a testament to strong female friendships that last over a series of failed relationships with men.

SIGNIFICANT COMEDY SERIES

Several situation comedies of the 1990s made significant strides in the portrayals of women on television. In *Home Improvement* (ABC, 1991–1999), although primarily a showcase for comedian Tim Allen, the depiction of the traditional nuclear family is occasionally rocked as wife Jill struggles for her own career in an all-male household. *Grace Under Fire* (ABC, 1993–1998) depicts a woman who left an abusive relationship to raise her three children on her own. *Living Single* (FOX, 1993–1998) is about four African American single women who seek both careers and mates. *Friends* (NBC, 1994–) is about six New Yorkers, three men and three women, who help each other through both their failures and successes. *Ellen* (ABC, 1994–1998), although the series didn't start out with this intention, features the first prime-time lesbian character. *Will & Grace* (NBC, 1998–) is about the close friendship between a homosexual man and heterosexual woman.

Home Improvement

Home Improvement debuted on ABC in 1991 in the top-10 Nielsen ratings and stayed there throughout its entire eight-year run. That year, thirteen of the top-20 shows were sitcoms, but only three, including *Home Improvement,* revolved around a traditional nuclear family of two parents and their biological children. Like the stars of the other family sitcoms, *Roseanne* and *The Cosby Show,* the star of this show is a standup comedian, Tim Allen, whose character in the series is based on his comedy routine. Allen had become famous as a comic who specialized in macho male humor with talk of "more power" in relationship to tools and cars, and a "men are pigs" mentality in relationship to women. Both Tim Allen in his comedy routine and Tim Taylor, his character on *Home Improvement,* frequently communicated with grunts and howls, as modern wild men following Robert Bly's Iron John.[8] While the "more power" that both Tims sought was literally for their cars and tools, it also could be read as a cry for more power for men and from women, in a post-feminist battle of the sexes.[9] The title of the series, *Home Improvement,* also has at least two meanings. Tim Taylor has a cable show, *Tool Time,* in which he and his assistant, Al Borland, in a mixture of humor and practical advice, demonstrate how to build and fix things around the house. On another level, the series title could be a reference to Tim who needs improvement in his relationship skills, taught in endless lessons from his wife, Jill, and their neighbor, Wilson. While Tim Allen/Tim Taylor is definitely the star of the show, Jill is a crucial part of it as Tim's primary civilizer.

At the beginning of the series, Jill Taylor is in her mid-thirties, the mother of three boys (ages ten, nine, and six) and a housewife in a middle-class suburb of Detroit. In the pilot, she unsuccessfully applies for a job after many years of staying home; a few episodes later, she attends a job search seminar. Early in the second season, Jill begins working at a magazine, *Inside Detroit,* as both a researcher and a writer. When she is laid off two years later, she decides to study psychology in graduate school to pursue a career as a family counselor. Before she finishes her master's degree, Jill becomes a research assistant to one of her professors and does some family counseling. Throughout the years, Jill is also active in many volunteer capacities, including the PTA as well as fund-raising for the library and opera.

One of five daughters of a career military man, Jill met Tim at Western Michigan University and they married soon after graduation. She was a good student while Tim was a party boy who barely graduated. In the battle of the sexes between Jill and Tim, it is not much of a battle; she almost always wins. Tim readily admits that she is smarter than he is. In "Back in the Saddle Shoes Again," when Tim is nervous about Jill's decision to go to graduate school, he asks her if she ever wishes she had married someone as smart as she, a question the audience might well ask. Her response indicates the attributes an intelligent, nurturing, and good-humored woman might find as compensation for a less intelligent mate: "Why would I want to marry anyone else? You're funny, you're sexy, you're creative, you take chances, and you're definitely not afraid to be wrong. I'm perfectly happy being married to a man who thinks that PBS is something women get once a month." Jill also has bested Tim in more traditional male pursuits as well, including bowling, driving a tank through an obstacle course, and building a house.

Conflict between Jill and Tim often stems from his unwillingness to discuss things. For example, when Jill's sister gives birth to a daughter, Jill thinks she might like to try for a girl in her household of males. Despite the fact that she ultimately decides she is too busy for a baby now, she explains to Tim that his early protests against another baby precluded any discussion. Tim, of course, does not seem to learn from episode to episode and gets in the same kind of trouble when he discourages Jill about returning to school. He not only has problems with intimate conversations with his wife, but he also does not share her interests. In "Let's Go to the Videotape," Tim accidentally records himself complaining to the guys at the hardware store about how boring he found Jill's speech to a library group and how bored he gets when she talks about her psychology classes. Naturally, she is hurt when she sees the tape. Tim apologizes, and is found later reading her psychology books to better understand her interests. What is particularly interesting about this and other episodes where Tim complains about Jill is Tim's notion of public and private space. The traditional notion of gender roles designates public spaces as male territory and private spaces (i.e., the home) as female territory. Tim explains to his sons in the "Videotape" episode that "there's a lot of stuff that can be said in the privacy of a hardware store that can't be said in public places, like your home." He also regularly complains about his personal life on *Tool Time*.

Space and possession are the focus of other episodes as well. In "A Battle of Wheels," Tim is upset when Jill places her pottery wheel in the garage where Tim frequently works on his hot rod. He considers the garage his space, even though it is where Jill washes clothes. In "Howard's End," Tim chastises Jill for referring to the station wagon as hers, not theirs. Later, however, she overhears Tim telling their son Mark that the car is his because he paid for it. The two end up in a big fight, with Tim admitting everything, including the house, is technically his because he paid for it. As in most episodes, Tim talks to next-door neighbor Wilson about his fight with Jill. The learned Wilson tells him how the Modock Indian tribe had no words for "yours" or "mine," just "ours." He explains how twentieth-century man, however, is measured by his possessions, which give him a sense of power as well as control over his mate. As he occasionally does, Tim makes a kind of apology to Jill on his show by talking about the power of ownership and that "in a relationship you've got to be equal, no matter who makes the money." Later he apologizes to Jill in person. Although in typical fashion Tim confuses some of what Wilson has told him, he does confess he judges himself by possessions. He also tells Jill that she does so much that it is hard to put a price on it. She challenges him to do so, and he is ready. For 12-1/2 years of housework and the pain of childbirth he figures he owes her 58 million dollars—a figure many feminists and housewives might be pleased with in recognition of "women's work" at home.

The two other significant adult males in *Home Improvement* are quite different from Tim in terms of sensitivity and intelligence. Al is Tim's coworker and actually quite competent with fixing and building things. He continually defends women and appreciates Jill's accomplishments (he not only liked her library speech, he also cried at the poem with which she concluded it). Wilson, too, is a liberated, sensitive male, and his knowledge goes far beyond the obscure subject matter in which he earned his Ph.D. While Tim constantly asks Wilson for advice, Jill occasionally seeks his counsel, and in her he has met his match. For example, in "Let's Go to the Videotape," where Tim unknowingly tapes himself complaining about Jill, Wilson tries to explain Tim's behavior to Jill:

Jill: He didn't even think he did anything wrong. He was just doing what all guys do when they get together.

Wilson: Well, Jill, the renowned psychiatrist Irvin D. Yalom postulated that men relieve their isolation by bonding over common fears and experiences.

Jill: Oh, please. Yalom was talking about universality as it applies to formal therapy, not about guys sitting around dumping on their wives.

In other episodes, however, Wilson is able to commiserate with Jill and quote feminists himself. In "The Flirting Game," Jill is upset about the idea of women flirting to get what they want, and she is afraid she has done it. Wilson says that "unfortunately, in many societies women are at a disadvantage so subconsciously or consciously they flirt in order to level the playing field." She says, "the whole thing stinks," and he replies, "I know who would agree with you—Charlotte Whitten, the Canadian feminist. She said that whatever women do they have to do twice as well as men in order to be thought half as good." It is also in this episode that Jill identifies herself as coming from "the old school of feminism" and says that she doesn't want to be wily. Jill says she does not mind working twice as hard; "it's these stupid games I don't want to have to play."

Jill is a loving mother who goes through the usual guilt about not paying enough attention to her kids once she starts working and going to school. Many episodes indicate that she understands her sons and knows how to both talk and listen to them. In "Maybe Baby," for example, youngest son Mark is upset when his older brothers tease him by saying that their mom wanted Mark to be a girl. When Mark confronts his mom, she tells him that a part of her did, but that she fell in love with him as soon as she saw him. She makes an analogy that a child his age will understand, getting him to remember when he wanted a puppy but got a turtle instead—he would not have traded his turtle for anything once he got it.

Various relatives of both Jill and Tim occasionally appear, but it is Jill's relationship with her parents that is the most complex. In "The Colonel," Jill's father visits and brings a book he has written about his career in the military for her and Tim to read and give him feedback. The book is boring, but Jill tells him it was good so he won't get upset. She tells Wilson that when the movie *Old Yeller* came out, she and her sisters thought by the title that it was about their dad, and that there was a house rule never to upset him. Encouraged by Wilson (as well as Tim earlier) to tell the truth, she finally confronts her father and says, "Dad, I love you so much and there were a million times that I needed to talk to you, but I couldn't." In "Some Like It Hot Rod," Jill blames her mother for her problem with apologizing to Tim for leaving his hot rod out in a snowstorm. She tells Tim, "To my mother, an apology was like an admission of guilt, which gave her the right to give me a nine-hour lecture on what a bad person I was." Jill has various female friends during the eight-year run of the series—including a feminist friend in the first season who teases Tim about being insecure and destructive—but none last for any length of time. Rarely is Jill seen at work or school, although it is clear both are important to her as probably are her implied friendships with other women. The focus of the series is her role in the family, particularly her relationship with Tim.

Jill is seen as superior to Tim in many ways, but not because she has been placed on a pedestal. Her flaws are several, as indicated over many episodes. For example, her husband and sons frequently make fun of her cooking skills. She can also come across foolishly, as she does when she interviews for a research assistant job and the professor catches her with her skirt rolled up and, in an attempt to "fluff" it, her hair in her face. After she excuses herself to fix herself up again, she babbles to the professor during the interview that she does not want to get the job based on how she flirts. He wants to know why she would think he would not base his decision on her qualifications. When she then flatters him, he says he does not hire on that basis either. On the whole, however, Jill is depicted as a woman who manages to do it all—that is, have both a loving family and career—despite obstacles. It is her choice to stay home until all three children are in school, and it is her choice to go back to school and seek a career. None of it is made to look easy.

In the last (eighth) season, several life changes take place, including Jill having an emergency hysterectomy because of a tumor on her uterus and then getting mood swings as a result. Perhaps the most life-changing development is Jill earning her master's degree and being offered a wonderful job in an adolescent development program in a family clinic—in Indiana. When she tells Tim of the offer, he immediately says he does not want to go, despite his having quit *Tool Time*. She tells Tim she doesn't necessarily want to move, but she wants to discuss it; he refuses. After talking it over with Wilson in the backyard, Tim decides it is Jill's turn and he convinces the boys that they should all move so she can take the job. According to television series chroniclers Brooks and Marsh, Jill accepts the job, Tim jacks up the house, and they move to Indiana.[10] However, a close look at the final scenes of the final episode shows Jill saying she is willing to give up this opportunity for Tim, that she does not want to give up her life where they are, and she can't imagine leaving their house. Tim replies, "Well, if we ever decide to move, maybe we wouldn't have to leave the house." When Jill asks him what he means, a cartoon balloon comes out of his head and, in Tim's imagination, we see Jill and Tim driving a flatbed with their house on it. In reality, it appears that Jill is once again sacrificing her career for Tim's. Or is she? If nothing else, Jill has succeeded in raising the consciousness of her husband, at least temporarily.

Grace Under Fire

Debuting in fall 1993, *Grace Under Fire* (ABC) is the first situation comedy whose main character had been an abused wife and whose story lines depict the daily struggle of this single, thirty-five-year-old working mother. The irony of her name is not lost. Grace Kelly is far from being a romantic movie star-turned-princess, and her "prince" tried to beat her into never-never land. The "fire" she is under includes fights with her ex-husband to get him to pay child support and the struggle she has getting treated fairly at work and raising her children. The war metaphor continues in the name of the Missouri town, Victory, to which she has moved.

She already has had two important victories, recently divorcing her abusive husband and giving up alcohol nine years earlier, but the struggle with both continues. The amount of "grace" she has in her battles varies, as does her success. With so many abused women and single, working mothers in the country, this sitcom did not gloss over the real struggles with money, child care, and complicated relationships such women faced. It apparently struck a nerve as it instantly became a top-10 hit and remained on the air until early 1998.

As the series starts, Grace, played by standup comic Brett Butler, is newly divorced and has just started a temporary job at an oil refinery. She has three children (Quentin, Libby, and baby Patrick) who rely on her for primary financial and emotional support. Grace copes with her situation with sarcastic humor, intelligence, and a small network of friends and family. Her relationship with her children is quickly established before the opening credits of the pilot episode. As they drive down the highway, the two older children are hitting each other with balloons. When Grace asks them what the rule is about throwing things in the car while she's driving, they reply, in unison with rolling eyes, "don't." To her query "And what's the punishment?" they reply, without fear, "death." When one asks why their dad isn't living with them, Grace replies, "because he won the coin toss." Despite her sarcasm, she encourages them to talk to her, ask her questions, and does her best to meet their emotional needs. Both children are troubled by the absence of their father, but particularly Quentin, who knows his father hit his mother but loves him nevertheless. Libby somehow was oblivious to the turmoil between her parents, and generally she is well-behaved and very smart. One episode, however, reveals that Libby has developed an ulcer from worrying about the family finances, among other things. Despite Grace's assurance that worrying is her job, not Libby's, and that she would take care of things, Libby continues to be a serious, concerned, but loving child. At the tender age of nine, Libby encourages her mom to go back to school, despite the fact it means they will be even poorer than they are now. Libby refers to a biography about Louisa May Alcott that said she didn't realize she was poor because she was happy; Libby says she could be just like her.

One of the most defining and complicated relationships Grace has is with her ex-husband, Jimmy. Although we do not see him until the second season, his presence is felt by the emotional scars and financial problems with which he has left Grace. We first see Jimmy when he shows up to help his family during heavy rains and the threat of flooding; he apparently hasn't seen his children in at least six months. It is clear that their relationship in their eight years of marriage was both passionate and violent, with alcohol playing a major role. Grace is tempted to sleep with Jimmy when he spends the night, but she doesn't, although she allows a long, lingering kiss. As Jimmy serves breakfast to his children the next morning, the kids beg him to stay and he says it is up to their mother. Angry, Grace sends Quentin and Libby to their rooms and asks Jimmy why he is making her the bad guy. Jimmy rants at her that she keeps bringing up the past and won't let him change, "so you tell me, Miss Holier than thou, blonde out of the bottle, Dixie bitch, who the bad guy is," and he pounds on the table. The tension is palpable, and Grace undoubtedly is expecting him to hit her as she slinks away. Sadly enough, in this and other episodes, Grace takes partial blame for Jimmy hitting her, claiming at times that she knew what to say to push him into it. Toward the end of the fourth season, Jimmy moves into Grace's garage apartment to be able to help more with the children. Grace has forgiven him for his previous abuse and neglect, but she has not forgotten as their relationship turns to friendship and she dates other men. In the case of Jimmy, she truly develops grace under fire. His reform, however, could send false messages of hope and redemption to other abused women. Although Grace's relatives, particularly her older sister, Faith, are shown in some episodes, her connection with Jimmy's mother, Jean, is the most constant. Their relationship is not an easy one, with Jean critical of Grace's life, including her non-church-going ways, and Grace with her sarcastic remarks. It is many years before Jean accepts that her son used to hit Grace. Nevertheless, Jean is quick to help Grace with the children and eventually moves in with her.

Grace actually has platonic friendships with several men in her life, including Wade, neighbor and husband to her best friend, and Russell, a pharmacist who has recently gone through a bitter divorce and later dates her older sister, Faith. Russell helps her out when she gets in trouble with the IRS because of Jimmy, and he is readily available when she needs a babysitter. It is fitting that she works at an oil refinery because she can be just as crude as the men with whom she works. She acts like "one of the boys," joking and teasing right back when they make sexual remarks to her. In the very first scene with the men at work, one man approaches her, calls her "Sweetpea," and says that the only reason she got the job is because she is a "chick." She replies, "Au contraire, Archimedes. The only reason I got this job (she moves closer) was because I promised to have sex with the smart guys. (In a tough guy accent) Too bad for you." The crudeness decreases over time, however, as the relationships are refined into caring, albeit gruff, friendships.

Grace has a serious relationship with two of the men she meets at work who are not part of her crew, including Ryan, an intelligent but sometimes awkward chemist. They break up primarily because he'd like to start a family with her and she wants no more children. Rick is a supervisor whom she dates and falls in love with, yet when he gets another job in Alaska and proposes, she turns him down. In "You Go Girl," Grace tells Rick she is tempted, but it has taken her four years to get the life she has and it is too soon to give it up: "I've got friends that I love, my friends love me, I've got a decent job...I can't just leave this for a man I've known for only eight months." Not all Grace's relationships are so serious, however, and some men she dates primarily for sex.

Although Grace is a strong woman, some of her strength comes from her best friend, Nadine, whom she has known since they were fourteen years old. They have been there for each other during both good and bad times, through rock concerts and proms as well as failed marriages and financial stress. Nadine works at a bar, and is on her fourth husband, with whom she desperately wants to have a baby. It is Nadine who usually watches Grace's children when she has to work overtime and for any other emergencies that evolve. It is Nadine who quickly brings Grace back to reality when Grace talks about how Jimmy is changing (she's heard it many times before). It is Grace who takes in Nadine when she leaves her husband, and it is Grace who pushes them to make up. The two do have their disagreements, however. When Nadine gets frustrated that she can't do anything right, including watching Grace's kids, Grace accuses her of whining and says, "just 'cause you can't win a fight with Wade, don't come pickin' one with me." Just before Nadine walks out, she tells Grace "it's not my fault you can't take care of your kids." The two quickly make up, however, as they remember how long they have been friends.

What we see Grace Kelly doing in this series is pursuing the American Dream. Despite her failed marriage, she is determined to work to not only care for her children, but also to better herself and their living arrangements. Throughout the series she continues to pursue a stable relationship with a man, but it is a secondary concern. In the fourth season she returns to college after many years with the thought of getting a better, more cerebral job. She also gets tired of renting, and buys a house. But the road to her dream starts with a temporary job as a crew member in an oil refinery, and she is soon given full-time work. After six months she is promoted to manager. The men she works with resent it because they feel it is a promotion based on affirmative action. When she asks her boss if she was promoted because she is a woman, he replies yes and her reply is "cool." Despite the fact that she has a potentially dangerous job (in "Ka-Boom," a coworker is killed), she can neither afford the lesser pay as a secretary nor does she want what she considers a boring job.

There is occasional tension at work because of male resentment and sexual harassment, as indicated earlier. Grace handles it matter-of-factly with humor while the rare female coworker takes it very seriously. For example, in the pilot episode the supervisor is talking to the crew about how it is now company policy that women must be treated with respect and must not be called demeaning names. When asked what she would like to be called, Wanda (who disappears after this episode) says, "Miss Honeycutt" until they get to know each other better. Grace's reply to the question is "How about throbbing mattress kitten?" and tells Wanda to shut up when Wanda says Grace is demeaning all women by allowing herself to be addressed in that manner. In the opening of the second season ("Good Ol' Grace"), Grace is in the lunchroom with the rest of the crew and there is the usual banter (Tony asks Grace to go behind the tank farm to have sex and she replies, "So I can pour you a cup of coffee and say, no, that's all right, it happens to all guys once in a while?"). Supervisor Bill walks in and introduces Tracy, a young woman who is uncomfortable with all the sexual talk and teasing. Grace encourages her to talk to Bill about it and later learns that Tracy has filed a sex grievance. Grace confronts Tracy, telling her that Bill is a good guy. Tracy explains that she wishes she could handle the guys like Grace does, but she can't, but that isn't why she filed—Bill said he wouldn't do anything about the men's language and he demoted her back to her old job. Grace apologizes and Tracy asks if she just assumed "I was some whiny, uptight, pseudo feminist?" "No," Grace replies, "that you were a militant, humorless, shrieking, back-porch harpy." Grace then confronts Bill, something she is known to do whenever she feels he is being unfair. He makes it clear that he will not change his mind and he is willing to lose his job over it. Like so many men in real life, he complains that "I'm a middle-aged white guy the only time in history it's ever been a bad time to be middle-aged, white, or a guy." Grace responds that "I'm a rapidly aging single mother. There's never been a good time to be that." While Grace has obviously benefited from the women's movement, she does not acknowledge it; she fights for what she gets on an individual basis despite the fact that she seems to believe in many of the same things most feminists do. At the end of the fourth season, Grace has earned her college degree and taken a job with an ad agency. When she is offered a job in St. Louis, her family encourages her to follow her dream, which she does, leaving the children in the care of their father, Jean, Wade, and Nadine. At the beginning of the fifth season, however, she has quit her job in St. Louis because she feels guilty leaving her children during the week, and she becomes an assistant at a construction company.

When *Grace Under Fire* debuted, the popular press ran many articles about Brett Butler's life, particularly about her abusive first marriage and alcoholism. The put-down humor in her standup comedy act, particularly of Southerners in general and men in particular, was brought to her television series, although both were toned down as the series progressed. She was often compared to Roseanne, with the anticipation that she, too, as a strong and forthright woman, would take control of her series after much conflict; she eventually did become executive producer. Whether the change in opening title song and visuals can be credited to Butler or not, the way the series is framed changed dramatically in the fourth season. Starting with the first season, Aretha Franklin is heard at the opening singing "Lady Madonna," a famous Lennon-McCartney tune, while a series of strobed-action scenes of Grace's children and friends are shown in a quick montage. The lyrics ask how Lady Madonna will make ends meet, a question Grace is struggling to answer for herself. The pictures are primarily domestic and internal. In the fourth season, however, the opening title visuals are desaturated and show Grace driving a car, pumping gas, picking up her kids, being greeted by Nadine and Wade, and ending with her sitting alone on her front porch. She now has a more separate identity with time to think; she seems more in control of her life. The lyrics of the new title song, "A Perfect World," are also more external, referring to walking down the street, and certainly more hopeful, envisioning a perfect world. Despite the abrupt ending of the series in 1998, we know Grace continues and hope it is with a brave and strong look to the future.

Living Single

The relatively new FOX network tried to establish its niche in the early 1990s with young, primarily African American audiences who were not well served on the other networks. From 1993 through January 1998, *Living Single* depicted the lives of four African American women in their twenties living in Brooklyn. With this series, Yvette Lee Bowser became the first African American woman to create a successful prime-time series for network television.[11] Using her own life experiences as a foundation for the series, Bowser created the four main characters as

extensions of different parts of herself: Regine (Kim Fields) is a materialistic fashion horse; Khadijah James (Queen Latifah) is a self-made entrepreneur who publishes her own magazine, *Flavor*; Synclaire James (Kim Coles) is Khadijah's dimwitted but adorable cousin; and Maxine Shaw

(Erika Alexander), the ever-present neighbor, is a ruthless attorney who thrives on large quantities of food and sex.[12]

Khadijah, her cousin Synclaire, and Regine share a brownstone apartment; Maxine, who is always there eating their food, lives nearby and is Khadijah's former college roommate. Also living in the brownstone and playing a significant part in their lives are roommates Kyle Bowser, a financial planner and Maxine's lover/adversary, and Overton Jones, the building handyman and Synclaire's boyfriend/husband.

The strength of this series is its focus on four independent women and their friendship, but some critics and viewers interpreted aspects of the program as harking back to black stereotypes. For example, media ecology professor Robin Coleman wrote that, although many black people loved the show, some disliked what they saw as "the series' reliance upon the same traditional White stereotypes of Blacks such as the use of black-voice (what the characters egregiously call 'Ebonics'), the use of ridicule in dealing with Black women (Regine is too mocked about her 'horse hair' in *Martin* fashion), and the presence of Oriole and Jim Crow character types in the dimwit Synclaire and the bumpkin Overton."[13] Despite some stereotypical aspects of *Living Single,* however, there also is pleasure to be had following the lives of these four women who are certainly not stereotypes physically. Three of the four are "full figured," and part of the pleasure is watching women whose body size is accepted and not an issue when it comes to attracting men.

Khadijah James is perhaps the most interesting character and the anchor among the friends. Played by rapper Queen Latifah (Dana Owens), the interpretation of Khadijah conceivably was enhanced by the extratextual information that many viewers would have had about her. Donald Bogle wrote that "she automatically represented a hip, postfeminist young African American woman, who was upwardly mobile and economically secure."[14] The connection between Khadijah and Latifah is strengthened further in an episode where a boss of Kyle's calls the women "bitches" after a poker game. In defense of his female friends, Kyle confronts his boss and orders him to leave, but it is Queen Latifah who gets the last word. The tag of the episode is the music video to "U.N.I.T.Y," her diatribe again sexism where she asks rhetorically, "Who you calling a bitch?" just before she throws a punch.

Founder and editor of her own award-winning magazine, *Flavor,* Khadijah struggles, and succeeds, in making a living for herself as well as the several people she employs. It is important to her to publish stories that matter, particularly to the black community. Besides her managerial skills, her reporting skills are sharp, and in "Who's Scooping Who?" we see her outwit a seasoned reporter in uncovering a story about a promoter who fixes fights. She also makes mistakes, but takes responsibility, as in "Scoop Dreams," when her desire to beat the competition leads her to publish an unverified story. In "Fatal Distraction," Khadijah makes a move on a handsome man she hired who seems interested in her. When she discovers he cannot write, he threatens to sue her for sexual harassment if he is fired, claiming she is just punishing him for rejecting her advances. Realizing her mistake of hiring him based on looks and not talent (and indicating women can be just as fallible as men), Khadijah fires him anyway, ready to suffer the consequences. When her employees threaten to sue for more money, she rearranges her finances to give them all a small raise. To get her employees a health plan, she sacrifices some of her independence by allowing a large publishing company to purchase a 25 percent share of her magazine. And when she is concerned that Maxine is spouting cliches rather than discussing issues in her bid for alderman, Khadijah risks their friendship by changing her endorsement to another candidate. Several episodes raise the question of how much Khadijah has sacrificed, particularly in terms of her love life, for the success of her magazine. It is a question often asked by many professional women in real life who have trouble balancing a career with a family.

Man-hungry, self-described diva Regine Hunter is another full-figured woman, who fancies herself as an expert in fashion and dresses accordingly. Shopping is her passion, second only to the pursuit of a rich man. At the beginning of the series, Regine works in a boutique, and later she becomes an assistant in the wardrobe department of a soap opera. She is a snob and prone to exaggerate her importance at work. When her soap is canceled, Regine starts freelancing as a party organizer, which suits both her need to be in charge and her preference for high society. She dates many men, but often gets discouraged that she'll never find the right one. In an episode where Regine is considering breast reduction for health reasons, it is revealed that, like many women, she considers her large breasts one of her greatest assets to attract men. Toward the end of the series run she still has not learned, as she instructs Khadijah, "God did not bless you with boobage so that you could carry office supplies. Girl, you've got to use them things to get a date!" By the end of the series, however, Regine has met and married her rich man, interestingly enough, by being honest with him.

Synclaire Jones is an upbeat innocent from the Midwest who is the heart of the group of women. She is known for her sing-songy "woo woo woo" to comfort those in distress, and her outlook is almost always optimistic. As her cousin Khadijah's secretary/receptionist at *Flavor,* her naivete and insecurity sometimes manifest themselves as incompetence. In "Quittin' Time," Synclaire leaves the magazine when Khadijah does not promote her. Khadijah is made to realize that Synclaire's cheerful personality makes up for any incompetence and rehires her as vice president of office affairs. Synclaire's burning ambition, however, is to be an actress, and several episodes depict her in a variety of roles as she struggles to reach that goal. While she may not be terrific at office work, she is shown to be a talented and confident performer.

Once Synclaire and Overton start dating, their romance blossoms and rarely do the two argue. In "School Daze," however, he enrolls in an art appreciation class that Synclaire is taking, and she asks him to drop the class. When he refuses, she explains to him that she needs a place to call her own because she is overshadowed at both home and work. "Obie," as she calls him, understands and drops the class. While the other women seem to have no problem sleeping with men early in a relationship, Synclaire and Overton date quite awhile before they have sex. In "Abstinence Makes the Heart Grow Fonder" in the second season, she tells an understanding Overton that she is afraid and is not ready; they decide to wait. The lesson about not allowing oneself to be pressured into having sex is clear. At the end of the fourth season, Synclaire and Overton are blissfully married.

In both 1995 and 1996, Erika Alexander won an NAACP "Image Award" for her portrayal of Maxine (Max) Shaw on *Living Single.*[15] Max is an aggressive, accomplished attorney who is suspended from her law firm after she independently tells a wealthy client to seek a prenuptial agreement and her fiancé dumps her. When she is called back to work, she is not treated well and quits, leading to several weeks of unemployment and a loss of confidence. In "Double Indignity," Max is unaware that her telemarketing boss is a scam artist and is arrested on the job. When she ends up representing herself after it becomes evident her lawyer is incompetent, she is offered, and accepts, a job as a public defense lawyer. In the fourth season, Max withdraws from her bid for alderwoman when she realizes her reasons for running are selfish, but she wins by write-in votes because of her honesty. In one of the last episodes of the series, "Forgive Us Our Trespasses," Max has her most thought-provoking client, a man arrested for trespassing at a hospital who claims to be the Son of God. Max finds the man upsetting not only because she doesn't believe she can win his case, but also because he knows things about her that he has no earthly way of knowing. He tells her that she has relied on her career as a crutch because she doesn't know who she is. Two episodes later, Max figures she was a man in previous lives and must have a child in this one. Her solution of having a child to find herself is a rather disturbing one.

Max is what some might call a "man-eater," and her dating life primarily consists of a series of one-night stands. When Regine tells her she never has a man because she is obsessed with revenge, Max replies, "It's not revenge; it's prevenge. Getting to them before they get to you." Throughout the series, however, she and self-proclaimed ladies' man Kyle Barker have a love/hate relationship, which escalates after a night of drunken love-making at the end of the first season. A typical exchange between the two is found in "Working Nine to Nine-Fifteen":

Max: You got to get up pretty early in the morning to get one over on me.

Kyle: Yes, because evil never sleeps.

Max: But ugly gets plenty of rest.[16]

Donald Bogle interpreted their verbal sparring as Shakespearean, "a pop/hip-hop version of Beatrice and Benedict."[17] Toward the end of the sixth season, the two admit they really love each other, but neither is willing to give in and stay with the other when Kyle is offered a job in London, England. In a kind of deux ex machina, the two get together at the end of the series, Max fighting almost all the way, when it is discovered that the sperm bank donor who impregnated Max is Kyle.

Initially, creator Yvette Lee Bowser called her series *My Girls,* but FOX network executives, afraid of alienating males, changed the name to *Living Single.*[18] More than the name changed, however. According to researcher Kristal Zook, "contrary to Bower's intentions, the show went from being a slice-of-life comedy about girlfriends to a narrative about the 'male quest,' or the 'Fight for Mr. Right' as one two-part episode was dubbed. From its inception, *Living Single* charged head-on, at Fox's urging, toward the imagined *Waiting to Exhale* audience."[19] *Waiting to Exhale* was a book (and later a movie) by Terry McMillan about four African American women, each searching for a man to complete her life. Indeed, the majority of episodes at least partially deal with the love lives of the women, but they never lose sight of their own interests and careers. Synclaire, who early in the series has a steady love interest in Overton, continues to strive to become a successful actress. While Overton occasionally resents how much time she spends working at her craft, he still supports her dream and, in fact, agrees to move to California with her when she is offered a television role. Being a lawyer is so much a part of Maxine (as is her defensiveness and pride) that one cannot imagine her giving it up, even with impending motherhood. Occasionally Khadijah is shown to feel that she sacrifices too much of her social life to make her magazine a success, and she also is chastised by friend-turned-lover Scooter, who asks that she pay less attention to her career and more attention to him. But the reality is that sometimes women do have to sacrifice some of their personal lives for success in business, at least until they get established. It is only Regine who might easily give up her work as a party organizer when she marries the rich, handsome man she had been seeking all her life, yet fashion and organizing social events are so much a part of her she would probably continue to do it. Perhaps the women's pursuit of love is better interpreted as just a normal desire for a well-rounded life with both career and family.

Despite the title change which initially emphasized female friendship, the opening title song is a tribute to the bonds of women, sung by Queen Latifah in a call-response, rap style. Although the women are close, they do not always get along and frequently snipe at each other. True to form, Max tends to be the meanest. In "Moi the Jury," Regine is concerned that she talks too much and asks her friends what they think. Khadijah tells her she is family and that it is not fair to ask that question. Maxine, however, tells her, "Regine, you're a gossipy, dirt-dealing human bullhorn." In a two-part episode in the first season, Khadijah, Regine, and Max compete for the affections of a handsome new man in their building. A story arc over three episodes concerns an argument between Khadijah and Regine in which Regine moves out. Regine eventually admits she feels lost without Khadijah in her life, and the two reconcile. Regardless of the fights, in the end *Living Single* is about female friendship. In "Love Is a Many Splintered Thing," Khadijah is spending all her spare time with a new love interest, and her girlfriends demand their time with her. Yet another episode, "Swing Out Sisters," has the women carving out time together, feeling that their friendship has been neglected. When Maxine becomes pregnant through artificial insemination and suddenly becomes scared, Khadijah assures Max that she will help her. Khadijah also encourages her cousin Synclaire in the final episode when Synclaire is afraid of leaving her behind, telling her they will always be close and that Synclaire can accomplish anything. Music is sometimes an important part of *Living Single,* often used to express the emotions of the characters. "My Girl" is of particular significance when sung by the women friends in both the pilot and the 100th episode. When they sing it, the lyrics can be interpreted as a celebration of their friendship.

Living Single rarely addressed any social issues, including racism; the series was most simply about four women friends. FOX's gamble in its appeal to African Americans paid off, and research indicated a big split in the most popular programs for black versus white people. In the 1994–1995 television season, for example, the BBDO advertising agency found *Living Single* was the most popular show with African Americans aged eighteen to thirty-four.[20] In the Nielsen ratings, *Seinfeld* was rated number one, and *Living Single* was not even in the top 30. That same year *Living Single* won the NAACP Image Award for Outstanding Comedy Series.

Ellen

Starring yet another standup comic, *Ellen* distinguished itself by becoming the first television series to feature a homosexual character, although it did not start out that way. Debuting on ABC in March 1994 as *These Friends of Mine,* Ellen DeGeneres portrays Ellen Morgan, an attractive woman in her early thirties who works in a bookstore in Los Angeles, lives platonically with a male friend, and shares her trials and tribulations of heterosexual dating with him and two female friends. ABC/Disney, which produced the series, changed the title to *Ellen* that fall to focus more on the talents of Ellen DeGeneres, made her the owner of the bookstore, and replaced her two women friends with no explanation. DeGeneres gained more creative control as the series progressed. In the summer of 1996, she was hinting that her character would go on a personal journey to find out who she is, and rumors abounded in the media.[21] Both actor and character were "outed" in the spring of 1997 with mixed reactions but high ratings.

Ellen Morgan is a funny, smart, likable woman who loves books and her bookstore, Buy the Book. Although story lines primarily focus on Ellen's relationships with her friends and family, she is shown to manage her business well. She initially refuses a chance to sell her store in the beginning of the fourth season, but relents when she finds she can still manage it and buy her dream house. By the last season, however, Ellen bravely quits her job to try other things, including hosting a radio show. While Ellen has moments of bravado, she is often insecure and self-deprecating. Perhaps more than anything else, it is important to Ellen Morgan to be liked. In "The Note," Ellen accidentally sees a note from someone in her book discussion group that says she is insufferable. When she finds out who wrote it, her insecurities show through, reminiscent of the "imposter syndrome" from which many successful women suffer. Ellen worries to roommate Adam, "I mean, these people are easy. But Phil—Phil obviously sees inside my soul. He knows. He sees. He sees the evil Ellen that no one ever sees. Gotta make things right. Gotta get back on track with Phil." Ellen tries to change herself on other occasions to fit in. When she dates a college professor who invites her to a jazz club, she studies books on it, then learns about opera when he takes her there. Her friend Paige doesn't understand why Ellen is "cramming" for a date, but we do—she wants to be liked and she wants to fit in, desires that are not exclusively female but are certainly expected more from them in terms of accommodating others.

In the beginning of the series, Adam is Ellen's roommate and has been for the past twelve years, two of them during college. They sometimes finish each other's sentences, spontaneously break into song together, laugh together, and comfort each other during times of crisis. Although Ellen, in her deep desire to be liked, rarely yells at others, she will to defend Adam. During a college reunion, Adam compares his life as a sometime employed photographer to his more successful peers and decides he needs to move. Although he tries to separate more completely, he ends up across the hall from Ellen and continues to spend a lot of time with her. Ellen is happy at this, because she has never lived alone before. In the 1995–1996 season, Adam has moved to London and Ellen's cousin Spence Kovak arrives at her doorstep in the aftermath of an earthquake. The two were close as children and quickly revive their friendship. When Ellen's current friends seem more involved in their own problems than the fact that her bookstore is in shambles after the earthquake, Spence steps in and tells them they should be ashamed of themselves and they need to rally for her. They rally. Spence stays with Ellen and she helps him as he struggles to find himself.

When the series started in March 1994, Holly and Anita are Ellen's close female friends. Anita is oversexed and Holly is underconfident. They are replaced with Paige Clark, Ellen's close childhood friend, and Audrey, an annoying and energetic new acquaintance. Paige is pushy, shallow, and self-centered, but actually does take time to listen to Ellen and help her occasionally. She tells Ellen she doesn't "get" books when Ellen wants her to join her reading group to find out who doesn't like her. Paige readily admits that she has "dated about a hundred guys and I don't know anything about any of them." She pushes her way through a career in the movie industry, however, stepping even on Ellen along the way. Audrey is also a pushy friend whom Ellen initially tries to avoid, but out of guilt she develops a friendship with her. Audrey speaks in a whiny, animated voice that can be grating. She is always giving Ellen advice (even on how to be gay!) and is highly critical about what Ellen wears and does. When Audrey loses her job, however, Ellen hires her at the bookstore. Clearly Ellen's male friends are more nurturing than either Paige or Audrey, yet they all are important in her life.

Ellen's parents, Lois and Harold Morgan, have played a large role in her life and occasionally are important parts of story lines. Ellen sums up the feelings of many children when she remarks to her friend and employee, Joe, that "isn't it strange how you can love your parents and want to strangle them at the same time?" Lois is constantly nagging Ellen to get married. In "The Therapy Episode," Ellen finally loses her temper when her mother again expresses her wish for Ellen to marry: "Oh, my God, I will then. You say that every time we talk. But here's the thing. I don't need a man to make my life complete. I am not gonna have the job you want me to have. I'm not gonna date the men you want me to date. I'm not gonna wear the clothes you want me to wear. It's my life, I want to live it my way. Just face it—I'm not you, Mom."

For most of the series, Ellen is presented as heterosexual and is shown as being attracted to a number of men, but no relationship lasts long. She quits dating a college professor because she introduces him to television and he becomes addicted. She quits dating another guy because he is too nice. When Ellen's mom accuses her of being too picky, Ellen agrees, but says she doesn't want to be with someone unless they are perfect for her. Ellen herself does not realize yet that part of the problem is she is pursuing the wrong gender. In a hint of things to come, shortly after the leak of Ellen's imminent outing in fall 1996, in "Give Me Equity or Give Me Death," a real estate agent is showing Ellen slides of potential homes to buy and uses a little doll to get Ellen to imagine walking up to her new home. When she pulls out a male figure to illustrate her husband coming home from work, Ellen says, "Oh, I think that puppet's in the wrong show." The opening titles starting in the third season (1995–1996) can also be seen as a metaphor for Ellen's search for identity, although not specifically for sexual preference, as she struggles for a title sequence. In many of these openings there is a simple set, sometimes just a chair with a table next to it in front of a curtain. In one she comes to the forefront and speaks to the camera (audience): "Okay, no opening sequence again and I am furious. I found the guy responsible and had him fired. Well, I sent him home...early...cause he was sick. And I gave him a ride. And made him soup. But after I did it everybody was like 'Ooh, we better get those titles done.' So next week. I don't want to have to do that again." Then someone off camera hands her a title card to hold. Part of the struggle for both her personal and series identity is her desire to fit in and not offend.

In "The Puppy Episode," a special hour-long program filled with guest stars and broadcast in April 1997, Ellen finally realizes she is a lesbian, but it is hard for her to admit it. When she meets an old boyfriend, Richard, and he introduces her to his television news producer, Susan (Laura Dern), the two bond instantly. When Ellen walks out of Richard's hotel room after an awkward, but gentle refusal of his sexual advances, Susan sees her and invites her into her hotel room. As Ellen is telling Susan about the awkwardness with Richard, Susan tells her she does not date men. Ellen is stunned even further when Susan says she thought Ellen was gay. Ellen strongly denies it and hurriedly leaves. Ellen later is shown with a therapist (Oprah Winfrey), and when asked if there is anyone she has ever "clicked" with, Ellen tells her, "Susan." When Ellen thinks Susan is leaving town, she hurriedly rushes to the airport to say goodbye. It is there she finally says it out loud: "You're right. This is so hard. I think I've realized that I am...I can't even say the word. Why can't I just say...I mean what is wrong? I mean, why can't I just say the truth? I mean, I'm thirty-five years old. I'm so afraid to just tell people. Susan (she unknowingly leans over the counter microphone), I'm gay." In the second half of the episode, Ellen goes back to her therapist and tells her that she thought if she ignored it, it would just go away and she could live a normal life. Her next hurdle is to tell her friends, who, she finds out, have had a bet about whether she is gay. While Audrey and Spence are very accepting, Paige is upset, hoping that this is just a phase Ellen is going through, but after a few more episodes, she finally accepts it.

In the episode that Ellen tells her parents she is gay, they both get very upset, and her dad walks out. Later at her parents' home, Ellen confronts her dad, who does not want to talk about it. Ellen asks her parents to attend a support group, but only her mother comes. Lois tells the counselor (Chastity Bono, then entertainment media director for the Gay & Lesbian Alliance against Defamation) that she is "heartbroken, confused, sad" and she misses the old Ellen. But when a man there with his gay son decides to walk out and calls Ellen "sick," Lois speaks up for her and says, "She is not sick. And sure I'm not happy about this, but I love her and I don't want to lose her." Her dad suddenly walks in to join the fight. Ellen claims to not be ready to date yet, a convenient evasion for family-friendly producer Disney. She tells her old boyfriend Dan in the beginning of the series' last season that things are the same as before, "but now instead of not having sex with men, I'm not having sex with women." She does find a steady girlfriend, however—an attractive real estate broker, Laurie, who has a twelve-year-old daughter. On their first date Ellen is so insecure she doesn't even know if it is a date; Laurie kisses her and removes all doubt, although physical contact between the two of them is primarily left to the imagination. In July 1998, in the last original episode aired, however, Ellen is considering marriage to Laurie.

According to *TV Guide,* the "coming out" episode of *Ellen* "was greeted with enthusiasm in the gay community, with boycotts by religious groups, and temporary withdrawals by corporate sponsors Chrysler and JC Penney."[22] Ellen's revelation brought the series back from number 44 in the Nielsen ratings the year before to number 29, and it was nominated for five Emmys, winning for best comedy writing. Certainly the series can be lauded for a positive role portrayal of a lesbian who is both charming and funny, a lesson perhaps for heterosexual audience members and encouragement through sheer recognition for the gay community. Despite the freedom both DeGeneres and her character felt after their "outing," DeGeneres did not want the series to focus on her sexuality, and she was eager for ABC to not renew the series another year. She says she "never wanted to be the poster child for lesbianism" and that being gay is only part of who she is.[23]

In her extensive discourse analysis of the three episodes that depict Ellen's "coming out" in spring 1997, feminist critic Bonnie Dow found that the treatment of Ellen's homosexuality "operates repeatedly to emphasize personal issues over political ones; that is, it presents acceptance by family and friends as the most crucial issues Ellen faces."[24] Dow pointed out instances where "at the same time that it dismisses the possibility or relevance of the material effects of homophobia, *Ellen* takes pains to establish gay political awareness and activism as oppressive."[25] The danger with positive portrayals that downplay systemic oppression and political struggles is that viewers may surmise that there has been concomitant social and legal change in real life and nothing need be done. But *Ellen* is a comedy and an angry, politically active Ellen would probably not be very funny. It also would be a major personality change in view of her deep desire to be liked and not confront people.

Friends

Created by Marta Kauffman and David Crane, *Friends* has been among the top-10 rated programs every year since its introduction on NBC in September 1994. Kauffman has said the series is about "that time in your life when your friends are your family."[26] The six main characters are all in their mid-twenties as the series begins, living in Manhattan and struggling to establish and maintain satisfying careers and romantic relationships. Parental relationships are a problem, but rarely, if ever, do current events intrude on their lives. The opening title sequence includes the song "I'll Be There for You" by the Rembrandts, which subsequently became quite popular, obviously touching a nerve in its expression of youthful struggle and the importance of friendship.

The six friends on the series consist of Monica Geller, a cleanliness/ neatness freak whose dream is to be a chef; her older brother, Ross, a nerdy paleontologist with a Ph.D.; Rachel Green, an initially spoiled runaway bride who aspires to a career in fashion; Chandler Bing, a data processor with a sarcastic sense of humor; Phoebe Buffay, a new-age space cadet with creative urges; and Joey Tribbiani, a dumb but kind and sexy, often out-of-work actor. The series focuses primarily on relationships, among the six friends as well as a series of boyfriends/girlfriends who come into their lives over the years. Their jobs frequently come up in conversation and occasionally we see them at work, but most of the action takes place in one of their apartments (usually Monica's or Chandler/Joey's across the hall) or the coffeehouse, Central Perk.

One of the laudable aspects of this series is the close, platonic friendships it initially depicts between men and women, although that line is eventually crossed between Ross and Rachel as well as Monica and Chandler (with the potential of a Joey/Rachel affair at the end of the 2002–2003 season). Most of the romantic relationships are heterosexual, but the series begins with Ross's wife leaving him for another woman whom she later marries. Several episodes hint at latent homosexuality in Chandler, including one where he is assumed gay by a coworker. His close friends admit they thought he had that "quality" initially, and his identity problem is understandable with an oversexed mother and cross-dressing father. Relationships with all the friends' parents are depicted in several episodes as crucial, personality-shaping explanations of character behavior.

Monica Geller is an attractive, slender young woman who is haunted by the fact that she was fat as a teenager. She is also insecure, a fact at least partially attributed to her parents' obvious preference for her brother, Ross. Her mother constantly criticizes her and refers to making mistakes as "pulling a Monica." Monica can be neurotic, particularly when it comes to cleanliness and neatness. On the positive side, Monica is an excellent cook and a loving friend. Her career ambition is to be head chef at a good restaurant. At the beginning of the series she is cooking at an elegant restaurant, but she eventually loses that job. For several episodes in the second season she works as a waitress in a '50s theme diner where she must wear poodle skirts and large fake breasts. Ultimately, however, Monica becomes head chef at a nice establishment, and there is no doubt she is good.

Monica's other ambition is to get married, and she realizes that dream too, in May 2001 when she marries longtime friend, Chandler. Before that, however, she dates a variety of men, and two are particularly important. Pete is a millionaire who falls for Monica when she is working at the '50s diner and buys her a restaurant so she can pursue her dream of being a chef. She refuses the job at first when she does not feel the attraction is mutual; when he sneaks a kiss later she discovers she likes him after all. Their relationship breaks up, however, when he refuses to quit pursuing his bid to become the "ultimate fighting champion." In her most serious romance before Chandler, Monica falls in love with a longtime friend of her parents, Richard (Tom Selleck), a charming man more than twenty years her senior. Her heart is broken, however, when he tells her he does not wish to have any more children, and so they break up.

The romantic relationship between Monica and Chandler begins when they are in London, England, for Ross and Emily's wedding at the end of the 1997–1998 season. After her brother's doomed ceremony, she is feeling lonely and forlorn; Chandler is more than happy to comfort her, and they make love. Once in New York, they still cannot keep away from each other and, one by one over several episodes, their friends find out; the two then decide to live together. By the end of the 1999–2000 season, Chandler's plan to ask Monica to marry him is complicated by the return of Richard, who tells Monica he stills loves her and now wants to marry and have children with her. True love triumphs, however, and Chandler and Monica become engaged. The next season, Monica is wedding obsessed, determined to have an expensive, showy event. She becomes somewhat shallow in her pursuit of the perfect wedding and honeymoon, even lamenting to Chandler after the wedding that now she is no longer a bride; she is just someone's wife. But the insecure, fat girl is still inside her, wondering if Chandler would leave her if she gained weight.

Rachel Green has been Monica's best friend since they were six years old, but they drifted apart after high school. Rachel got a nose job and was content to let her rich father support her until she found an equally successful husband. In the pilot episode, however, she appears at Central Perk in her wedding gown, having left Barry, an orthodontist, at the altar because she really does not love him. She moves in with Monica, and the friends take on the challenge of teaching Rachel about being independent. After a day of job searching and being laughed at because she is trained to do nothing, Rachel consoles herself with buying a pair of expensive boots and says she doesn't need her parents. When it is pointed out to her that she bought the boots with her dad's credit card, her friends get her to ceremoniously cut up all her cards. In the tag (last scene), Rachel is shown serving coffee at Central Perk, a job she will have for more than two years.

Of all the friends, Rachel grows the most in status over eight years of episodes. Early in the third season, she quits her job at Central Perk after she is told she is not doing well and will have to retrain as a waitress. In the next episode, she meets Mark, a man who helps her get a job at Bloomingdale's, long her favorite place to shop. To get in the good graces of her unpleasant boss, she fixes her up with Chandler. Rachel is later transferred to the personal shopping department. In the fifth season, Rachel gets a job at Ralph Lauren where she takes up smoking to fit in with yet another female boss. In the seventh season (2000–2001), she gets a promotion that includes her own large office and a personal assistant. Rather than hire a highly qualified woman, however, she hires a young, handsome man, Tag Jones, with little experience, and she proceeds to pursue him in a way that could be considered sexual harassment, if not for his willingness. While Rachel is quite competent in her job, her obsession with sex and occasional unprofessional behavior do not speak favorably about women in the workplace.

Throughout the series, Rachel has a number of boyfriends, including some who last a few episodes. The most crucial male relationship Rachel has throughout the entire series run is with Ross Geller, however, a relationship that has many twists and turns. Early in the first year of *Friends,* we learn that Ross had a crush on Rachel in high school. The two get together in the second season, but after awhile Rachel wants to take a break because Ross is constantly around her (the last straw is when he brings a picnic basket to her job when she is very busy). When a distraught Ross sleeps with another woman, Rachel sees it as a betrayal, despite Ross's constant cry of "but we were on a break!" The two get together again and break up again. At Monica and Chandler's wedding at the end of the seventh season Rachel learns that she is pregnant, and in the eighth season (2001–2002) we learn the father is Ross, after one night of passion. To Rachel's credit, she is willing to let Ross participate in their child's life, but she does not marry him just because she is pregnant. Their troubled past is indicative of the complexity of romantic relationships. Most important, perhaps, is Rachel's growth from a young woman dependent on her father for support to a person able to care for a child on her own. Nevertheless, the cliff-hanging episode at the end of the 2001–2002 season has a worried Rachel, contemplating the idea of raising her newborn daughter alone, say yes to Joey when she mistakenly thinks he is proposing (he had confessed his love for her several episodes earlier, but she turned him down). Although the confusion is cleared up early in fall 2002, by the end of the season Rachel indicates that she is indeed attracted to Joey, and the two may just be suited for each other after all.

Phoebe Buffay's troubled past can at least partially explain her flaky, new-age yet street-smart ways. She came to New York City when she was fourteen, after her mom killed herself and her dad was sent back to prison. She ended up living with an albino who cleaned windshields outside the Port Authority bus station, and she discovered aromatherapy after he killed himself. Phoebe has a twin sister, Ursula, who is a waitress and who Phoebe claims has always stolen things from her. At the end of the third season, Phoebe learns she was conceived during a "menage a trois" and meets her real mother, Phoebe Sr. In a search for her dad, she discovers she has a half brother, Frank Junior. A dim-witted underachiever, Frank marries his much older home economics teacher, and the two convince Phoebe to carry their child. The storyline was developed to accommodate Lisa Kudrow's real-life pregnancy, but it is also a chance to watch Phoebe's maternal instincts grow as she eventually gives birth to triplets. As hard as it is, she does give up the babies and they disappear out of her life, as did other members of her family. Phoebe's most consistent family relationship is with her grandmother, whom we see only once and who dies in the fifth season. Unlike Rachel and Monica, Phoebe has no long-term romantic relationships until the ninth season. In the first season, she falls for a scientist, David, who must go to Minsk for long-term research. When he returns in the seventh season, Phoebe's heart is broken because he can't stay; she claims he is the only guy she was ever crazy about. One of the most romantic episodes with Phoebe is "The One with the Chicken Pox," where a navy man she sees about every two years when he is in port purposely gets chicken pox with her so they can be together. She also has an affair with Gary, a police officer who wants her to live with him, but she is reluctant, and they part. Finally, in the 2002–2003 season, she falls in love with Mike, a younger man, and the two seem to have a future together when she turns down the marriage proposal of long-lost love David.

Phoebe's new-age philosophy and flakiness is revealed in several ways, including when she attempts to cleanse Ross's aura in the pilot episode, but it is most apparent in the several jobs she has over the years. She is a massage therapist until she gets fired for sexually attacking a client, who turns out to be willing, but married. She also sings her bizarre songs about life accompanied by her questionable guitar playing at Central Perk. Her signature song is "Smelly Cat." Phoebe's short-lived jobs include working as a temporary secretary at Chandler's work, a caterer with Monica, a bell ringer for Christmas donations, and a telemarketer. At one point she considers a new business venture she'd call "Relaxi Taxi," a massage/cab service for which she'd use her grandmother's cab. It is easy to see why Phoebe has a hard time finding a career because she is not the brightest of people. In the fourth season, for example, she learns that "Pheebs" is her nickname, not just "something that we call each other." Despite her spaciness, Phoebe's life on the street and struggle for survival during her teens manifest themselves occasionally in an instant flash of temper, which can go as quickly as it comes.

As the title of the series indicates, the most important aspect of the show is the friendship among the six main characters. Before Rachel becomes Monica's roommate in the pilot episode, Phoebe had lived with Monica. In a later episode, we learn that Phoebe had slowly moved out because Monica's manic urge for cleanliness was driving her crazy ("I need to live in a land where people can spill," she says), but she didn't want to hurt her feelings. The specialness of female friends is indicated early in the first season when Phoebe's overnight stay at Monica and Rachel's apartment is turned into an adult version of a girls' pajama party. The women surround themselves with trashy magazines, cookie dough, and the games Twister and Operation while they get drunk and gossip. Earlier in the episode, Rachel was feeling like a failure after a visit from her snobby, rich former girlfriends; by the end of the episode, with the help of Monica and Phoebe, she is fine. In another episode, the male friends are appalled to learn that the women tell each other everything, including details about sex. Occasionally the women will admit jealousy of each other, usually over relationships, and have vied for the same man on at least two occasions. When Monica refuses to choose between Rachel and Phoebe to be her maid of honor, she lets them choose and it becomes a real contest. Phoebe finally concedes to Rachel because it means more to her, as Rachel shows her the things she has collected for Monica since her engagement. Monica and Rachel have had the worst fights, including when Monica accuses Rachel of "stealing her thunder" from her engagement to Chandler when Rachel kisses Ross. After Rachel explains that she was feeling a little sad for herself because she's not getting married and had turned to Ross for comfort, all is forgiven. In the eighth season debut in September 2001, the friendship of the women is particularly evident during Monica's wedding. Putting aside her own obsession with her desire for the perfect wedding, Monica is concerned about Rachel when she realizes she might be pregnant. She insists that Rachel take another pregnancy test during the wedding reception, and the three friends wait in the women's room for the results.

The popularity of *Friends* was immense from the beginning and many fans wanted to be like them. "The Rachel," which described an early hairstyle of the character on the show, became popular with women of many ages. Apart from fashion and relationships, however, *Friends* has had little connection to issues. In a second-season episode, the women get excited about a feminist book called *Be Your Own Wind-Keeper,* but it becomes more a jab at new-age wisdom. Despite all the sex on the show, birth control is rarely addressed. Condoms do seem to be the method of choice, however, as we see Rachel and Monica fighting for the last condom in the apartment in a second-season episode. In the largest city in the country it is also odd that people of color are rarely seen. Nevertheless, the series theme of friendship is particularly appealing during troubled and unsettling times when terrorist attacks in the very neighborhood the friends live in have become a horrific reality.

Will & Grace

Unlike previous sitcoms, there has never been any doubt about the homosexuality on *Will & Grace,* which made its debut in September 1998 on NBC. Will Truman is a successful Manhattan attorney in his early thirties who did not realize he was gay until he was in college. Will's best friend is Grace Adler, an interior designer who was in love with Will at the time he admitted his homosexuality. When the series starts, Will is still getting over the end of a seven-year relationship with Michael and Grace leaves her boyfriend of two years, Danny, at the alter. To help each other heal emotionally, Grace moves in with Will. Complicating their lives are Karen Walker, Grace's incompetent, rich assistant, and Jack McFarland, who considers himself an entertainer but is usually unemployed. A popular series, *Will & Grace* has won multiple awards, including a People's Choice Award as Favorite New Comedy Series and an Emmy in 2000 for Outstanding Comedy Series.

Grace Adler is a beautiful, sexy young woman who is an interior designer and owns her own company, Grace Adler Designs. Although she is good at what she does, she is often insecure. In "The Buy Game," Will represents Grace when she has a chance to buy her office space, but he accuses her of being a bad businesswoman when she settles for what he considers less than "rock bottom." He proceeds to get her a lower price by bullying the owner and presenting Grace as a bad businesswoman of whom the owner took advantage. Grace refuses to sign the contract, however, crying that her life is a mess. Feeling sorry for her, the owner offers her an even lower price and after he leaves, Grace stops crying and tells Will to now tell her she's not a good businesswoman. Although her crying was not as loud as Lucy's wailing from the 1950s, the female stereotype of using tears to get one's way was both regressive and progressive (she bought property for a bargain price instead of fighting to be allowed to work or buy a dress). A Freudian therapist might diagnose Grace as anal retentive, both literally and figuratively. On many occasions Grace mentions that she has trouble pooping. She also has trouble letting go of her dependence on Will and family squabbles. In true psychotherapy fashion, many of Grace's less attractive characteristics are blamed on her mother, Bobbi, seen in only a few episodes. Both always have to be the center of attention, are very competitive, and must always be right.

Will and Grace are so close that they do not have to complete sentences to know what the other means. A date is not complete until one has told the other all about it. They nurse each other's heartaches and seek each other's advice. Grace has dumped more than one man because Will thought he wasn't right for her and has continued to stay with others because of his encouragement. Throughout much of the series they live together, despite many attempts to live apart. Their fights can be as intense as their love, however, and they know how to hurt each other. In "Polk Defeats Truman," Grace is angry at Will for dropping longtime clients to concentrate on a new, rich one. Will claims that is how business works and she responds, "not hers." His response is quite cutting when he says, "That's because your job is shopping for pillows and tassels. My God, a gay guy could do your job in his sleep." She accuses him of becoming the incarnation of pure evil, but not to take it out on her. They always make up, however, and are each other's backup in case a long-term romance does not happen during their fertile years. As Will told Grace, "if there's gonna be a little Will running around out there, I want him to be a little Will and Grace." Toward the end of the 2001–2002 season, Will convinces Grace that it is time for them to have a child together, but they cannot get themselves to have sex. The cliffhanger for the season has Grace running to her gynecologist's office with Will's sperm in a cup. The next season starts with Grace's rescue by a handsome doctor, Leo. When Grace decides she no longer wants to have Will's baby because she is interested in Leo, it almost ruins their friendship.

Over several episodes in the second season (1999–2000) Grace dates Josh, a man who cannot seem to go five minutes without saying he loves her. When she starts dating Will's African American boss, Ben, she eventually decides she needs to choose between him and Josh. Her mind is made up for her, however, when Jack confesses that he and Josh had sex. Traumatized by Will when in college because of his "coming out" when she was in love with him, Will teases her when yet another of her boyfriends turns out to be gay. In "Loose Lips Sink Relationships" aired in the early part of the fourth season, we learn that Grace has had sex with twenty-three people for a total of 282 times. She has a significant romance with Nathan, a low-class man whom she initially can't stand. Despite his demeanor, Grace is sexually attracted to Nathan and continues to date him, but is ashamed to tell Will. After Will, Nathan, and Jack bond over the death of Jack's father, however, Nathan moves in with Will and Grace, and they all get closer. After Grace turns down his marriage proposal because it was not done as she thought it should be (they were having sex), she decides she really wants to marry him, but Nathan turns her down and breaks her heart. In the fifth season (2002–2003), Grace meets and marries Leo, her dream Jewish doctor, who conveniently spends much time working oversees, allowing Grace to continue to spend most of her time with Will, Karen, and Jack.

Karen Walker is the closest that Grace comes to having a female friend, a woman who constantly drinks alcohol and pops pills to get through the day. Although Karen is useless and often absent in the office, Grace hired her for her social contacts; Karen feels working keeps her "down to earth." At first Grace tries to train Karen, but she eventually gives up. Karen married the unseen Stan because he is very rich, although he is also evidently fat and much older than she. Stan also has two children from a previous marriage (to which Karen cannot relate), and he ends up during the fourth season in prison for tax evasion. Nevertheless, on several occasions Karen admits she really loves her husband. She also loves spending his money and finds shopping a key to happiness. At the end of the 2001–2002 season, however, Karen is fed up with Stan being in prison and contemplates divorce. In the next season, Stan is released from prison and has an affair. Before Karen can divorce him, however, he dies and she is left squabbling with his mistress.

Will refers to Karen as the "local insensitive drunk," and she usually is. On some occasions Grace reluctantly has asked Karen for advice when she is troubled, and Karen can be quite cruel. She tells Grace, for example, that Grace has had more lovers and less sex than Nathan because guys don't like to have sex with her. In addition to chipping away at Grace's self-confidence by constantly criticizing her wardrobe and hair, Karen buys Grace's boyfriend Nathan an expensive present (a motorcycle) to put

Grace's thoughtfully chosen present (a signed first edition of *The Zen of Motorcycle Maintenance*) to shame. Karen also laughs when she sees Grace hurt herself. In an episode where Grace has overstayed her welcome to comfort Karen while Stan is in prison, she actually pushes Grace down the steps. There is a long history of slapstick comedy where audiences laugh at the misfortunes of others, but a major character deliberately causing physical pain to another does not seem so funny. Sometimes Karen can be insightful, though, such as when she tells Grace that she is upset about another woman getting Will's sperm because he was her backup plan. Mostly, however, Karen shows whatever affection she has through money.

Karen has two best friends who share her joy of fighting and laughing at others. Rosario is Karen's immigrant housekeeper, with whom she is constantly arguing and threatening. A typical exchange can be found in "Object of My Rejection," where Karen tells Rosario, "If it wasn't for this, you'd be flying back to Cucaracha on Air Guacamole with live chickens running up and down the aisle!" Rosario responds with, "Listen, lady, I'm gonna snap you like a twig and throw you in a bush." Their arguments often overlap each other in their anger, but when there is the possibility that Rosario may be deported, the two exclaim their love for each other and desperately try to find a solution. In the second episode of the series, Karen and Jack meet and become fast friends. Jack thinks she is a "hottie," and Karen revels in the flattery. The two bond in their cruel sense of humor, including laughing at Grace's occasional clumsiness and painful slips. They also have a reckless disregard for others' property, like when they consciously leave Grace's office unlocked and vulnerable to theft. Karen calls Jack "poodle" and lavishly spends money on him (what she calls buying him a little "happy"). Jack is there for Karen when she thinks she's pregnant (he even takes a pregnancy test with her), and Karen helps Jack to adjust to being the dad of a twelve-year-old boy.

Most of the humor in *Will & Grace* stems from relationships and takes the form of wordplay and put-down humor. Some of the humor is physical, particularly from Grace's clumsiness and Jack's flamboyant antics. Social issues are rarely addressed directly, and unfortunate assumptions could be made because of it. For example, Will and Jack seem to have few problems because they are gay, indicating that homophobia is a personal, not social, problem. In the episode where Grace is appalled at Will's tough negotiating methods, he explains that he has to be tough because he's gay; it's harder for him because of that. Belittling his stance, Grace tells him not to "pull out the gay card" because she'll have to pull out the "girl" card and "we both know the girl card trumps the gay card." It then evolves into a contest that ignores serious issues concerning homophobia, sexism, and other forms of prejudice. Kathleen Battles and Wendy Hilton-Morrow have claimed that homosexuality in this series has been made safe for broadcast television audiences

> by framing its characters within the familiar popular culture convention that equates gayness with a lack of masculinity and through the familiar situation comedy genre conventions of romantic comedy and delayed consummation, infantilization, and an emphasis on characters' interpersonal relationships rather than the characters' connections to the larger social world.[27]

Voting behavior based purely on sexual preference or ethnicity is lampooned, however, in "Star Spangled Banter." Will pushes Grace to vote for a gay man for city counsel. When she asks how he stands on various issues, Will doesn't know, and Grace chastises him. Soon thereafter she learns of a Jewish woman who is running for city council and, since Grace is Jewish, she proceeds to support her without question. The two hold a fundraiser for their candidates at their apartment and learn that neither is appropriate based on issues of equality and freedom. Disgruntled, they decide not to vote until they learn an African American man is running for council—and they rush out to vote for him.

Karen's problems with alcoholism and pill addiction are accepted, and none of her friends try to help her. With the amount and mixture of booze and pills she ingests, another person would be seriously ill and dysfunctional, yet Karen is able to cope. She is mean and lazy, but that is attributed to her general personality, not her addictions. Addicts are funny, and sexual harassment is a solution, not a problem. Karen says to her lawyer, Ben, "Why are you here? Is Stan in trouble again? 'Cause listen to me, you tell that secretary of his, one woman's sexual harassment is another woman's night off." Like many other sitcoms, however, *Will & Grace* have endless lessons about the importance of love, friendship, and accepting one another as we are.

OTHER SITUATION COMEDIES IN THE 1990s AND BEYOND

Approximately a hundred sitcoms were introduced in the 1990s on six broadcast networks. Media studies critic Michael Tueth has written about how many of these programs are urban comedies, noting that "comic situations are allowed to remain frustrating or confused in accordance with the general indeterminacy and unpredictability of modern life" and that "the

1990s television comic heroes need not be admirable."[28] A good example of such a comedy is *Seinfeld* (NBC, 1990–1998), which spent much of the 1990s as the most popular sitcom. Based on the standup comedy of Jerry Seinfeld, this self-proclaimed show about nothing portrays four self-absorbed single friends who live in New York City. In the series, Jerry makes a living as a standup comic, his friend George Costanza works at several jobs, and neighbor Cosmo Kramer is always developing new ways to make money. Their platonic friend, Elaine Benes (Julia Louis-Dreyfus), works as an editor in a publishing house in the beginning of the series and later becomes a copywriter for catalog magnate J. Peterman. In an interesting essay that considers whether Elaine is a feminist by evaluating her by feminist ethics related to care, Sarah Worth concluded that "not only does Elaine not particularly care about her three close friends, she doesn't care about the men she dates either.... She is fickle, breaking up with men for petty reasons, refusing to care about them for any length of time."[29] Elaine has no close female friendships throughout the series either. There is no pretense that the characters are nice people, and there is satisfaction in the series finale when all four are jailed for breaking a good Samaritan law in Massachusetts when they do not help a man during a robbery.

There are a number of strong, caring sitcom women in the 1990s, however, including the title character in *Cybill* (CBS, 1995–1998). Cybill Shepherd portrays Cybill Sheridan, a wisecracking middle-aged actress in Los Angeles who plays mostly small parts in an industry notorious for its emphasis on youth, particularly in women. She has a daughter from each of her two marriages and becomes a grandmother early in the series. She is still friends with her ex-husbands, but her best friend is Maryann, a rich alcoholic who endlessly seeks retribution against her ex, "Dr. Dick." Cybill and Maryann are involved in a series of slapstick adventures, often involving some scheme against Dr. Dick. Many other single career women appeared in the 1990s, often paired with a potentially romantic male counterpart. In *Wings* (NBC, 1990–1997), Helen Chappel runs the lunch counter at a small airport in Nantucket. Her childhood friends, brothers Joe and Brian Hackett, run a one-plane commuter service. Fat as a child, Helen has become beautiful and slender, and the on-again, off-again romance with Joe results in marriage after a few seasons. The final episode depicts the brothers giving Helen their hard-earned inheritance to pursue her dream as a professional cellist. The popular and critically acclaimed *Frasier* (NBC, 1993) features two strong women. Roz Doyle is the producer of Frasier's radio show who, when she accidentally gets pregnant, decides to raise her child on her own. Daphne Moon is the live-in physical therapist, sometime psychic and longtime secret crush of Frasier's brother, Niles, who eventually marries her. *The Nanny* (CBS, 1993–1999) is the Queens version of the Cinderella story, although it takes Fran Fine several years for her rich employer, Max Sheffield, to marry her.

As discussed earlier, the development of new broadcast networks led to a proliferation of black sitcoms to counterprogram the more mainstream networks, in what academic critic Robin Coleman has referred to as the "neo-minstrelsy era" containing stereotypes of decades ago. Coleman said that

> the blackvoice has remained, laden with gross malapropisms.... The voices seem louder, more shrill, and more bossy and sassy. Dialogue is often accentuated by ample finger snaps, eye rolling, neck swaying, and tongue clucking. Physical comedy is now far more prevalent and more ridiculing.... [30]

Although Coleman found the newer networks—FOX, UPN, and WB— had the most racist comedic images, even the popular *Fresh Prince of Bel Air* (NBC, 1990–1996) with rapper Will Smith was interpreted as "the equivalent of Blacks in blackface—traditional White stereotypes of Blacks enacted by Blacks."[31] Perhaps the most offensive sitcom starring African Americans is *Martin* (FOX, 1992–1997) because of the misogynism of both the series and the series star, standup comic Martin Lawrence. Lawrence plays Martin Payne, a Detroit radio talk show host, and Gina is his girlfriend (later his wife) who is a marketing executive. Pam, who hates Martin, is Gina's coworker and best friend. Martin is constantly ridiculing Pam, particularly about her looks. Gina, however, does not escape Martin's hostility. As Kristal Brent Zook explained, "As Gina strives for personal and professional autonomy, she too is subjected to Martin's wrath. This tension is often played out in episodes that pit Gina the 'career woman' against Martin's mother, who is played by Lawrence in drag. A 'legitimate' matriarch, Mrs. Payne is known for tending to her son's every need."[32] Tisha Campbell had her own real-life conflict with Lawrence, as was revealed when she walked off the set of the series during its fifth season and later filed a lawsuit, charging him with "repeated and escalating sexual harassment, sexual battery, verbal abuse, and related threats to her physical safety."[33] But not everyone agrees that *Martin* had such bad images on it. The NAACP Image Award, given to those who have helped promote "positive images of people of color,"[34] was given to Martin Lawrence in 1996 for "Outstanding Lead Actor in a Comedy Series." The series itself was nominated in 1997, a move that resulted in discord in the NAACP.[35]

When the WB and UPN networks debuted in 1995, most of their shows were centered on young urban males, such as *Malcolm & Eddie* and *The Jamie Foxx Show,* as they attempted to appeal to a black audience. Bogle described most of the older women on the shows as "heavy, nurturing mamas," while the younger ones strutted around in sexy clothing.[36] According to Bogle, "Sometimes they had attitude as they peddled the independent woman line. But after one look at the young women, you knew what they were there for."[37] But there are exceptions. *Sister, Sister* (ABC, 1994–1995; WB, 1995–1999) focuses on twin girls separated at birth who are reunited as teenagers. The series follows their typical teen problems and family adjustments, including the gradual attraction of their parents. Singing star Brandy Norwood plays the title role in *Moesha* (UPN, 1996–2001), about a teenage girl who has the usual problems with boys, school, and parents, including her stepmother.

Showcasing the friendship of four African American women in Los Angeles, *Girlfriends* (UPN, 2000) inevitably evokes comparisons with *Living Single.* The most obvious difference between the two sitcoms is that the newer friends are slender and fashion conscious, with looks difficult to emulate, while the "full figure" women on *Living Single* were not self-conscious of their larger bodies and still had no trouble getting dates. There is also a nastier tone to *Girlfriends,* with the relationship between the two oldest friends the most explosive. Joan Clayton is a twenty-nine-year-old junior partner in a law firm, and Toni Childs, an initially unsuccessful real estate agent, has been her best friend since fifth grade. Lynn has five college degrees yet has not found a career; in the beginning of the second season she is bussing tables at a restaurant. Maya is Joan's secretary and the only one of the friends who is married and working class. When the series starts she has a nine-year-old son and got married when she was seventeen.

In the first episode of the series, Toni has a date with Charles, Joan's rich ex-boyfriend. Lynn insists that Toni tell Joan about it to see if it is okay with her. Joan agrees to their date, and Toni brings Charles to Joan's twenty-ninth birthday party. At the party, Maya tells Toni that "you nasty" for dating Joan's ex-boyfriend, that black women don't do that. Evidently Maya, as a working-class black person, presents herself as more in touch with what it is to be black—she frequently makes references to what is acceptable for black women in particular to do. Toni corrects Maya's English on a couple occasions and refers to Maya as low rent. The two get into a fight, then Joan gets into a fight with Toni. Although the women all make up by the end of the episode, Joan and Toni later have an extended feud over several episodes into the second season. On vacation together in Jamaica, Joan unknowingly reveals to Toni's true love that Toni has gotten engaged to another man. Toni "bitch slaps" Joan as Maya describes it, yet Joan tries to salvage the friendship, even after Toni makes a play for Joan's boyfriend for revenge. Joan even goes to therapy; her hair is falling out because of the stress between her and Toni. The final straw for Joan, however, is when Toni reveals to Joan's boss that Joan's boyfriend, Sean, is a sex addict. She tells Toni, "You're no longer my friend. How dare you tell my boss about my personal life. I'm tired of turning the other cheek. I'm tired of trying to understand you. I'm tired of being your whipping dog. I'm tired of explaining to people what's good about you when I'm not even sure myself." Toni begs her forgiveness, but Joan initially refuses. After Toni loses her job and she is desperate, Joan's deep love for her eventually prevails. A survivor, Toni opens her own real estate agency, and the friendships continue.

A number of other series through the 1990s into the twenty-first century focused on young, primarily Caucasian, people. *Blossom* (NBC, 1991–1995) is about a teenage girl living with her divorced dad and two brothers. She often demonstrates more wisdom than the men in her house and is constantly seen in the company of her best girlfriend, Six. *Sabrina, the Teenage Witch* (ABC, 1996–2001; WB, 2001–2003) is about a young woman who discovers on her sixteenth birthday that she is a witch. Living with her two attractive and loving witch aunts, her normal teen activities are often complicated by her attempts to master her new powers. A bit more down-to-earth even if it takes place in the disco days of the 1970s, *That '70s Show* (FOX, debuting in 1998) features six teenage friends who spend a lot of time hanging out in the basement of one's home. Two of the friends are girls. Jackie, who needs constant reassurance that she is the most beautiful girl around, has an on-again, off-again love relationship with Michael, who is equally enthralled with his own beauty; both are equivalently simple. Donna is perhaps the smartest and most ambitious of the friends, and has had a long relationship with Eric, whose parents have seemingly adopted all the kids as their own. Unlike sitcoms broadcast in the '70s, the teens in this show about '70s culture are much more realistic—these characters have sex, drink beer, and smoke pot.

Married life is the focus of several other series. *Mad About You* (NBC, 1992–1999) stars standup comic Paul Reiser as newlywed and documentary filmmaker Paul Buchman; his wife, Jamie (Helen Hunt), specializes in public relations. Early in the series, Jamie returns to college, but she eventually starts a public relations business with her best friend, Fran. Although the couple have their disagreements and nearly break up in the fourth season over attractions to other people, they eventually reunite and have a daughter. Jamie is generally a strong and smart woman who is loyal to her somewhat ditzy sister and Fran. Both Paul and Jamie have trouble with their parents, and Paul's mother is particularly critical of Jamie, perpetuating the obnoxious mother-in-law stereotype. The humor is generally gentle, however, and scenes are often stolen by their pet dog (their first child), Murray. *Evening Shade* (CBS, 1990–1994), created and written by the prolific Linda Bloodworth-Thomason, is about Wood Newton (Burt Reynolds), the football coach of the high school in a rural Arkansas town, and his family. His wife, Ava (Marilu Henner from *Taxi* of the 1970s), is pregnant with their fourth child when the series begins and is elected as the town's prosecuting attorney. Although it is not shown to be easy, her dual role of mom and attorney is accomplished within the confines of the close-knit town.

King of Queens (CBS, 1998) depicts a chubby man's fantasy of marrying a beautiful, slender, sexy woman. Doug drives a truck for a delivery service, and Carrie is a secretary in a law firm. When Carrie accidentally gets pregnant, she is at first upset because of the timing, but when she miscarries, the couple are clearly heartbroken and brought closer together. Carrie is a strong woman and she would clearly win in any battle of the sexes, although she is neither shrill nor mean. The series, however, is a good illustration of our acceptance of chubby men with beautiful women and a reminder that such a situation would not be so easily accepted if the roles were reversed.

The most popular family sitcom into the twenty-first century is *Everybody Loves Raymond* (CBS, 1996–), starring standup comic Ray Romano as Ray Barone, a successful sportswriter for a New York City newspaper. Debra is his stay-at-home wife (she used to work in public relations) who tends to their three young children, twin boys and a girl. The bane of Debra's existence is her in-laws who live across the street. Particularly annoying is her mother-in-law, Marie, who is passive/aggressive in her criticisms of Debra's housekeeping and cooking skills. Both of Marie's sons are somewhat intimidated by her, including her cop son, Robert. Marie keeps a plastic cover on the couch so it doesn't get dirty, and she takes great pride in besting Debra at domestic skills. Marie desperately (and pathetically) wants to remain the most important woman in both Ray and Robert's lives. Debra is a strong woman, however, and is up to the challenge. She readily expresses her anger to Marie when provoked, and their feuds are not always quickly resolved. Ray is somewhat intimidated by Debra because she is quick to express her dissatisfaction whenever it arises, and the two frequently argue. They have a solid relationship, how-ever, and Ray is still quite attracted to her. Marie's husband, Frank, though, frequently indicates he is no longer attracted to Marie, freezing up when she tries to hug him and occasionally making cutting remarks when provoked. The primary conflict in this series, however, comes from the constant interference from Ray's family in his and Debra's married life.

As the twenty-first century approached, the NAACP and other minority-based groups threatened to boycott the major broadcast networks because of a dearth of roles for people of color. While UPN and WB had several sitcoms of questionable taste targeted toward African Americans, there were few people of color on the other networks. Latino and Asian charac-ters hardly existed. The one Asian family, seen in *All American Girl* (ABC, 1994–1995), starring standup comic Margaret Cho, was full of shallow and stereotyped depictions of Korean Americans and did not last long. Cho played a twenty-something with no direction other than she wanted to be creative. She continually made fun of her Korean family by imitating their accent and attitudes. Bill Cosby returned in *Cosby* (1996–2000) with his former television wife, Phylicia Rashad, but did not experience the phenomenal success of his first series (the cute little kids were gone and he had a grown daughter in this series). There were certainly a new variety of roles for Caucasian women, some shallow and demeaning, some strong and smart, but for women in general, and women of color in particular, there is still room for improvement, despite all the new broadcast and cable networks.

NOTES

1. Editors of Time-Life Books, *The Digital Decade: The 90s* (New York: Bishop Books, 2000), 22.

2. National Organization for Women website, "Intense Efforts to End Wage Gap Underway" (August 22, 2001, http://63.111.42.146/news/article.asp?articleid=7653).

3. *Digital Decade,* 141.

4. *Entertainment Weekly.* 10th Anniversary Issue (Spring 2000): 90.

5. Bonnie Dow analyzed this series as an example of maternal feminism in *Prime-Time Feminism: Television, Media Culture, and the Women's Movement Since 1970* (Philadelphia: University of Pennsylvania Press 1996), 164–202.

6. For a good summary of the characters and the first two seasons, see Tim Appelo, *Ally McBeal: The Official Guide* (New York: HarperPerrennial, 1999).

7. Brenda Cooper, "Unapologetic Women, 'Comic Men' and Feminine Specta-torship in David E. Kelley's *Ally McBeal*," *Critical Studies in Media Communication*

18 (2001): 416. For a consideration of *Ally McBeal* in relationship to third-wave feminism, see Helene A. Shugart, Catherine Egley Waggoner, and D. Lynn O'Brien Hallstein, "Mediating Third-Wave Feminism: Appropriation as Postmodern Media Practice," *Critical Studies in Media Communication* 18 (2001): 194–210.

8. Charmaine McEachern explores *Home Improvement* in relationship to the spiritual strand of the men's movement as found in Robert Bly's *Iron John* in "Comic Interventions: Passion and the Men's Movement in the Situation Comedy, *Home Improvement*," *Journal of Gender Studies* 8 (1999): 5–18.

9. Robert Hanke considered *Home Improvement* a "mock-macho" situation comedy, claiming that it actually reinforces hegemonic masculinity and induces pleasure in the realization of masculinity as a gender performance, in "The 'Mock-Macho' Situation Comedy: Hegemonic Masculinity and its Reiteration," *Western Journal of Communication* 62 (1998): 74–93.

10. Tim Brooks and Earle Marsh, *The Complete Directory to Prime Time Network and Cable Shows 1946–Present,* 7th ed. (New York: Ballantine, 1999), 461.

11. Kristal Brent Zook, *Color by Fox* (New York: Oxford University Press, 1999), 67.

12. Zook, 66.

13. Robin R. Means Coleman, *African American Viewers and the Black Situation Comedy: Situating Racial Humor* (New York: Garland, 2000), 118.

14. Donald Bogle, *Prime Time Blues: African Americans on Network Television* (New York: Farrar, Straus and Giroux, 2001), 424.

15. Coleman, 127.

16. Pam Mitchelmore, *Living Single: An Episode Guide* (epguides.com/LivingSingle/guide.shtml), 23.

17. Bogle, 423.

18. Zook, 67.

19. Zook, 67.

20. Rob Owen, *Gen X TV: The Brady Bunch to Melrose Place* (Syracuse, NY: Syracuse University Press, 1997), 89.

21. A.J. Jacobs, "Out?" *Entertainment Weekly,* 4 October 1996: 20.

22. Hilary De Vries, "Out & About," *TV Guide,* 11 October 1997: 20.

23. De Vries, 22.

24. Bonnie Dow, "*Ellen,* Television, and the Politics of Gay and Lesbian Visibility," *Critical Studies in Media Communication* 18 (June 2001): 132.

25. Dow, "*Ellen,*"134.

26. Hilary de Vries, "You Gotta Have Friends," *TV Guide*, 28 January 1995: 40. For an introduction to the series and thorough summary of its first season, see David Wild, *Friends: The Official Companion* (New York: Doubleday, 1995).

27. Kathleen Battles and Wendy Hilton-Morrow, "Gay Characters in Conventional Spaces: *Will and Grace* and the Situation Comedy Genre," *Critical Studies in Media Communication* 19 (2002): 101.

28. Michael V. Tueth, S.J., "Fun City: TV's Urban Situation Comedies of the 1990s," *Journal of Popular Film and Television* 28 (2000): 107.

29. Sarah E. Worth, "Elaine Benes: Feminist Icon or Just One of the Boys?" *Seinfeld and Philosophy,* ed. William Irwin (Chicago: Carus, 2000), 31.

30. Coleman, 107.

31. Coleman, 109

32. Zook, 56–57.

33. Zook, 59.

34. NAACP Image Awards website, www.naacpimageawards.org.

35. Robin Coleman reported that the Beverly Hills/Hollywood chapter of the NAACP in 1997 parted ways with the national organization and lashed out at *Martin* and seven UPN and WB black sitcoms, calling the portrayals "buffoonish" (Coleman, 123).

36. Bogle, 431.

37. Bogle, 431.

Chapter 7

LOVING AND NOT LOVING LUCY

Although one tries not to have predetermined conclusions going into research, it is hard to be neutral about images that have been a part of one's life since childhood. For almost all of the series discussed in this book, I have watched nearly every episode, many of them several times, and most of them at least once when they were initially broadcast. As I approached revisiting these sitcoms, I fully expected to be righteously indignant about most images of women and girls on television throughout the past fifty years, but I was not. While the quantitative research summarized in the first chapter indicated what to expect in terms of numbers of women and the roles they have played, a closer look at the series themselves offers rich and meaningful interpretations of some characters not revealed in statistics, as well as clues to our culture and who we are. For example, I was pleasantly surprised to realize that Susie on *Private Secretary* in the 1950s was quite content with her job and to live by herself when the dominant culture was pushing women to marry, stay home, and have babies. I was rather shocked, however, to revisit *I Love Lucy* and realize that Lucy's occasional fear of Ricky was real, that he actually spanked her at least twice, and that it was acceptable to their best friends. In some series there was a disconcerting connection of sex and violence, such as in *Roseanne* when the Conners get sexually excited during a fight. Starting in the 1970s, some sitcoms occasionally got serious about important issues, bringing tears and a dose of hard reality instead of laughter, such as when Edith is threatened by a rapist on *All in the Family* and Grace is clearly afraid her ex-husband will hit her during an argument on *Grace Under Fire*. Feminism was found in unexpected places, including the mock-macho *Home Improvement*. I enjoyed revisiting these sitcom women and girls, and I missed them when I moved on to other topics. I found it rewarding to compare sitcoms today with those of earlier decades, and to re-view and reevaluate them with the perspective from another century.

In the 1950s, many people in the United States were starting to enjoy post-war prosperity, purchasing cars and homes in the suburbs, and trying to convince wives to become "homemakers" and mothers outside the workforce. The American dream seemed obtainable to many if you just worked hard enough. While the Korean War, the Red Scare, and the cold war put a damper on these "Happy Days," rock 'n' roll and the proliferation of television made them enjoyable. On *I Love Lucy,* it is fun to see Lucy Ricardo defy her husband and pursue her dream of being in show business. In retrospect, however, it is also a nightmare to see her fear of Ricky and truly appalling when he spanks her. I see no redeeming social value in the scatter-brained Oriole character on *Beulah,* particularly when there were few if any images of black people available on television to counteract her stereotype. Seeing Beulah as a maid is certainly reflective of the service roles many black women have played in supporting their own families, and it is not offensive in itself. What is insulting is that there weren't other roles for African American women (and men) on television. In terms used by Cedric Clark, there was neither recognition nor respect for them. There is also nothing inherently offensive about portraying women as housewives, such as in *The Donna Reed Show* or *Mama.* What is offensive and dangerous, however, are the lessons that daughters are taught, such as Betty in *Father Knows Best* being discouraged about becoming an engineer. Connie Brooks in *Our Miss Brooks* is witty and a good teacher, yet her constant and desperate pursuit of a husband makes her a somewhat pathetic character. At least in the 1950s most women weren't unhealthily slender. Susie MacNamara in *Private Secretary* is not only hefty, but she also has men fighting over her, men she turns down because she likes her life as it is, as a single career woman living alone in New York City.

War, race riots, and feminism helped to make the 1960s a turbulent and unsettling decade. Laura Petrie on *The Dick Van Dyke Show* chose to be "just" a housewife, even though her husband would have (reluctantly) supported her decision to continue as a dancer. Significantly, however, she had a choice. Darrin's chauvinistic insistence that Samantha not use her witch powers on *Bewitched* could be construed as a metaphor to contain feminism, but neither could be repressed. Jeannie on *I Dream of Jeannie* is perhaps a male fantasy of being master to a beautiful woman, but even she could not be controlled. No one could tame Elly May on *The Beverly Hillbillies* either, and Granny's solutions to illnesses were "new age" before the age was new. Despite the fact that she has a steady boyfriend and nosy father, Ann Marie on *That Girl* makes the single, working life in a big city look like fun and, more important, a reasonable goal for girls. *Julia,* despite the criticism of it not being realistic, is also a step forward in presenting an educated and successful African American woman supporting her child on her own.

With second-wave feminism in full force, sitcoms of the 1970s finally started to reflect diverse roles for women and feminist attitudes in some of the characters. Mary Richards on *The Mary Tyler Moore Show* is hesitant in expressing her rights for equal pay, but she does express them. On *All in the Family,* Gloria can be a strident feminist and a whiney little girl at the same time. What is particularly interesting to watch, though, is the growth in Edith over the years as she learns to tell husband Archie to shut up and finds herself valued working outside the home. Maude Findlay is very vocal in expressing herself as an upper-middle-class feminist, and *Maude* is perhaps the only sitcom in which a main character has an abortion. The African American family that "moved on up" on *The Jeffersons* has a sassy black maid and indicates that the American dream is obtainable if you just work hard enough. Other comedies focusing on black characters, such as *Good Times,* however, indicated that that might not be the case. In *One Day at a Time* divorcee Ann Romano is perhaps the first female character who insists on being called "Ms." as she faces financial and identity problems while raising her two daughters. The title characters in *Laverne & Shirley,* set primarily in the 1950s, are not part of second-wave feminism, although their work at a factory and modest apartment living showcased the working class and made single life look like fun. Mostly, however, the two women illustrate the importance of close female friendships. Unfortunately, *Three's Company* changed the emphasis of female friendship in single life to sexual double entendres and pratfalls.

The 1980s witnessed a recession and a decline of women's rights. One of the joys of the decade is to be found in a television sitcom, however, in the close friendship of single parents *Kate & Allie* (in drama, *Cagney & Lacey* are a similar pleasure). *The Golden Girls* gives a rare look (for television) at the lives of women over fifty and depicts their dating lives that most real women might envy. It also depicts these women friends as family, as did *Designing Women.* In the latter, Julia is often the feminist mouthpiece for producer/writer Linda Bloodworth-Thomason. *The Cosby Show,* although it received criticism by some for not being "black enough," often addresses sexism and is a pleasant depiction of an upper-middle-class African American family. Although Clair sometimes refers to her work as an attorney, she is rarely seen working, and housework seems miraculously to take care of itself. *Roseanne,* however, depicts a working-class family where money is scarce, children misbehave, and housework is truly a chore. Roseanne is sarcastic to her children, bossy to her sister, and does not hesitate to fight with her husband if he makes her angry, yet she clearly loves them all. *Murphy Brown* can be seen as a warning to single women that they must be abrasive and gruff to succeed in a "man's world," sacrificing their personal life along the way. Murphy also does not have close women friends; they are the competition to beat or belittle.

In the 1990s and into the early twenty-first century, we have witnessed a lot of violence with Operation Desert Storm, war in Iraq, school mass killings, and terrorism. Sitcoms have been a bright spot, however. *Home Improvement* introduces feminist Jill Taylor, married to Tim, the Tool Man. Tim is the grunting wild man that Jill has to tame (or at least bring back to civilization in one piece). Like many housewives, Jill grows tired of staying at home and earns her master's degree in psychology. It is not effortless, however, and her struggle with household chores and getting husband and kids to help are shown on a regular basis. *Grace Under Fire* depicts another struggling single mom with a twist—Grace is a recovering alcoholic, her ex-husband used to beat her, and she works hard to keep her job and pay her bills. She, too, goes back to college to prepare herself for a more fulfilling job (and better money). She also has a best friend, Nadine, who helps her emotionally and with child care. With *Living Single* it is a pleasure to watch the friendship of four African American women as it is tested and grows. Khadijah is particularly interesting as the owner of a magazine targeted toward a black audience. Through all their dating and career woes, the women turn to each other for the talk that binds. *Ellen* depicts the coming out pains of the first primary gay female character, and *Will & Grace* introduces the close friendship of a male homosexual and a heterosexual woman. We follow the six characters on *Friends* as they struggle through dating and careers, untouched by terrorism in their Manhattan neighborhood. Rachel in particular shows much growth from the runaway, spoiled bride she is at the beginning of the series in 1994 to her single-career-mom status at the end of the 2002–2003 season.

Life has changed dramatically since the late 1940s when network television began, including gains in both civil rights and women's rights.

There are still struggles for equal pay and job opportunities, and abortion rights are continually threatened, however. In sitcoms, sex has moved from married couples in twin beds to homosexuals kissing. Characters of all persuasions discuss sex endlessly, but they very rarely mention birth control or sexually transmitted diseases. A big improvement, however, is that individual problems are often not solved in one episode. For example, Darlene's depression on *Roseanne* lasted over several episodes and the family's struggle for money lasted years. Sitcoms have addressed social issues with more frequency over the past two decades, sometimes in dramatic ways, but the solutions offered continue to be based primarily on individual effort, not on collective and political action. As Bonnie Dow explained in her work on prime time feminism, this view fits well with the commercial base of television:

> The medium's individualistic view of the world implies that most problems can be solved by hard work, good will, and a supportive family. Television programming does not deal well with complex social issues; it prefers the trials and tribulations of the individual. This logic works well with advertising, which operates on the presumption that an individual's purchasing decision can make an enormous change in his or her life.[1]

In the world of sitcoms, the political is personal and the personal is marketable.

Jill Taylor on the testosterone-filled *Home Improvement* is an exception to the rule that women in sitcoms do not identify themselves as feminists, even though many since the 1970s espouse rhetoric about equality and equal rights. Even Lucy and Ethel demanded equal rights in the 1950s, but in typical sitcom fashion the notion was belittled, this time by equating equality to paying one's own restaurant bill. It is refreshing to see a 1960s program depict a man unthreatened by strong women (Andy Taylor in *The Andy Griffith Show*), but the battle of the sexes in sitcoms is still common, often depicted as a wife trying to civilize or educate her sexist husband (e.g., *Home Improvement* and *Everybody Loves Raymond*). Television into the twenty-first century is primarily a post-feminist world, where equal rights are assumed and problems are between individuals, not systemic. It is also seemingly a post-racist and post-classist world, rarely addressing either racism or class bias.

All in all, however, the picture of both white (European American) and African American women and girls in sitcoms has improved notably in both recognition and respect. Women are depicted in many more ways than in the 1950s, including divorced and gay. Both married and single women are shown in a variety of careers. Unfortunately, for some women—specifically Latina, Asian, and Native American—there is still what Gaye Tuchman called years ago "symbolic annihilation."[2] Television images of them are rare; thus, in the television world they do not exist. This could potentially harm the self-esteem of real underrepresented or absent groups of people and indicate to others that they are not important. The lines among classes have also been erased in one respect (only enough hard work to succeed is needed) and solidified in another respect (the rich are different—their values are not as good as ours—so why would we want to have money?). Most characters are still middle class and Caucasian.

In the introduction to her analysis of the images of women and girls in mass media, Susan Douglas wrote in the early 1990s that "American women today are a bundle of contradictions because much of the media imagery we grew up with was itself filled with mixed messages about what women should and should not do, what women could and could not be."[3] Sitcom women and girls now are depicted in a much larger variety of careers and marital/sexual situations, indicating to real females that they have choices, but there are still mixed messages. And, as theorized by Bradley Greenberg in his drench hypothesis discussed in the first chapter, one image can overwhelm a decade of images in its influence. I have a particular concern about body images in sitcoms. Compared to the mixture of body types in earlier decades, most lead female characters now are very slender, depicting potentially unhealthy and nearly impossible images to emulate, a concern as many real women and girls struggle with eating disorders and poor self-concepts. We need search no further than the long popular *Friends* to find a plausible drench effect in body shape and image.

While I was evidently not affected by the limited career choices portrayed on television as I was growing up (other influences were more powerful, particularly my mother), I was affected by the interpersonal relations depicted among women. I remember being pleasantly surprised at real-life close personal friendships among women and girls, after seeing petty jealousies and "cat fights" among women on television (even close friends Lucy and Ethel tore each other's identical dresses while singing "Friendship"). As an adult, I enjoyed immensely the female friendships on *The Mary Tyler Moore Show* in the 1970s and *Kate & Allie* in the 1980s, but I found the title character in *Murphy Brown* in the 1990s often a sad figure in her lack of closeness with other women. In the first episode of *Girlfriends* at the beginning of the twenty-first century, I found the catty, nasty attitude among the four women friends very unsettling, particularly between longtime friends Joan and Toni. In her disturbing research of aggression among girls, Rachel Simmons wrote about their use of "relationally aggressive behavior," which consists of acts such as "ignoring someone to punish them or get one's own way, excluding someone socially for revenge, using negative body language or facial expressions, sabotaging someone else's relationships, or threatening to end a relationship unless the friend agrees to a request."[4] Simmons found that "humor is an especially popular way to injure a peer indirectly. Joking weaves a membrane of protection around the perpetrator as she jabs at a target."[5] When the object of the joke would react in a very hurt way, the perpetrator could dismiss her reaction with a "just kidding," dissociating herself from the real pain and confusion of her victim. Freud recognized long ago the hidden (and not so hidden) aggression expressed in humor. Simmons also compared the expulsion of tribe members in the popular reality series *Survivor* to "a disturbing ritual in cliques of girls. With little or no warning a clique will rise up and cut down one of its own. For the targeted girl, the sheer force of this unexpected expulsion can be startling, unpredictable, and even devastating."[6]

The pursuit of popularity has been depicted in sitcoms throughout its history, but generally not to the extent where one person destroys the self-esteem of another and there is lifelong damage. Considering the importance of female friendships in real life, there is a danger in depictions of nasty relationships among women and girls. Interestingly enough, Simmons discussed the importance of girls being able to express their anger with each other, rather than hurting each other in covert ways, and she found African American and working-class girls more prone to do this. On *Girlfriends,* the four African American women are quick to express their anger and not so quick to forgive, yet they always eventually come back to each other. On *Friends,* the three Caucasian women often initially try to hide it when they are upset with each other, primarily to avoid hurt feelings. Eventually the truth comes out, though, and their friendship survives, despite the confrontation, an important lesson to young girls. On some sitcoms, however, the humor can be mean-spirited among friends, family, and coworkers (as sometimes found in *Will & Grace*); a "just kidding" would not erase the hurt in real life.

In their analysis of images of African Americans in mass media, Jannette Dates and William Barlow wrote about how "white domination of mainstream culture inevitably gave rise to African American cultural resistance, splitting the black image."[7] The image of women of all races and classes also has been split to some extent, with white males determining most of what we see on television throughout its history while women struggled to get their voices heard. When that struggle is successful, it has made a difference. Women such as Susan Harris *(The Golden Girls)*, Linda Bloodworth-Thomason *(Designing Women)*, Diane English *(Murphy Brown)*, Debbie Allen *(A Different World)*, Yvette Lee Bowser *(Living Single)*, Roseanne *(Roseanne)*, and Brett Butler *(Grace Under Fire)* have struggled as creators, producers, directors, writers, or artists to enrich the depiction of women and their realities on sitcoms. Of course, sometimes the stories and characters in sitcoms are affected more by business decisions than creative ones. The broadcast networks are concerned about offending audiences and losing advertisers, so they sometimes shy away from certain topics or characterizations. For example, married couples were relegated to twin beds and the word "pregnant" could not be used on *I Love Lucy*. Sometimes network executives also think they know how to increase the audience size in ways that contradict the vision of the creator of a series. On the other side of the television set, audiences can be unduly influenced in their interpretations of certain sitcoms by extratextual material, such as stories that have been published about the actors and behind-the-scenes fighting on a set. Rumors about Ellen DeGeneres "coming out" put a different spin on some of the dialog in her series before she officially announced she was gay, and the image of Roseanne as out of control in real life made her character in her series seem perhaps even more unruly. The influences on what we see in sitcoms and how we interpret them are many, but, whatever those images are, we are richer for them and the discussions they might inspire.

At home and at work, we have replaced typewriters with computers and albums with CDs. We now use e-mail instead of writing letters. Videocassettes are quickly being replaced by DVDs, and we can buy entire seasons of our favorite situation comedies. We can watch endless reruns of sitcoms from decades ago on cable networks such as TV Land and Lifetime, and discuss them with others in "chat rooms" on the Internet or with friends at lunch. We grow attached to particular sitcoms and develop parasocial relationships with the characters—seeing them is like visiting old friends. Sitcoms still allow us to explore characters and issues not found in drama, and laughter has allowed us a catharsis for our frustrations and anger. These images may affect us in a variety of ways as individuals, but they do affect us, both three-dimensional characters and stereotypes. As media effects researchers Grossberg, Wartella, and Whitney wrote:

> the fact is that stereotypes, even if they are only images, do have real and important consequences. They can affect self-esteem of those being stereo-

typed, and they can often come close to determining the way some people think of and behave toward members of the groups being stereotyped. And sometimes, if they are repeated often enough, people forget entirely that they are dealing with images; the images become the reality that determines the ways people, institutions, and even governments act in the world.[8]

Negative or stereotyped images are not as offensive or potentially damaging when they are counterbalanced by other images, and, of course, positive images can have healthy effects on viewers. Whether we love Lucy or not, her image and those of hundreds of other women and girls throughout the history of television sitcoms are part of who we are and how we treat ourselves and others.

NOTES

1. Bonnie J. Dow, *Prime-Time Feminism: Television, Media Culture, and the Women's Movement Since 1970* (Philadelphia: University of Pennsylvania Press, 1996), xxi–xxii.

2. Gaye Tuchman, "Introduction: The Symbolic Annihilation of Women by the Mass Media," *Hearth and Home: Images of Women in the Mass Media,* ed. Gaye Tuchman, Arlene Kaplan Daniels, and James Benet (New York: Oxford University Press, 1978), 3–38.

3. Susan J. Douglas, *Where the Girls Are: Growing up Female with the Mass Media* (New York: Times Books, 1994, 1995), 9.

4. Rachel Simmons, *Odd Girl Out: The Hidden Culture of Aggression in Girls* (New York: Harcourt, 2002), 21.

5. Simmons, 78.

6. Simmons, 88.

7. Jannette L. Dates and William Barlow, "Introduction: A War of Images," *Split Image: African Americans in the Mass Media,* 2nd ed., ed. Jannette L. Dates and William Barlow (Washington, D.C.: Howard University Press, 1993), 16.

8. Lawrence Grossberg, Ellen Wartella, and D. Charles Whitney, *MediaMaking: Mass Media in a Popular Culture* (Thousand Oaks, CA: Sage, 1998), 224.

SELECTED BIBLIOGRAPHY

Adler, Richard, ed. *All in the Family: A Critical Appraisal.* New York: Praeger, 1979.

Allen. Robert C., ed. *To Be Continued...Soaps Operas around the World.* London: Routledge, 1995.

Alley, Robert S., and Irby B. Brown. *Love Is All Around: The Making of* The Mary Tyler Moore Show. New York: Dell Publishing, 1989.

Alley, Robert S., and Irby B. Brown. *Murphy Brown: Anatomy of a Sitcom.* New York: Dell, 1990.

Andrews, Bart. *The "I Love Lucy" Book.* Garden City, NY: Doubleday, 1985.

Ang, Ien. *Living Room Wars: Rethinking Media Audiences for a Postmodern World.* London: Routledge, 1996.

Appelo, Tim. *Ally McBeal: The Official Guide.* New York: HarperPerrennial, 1999.

Asamen, Joy Keiko, and Gordon L. Berry, eds. *Research Paradigms, Television, and Social Behavior.* Thousand Oaks, CA: Sage, 1998.

Associated Press. "Quayle Offers Peace." *Times Herald Record,* 22 September 1991: 6.

Atkin, David. "An Analysis of Television Series with Minority-Lead Characters." *Critical Studies in Mass Communication* 9 (1992): 337–49.

Atkin, David J., Jay Moorman, and Carolyn A. Lin. "Ready for Prime Time: Network Series Devoted to Working Women in the 1980s." *Sex Roles* 25 (1991): 677–85.

Baker, Kathryn. "Prodigious Writer by Design." *New York Post,* 25 March 1988: 94.

Barker, Chris. *Cultural Studies: Theory and Practice.* London: Sage, 2000.

Battles, Kathleen, and Wendy Hilton-Morrow. "Gay Characters in Conventional Spaces: *Will and Grace* and the Situation Comedy Genre." *Critical Studies in Media Communication* 19 (2002): 87–105.

Berger, Arthur Asa. *Cultural Criticism: A Primary of Key Concepts.* Thousand Oaks, CA: Sage, 1995.

Beyer, Lisa. "The Women of Islam." *Time,* 3 December 2001: 50–59.

Bianculli, David. "The Real Thing." *New York Post,* 18 October 1988: 77.

Biddle, Julian. *What Was Hot! A Rollcoaster Ride through Six Decades of Pop Culture in America.* New York: Citadel, 1994, 2001.

Bogle, Donald. *Prime Time Television: African Americans on Network Television.* New York: Farrar, Straus and Giroux, 2001.

Brash, Sarah, and Loretta Britten, eds. *Rock & Roll Generation: Teen Life in the 50s.* Our American Century. Alexandria, VA: Time-Life, 1998.

Brooke, Jill. "On 'Murphy,' Sources are Everything." *New York Post,* 27 March 1989: 62.

Brooks, Tim, and Earle Marsh. *The Complete Directory to Prime Time Network and Cable TV Shows 1946–Present.* 7th ed. New York: Ballantine, 1999.

Brown, Jane D., Jeanne R. Steele, and Kim Walsh-Childers, eds. *Sexual Teens, Sexual Media: Investigating Media's Influence on Adolescent Sexuality.* Mahwah, NJ: Erlbaum, 2002.

Brown, Mary Ellen. *Soap Opera and Women's Talk: The Pleasure of Resistance.* Thousand Oaks, CA: Sage, 1994.

Brown, Mary Ellen, ed. *Television and Women's Culture: The Politics of the Popular.* London: Sage, 1990.

Brown, Rich. "Murphy Brown Gives Birth to Controversy." *Broadcasting,* 25 May 1992: 3.

Brunsdon, Charlotte, Julie D'Acci, and Lynn Spigel, eds. *Feminist Television Criticism: A Reader.* New York: Oxford University Press, 1997.

Bryant, Jennings, and Dolf Zillmann, ed. *Media Effects: Advances in Theory and Research.* 2nd ed. Mahwah, NJ: Erlbaum, 2002.

Bryant, Jennings, and Dolf Zillmann, eds. *Responding to the Screen: Reception and Reaction Processes.* Hillsdale, NJ: Erlbaum, 1991.

Butler, Jeremy G. "Redesigning Discourse: Feminism, the Sitcom, and *Designing Women.*" *Journal of Film and Video* 45 (1993): 13–26.

Butsch, Richard. "Class and Gender in Four Decades of Television Situation Comedy: Plus ca Change. . . ." *Critical Studies in Mass Communication* 9 (1992): 387–99.

Carbillo, Toni, Judith Meuli, and June Bundy Csida. *Feminist Chronicles 1953–1993.* Los Angeles: Women's Graphics, 1993.

Carruth, Gorton. *What Happened When: A Chronology of Life & Events in America.* New York: Harper & Row, 1989.

Carter, Bill. "Cosby Ready to Go on Despite the Inroads by Fox's 'Simpsons.' " *New York Times,* 22 February 1991: C13+.

Carter, Bill. "Television Gets on the Bandwagon of the Thomas-Hill Contretemps." *New York Times,* 4 November 1991: C15.

Chapman, Antony J., and Hugh C. Foot, eds. *Humor and Laughter: Theory, Research, and Applications.* New Brunswick, NJ: Transaction, 1996.

Christon, Lawrence. "Does 'Roseanne' Rise above It All?" *Los Angeles Times,* 11 December 1988, Calendar section: 8+.

Clark, Cedric. "Television and Social Control: Some Observations on the Portrayals of Ethnic Minorities." *Television Quarterly* 8 (1969): 18–22.

Cole, Stephen. *That Book about That Girl.* Los Angeles: Renaissance, 1999.

Coleman, Robin R. Means. *African American Viewers and the Black Situation Comedy.* New York: Garland, 2000.

Comstock, Jamie, and Krystyna Strzyzewski. "Interpersonal Interaction on Television: Family Conflict and Jealousy on Primetime." *Journal of Broadcasting & Electronic Media* 34 (1990): 263–82.

Condit, Celeste. "The Rhetorical Limits of Polysemy." *Critical Studies in Mass Communication* 6 (1989): 103–22.

Condry, John. *The Psychology of Television.* Hillsdale, NJ: Erlbaum, 1989.

Cooper, Brenda. "Unapologetic Women, 'Comic Men' and Feminine Spectatorship in David E. Kelley's *Ally McBeal.*" *Critical Studies in Media Communication* 18 (2001): 416–35.

Cox, Stephen. *The Beverly Hillbillies.* New York: HarperCollins, 1993.

Cox, Stephen. *The Hooterville Handbook: A Viewer's Guide to Green Acres.* New York: St. Martin's Press, 1993.

Cox, Steve, with Howard Frank. *Dreaming of Jeannie: TV's Prime Time in a Bottle.* New York: St. Martin's Press, 2000.

D'Acci, Julie. *Defining Women: Television and the Case of Cagney & Lacey.* Chapel Hill, NC: University of North Carolina Press, 1994.

Dates, Jannette L. and William Barlow, eds. *Split Image: African Americans in the Mass Media.* 2nd ed. Washington, D.C: Howard University Press, 1993.

Davis, Flora. *Moving the Mountain: The Women's Movement in America Since 1960.* New York: Simon & Schuster, 1991.

de Vries, Hilary. "Laughing off the Recession." *New York Times Magazine,* 3 January 1993: 24.

DiMatteo, Robert. "New Series." *Video Review,* September 1986: 114.

Donovan, Josephine. *Feminist Theory: The Intellectual Traditions of American Feminism.* New Expanded Edition. New York: Frederick Ungar, 1985.

Douglas, Susan J. *Where the Girls Are: Growing up Female with the Mass Media.* New York: Times Books, 1994, 1995.

Douglas, William, and Beth M. Olson. "Beyond Family Structure: The Family in Domestic Comedy." *Journal of Broadcasting & Electronic Media* 39 (1995): 236–61.

Dow, Bonnie. "*Ellen,* Television, and the Politics of Gay and Lesbian Visibility." *Critical Studies in Media Communication* 18 (2001): 123–40.

Dow, Bonnie J. "Femininity and Feminism in *Murphy Brown.*" *Southern Communication Journal* 57 (1992): 143–55.

Dow, Bonnie J. "Performance of Feminine Discourse in *Designing Women.*" *Text and Performance Quarterly* 12 (1992): 125–45.

Dow, Bonnie J. *Prime-Time Feminism: Television, Media Culture, and the Women's Movement Since 1970.* Philadelphia: University of Pennsylvania Press, 1996.

Downing, John D. H. "'The Cosby Show' and American Racial Discourse." *Discourse and Discrimination.* Ed. Geneva Smitherman-Donaldson and Teun A. van Dijk. Detroit: Wayne State University Press, 1988. 46–73.

Editors of Time-Life Books. *The Digital Decade: The 90s.* New York: Bishop Books, 2000.

Ehrenreich, Barbara, and Jane O'Reilly. "No Jiggles. No Scheming. Just Real Women as Friends." *TV Guide,* 24 November 1984: 6–10.

Ely, Melvin Patrick. *The Adventures of Amos 'n' Andy: A Social History of an American Phenomenon.* New York: Macmillan, 1991.

Entertainment Weekly. 10th Anniversary Issue. Spring 2000.

Faludi, Susan. *Backlash: The Undeclared War against American Women.* New York: Crown, 1991.

Feuer, Jane, Paul Kerr, and Tise Vahimagi, eds. *MTM 'Quality Television.'* London: British Film Institute, 1984.

Fiske, John. *Television Culture.* London: Methuen, 1987.

Fiske, John, and John Hartley. *Reading Television.* London: Methuen, 1978.

Foss, Karen A., Sonja K. Foss, and Cindy L. Griffin. *Feminist Rhetorical Theories.* Thousand Oaks, CA: Sage, 1999.

Fouts, Gregory, and Kimberley Burggraf. "Television Situation Comedies: Female Weight, Male Negative Comments, and Audience Reactions." *Sex Roles* 42 (2000): 925–32.

Freeman, Lewis. "Social Mobility in Television Comedies." *Critical Studies in Mass Communication* 9 (1992): 400–406.

Freud, Sigmund. *Jokes and Their Relation to the Unconscious.* Trans. and ed. James Strachey. New York: Norton, 1960.

Fujioka, Yuki. "Television Portrayals and African-American Stereotypes: Examination of Television Effects When Direct Contact is Lacking." *Journalism & Mass Communication Quarterly* 76 (1999): 52–75.

Gaar, Gillian G. *She's a Rebel: The History of Women in Rock & Roll.* Seattle, WA: Seal Press, 1992.

Gardella, Kay. " 'Murphy': Making It After All." *Daily News,* 14 November 1988: 70.

Gerard, Jeremy. " 'Murphy Brown' Stays on Top of the News." *New York Times* 16 Oct. 1989: C20.

Grauerholz, Elizabeth, and Amy King. "Prime Time Sexual Harassment." *Violence against Women* 3 (1997): 129–49.

Gray, Herman. *Watching Race: Television and the Struggle for "Blackness."* Minneapolis, MN: University of Minnesota Press, 1995.

Greenberg, Bradley S., and Larry Collette. "The Changing Faces on TV: A Demographic Analysis of Network Television's New Seasons, 1966–1992." *Journal of Broadcasting & Electronic Media* 41 (1997): 1–13.

Grossberg, Lawrence, Ellen Wartella, and D. Charles Whitney. *MediaMaking: Mass Media in a Popular Culture.* Thousand Oaks, CA: Sage, 1998.

Gruner, Charles R. *The Game of Humor: A Comprehensive Theory of Why We Laugh.* New Brunswick, NJ: Transaction, 1997.

Gunther, Mark. "CBS and the Steel Magnolia." *New York Times.* 3 March 1991: H30.

Hamamoto, Darrell Y. *Nervous Laughter: Television Situation Comedy and Liberal Democratic Ideology.* New York: Praeger, 1989.

Hanke, Robert. "The 'Mock-Macho' Situation Comedy: Hegemonic Masculinity and Its Reiteration." *Western Journal of Communication* 62 (1998): 74–93.

Haralovich, Mary Beth, and Lauren Rabinovitz, eds. *Television, History, and American Culture.* Durham, NC: Duke University Press, 1999.

Harris, Richard Jackson. *A Cognitive Psychology of Mass Communication.* 3rd ed. Mahwah, NJ: Erlbaum, 1999.

Heldenfels, R.D. *Television's Greatest Year: 1954.* New York: Continuum, 1994.

Hickey, Neil. "Decade of Change, Decade of Choice." *TV Guide,* 9 December 1989: 33.

Himmelstein, Hal. *Television Myth and the American Mind.* New York: Praeger, 1984.

"Inside Hollywood! Women, Sex & Power." *People Extra.* Spring 1991.

Irwin, William, ed. *Seinfeld and Philosophy.* Chicago: Carus, 2000.

Jacobs, A.J. "Out?" *Entertainment Weekly,* 4 October 1996: 18–25.

Jhally, Sut, and Justin Lewis. *Enlightened Racism: The Cosby Show, Audiences, and the Myths of the American Dream.* Boulder, CO: Westview, 1992.

Jones, Gerard. *Honey, I'm Home! Sitcoms: Selling the American Dream.* New York: St. Martin's Press, 1992.

Kelly, Richard. *The Andy Griffith Show.* Rev. ed. Winston-Salem, NC: Blair, 1989.

King, Coretta Scott. "Goodbye, Bill." *TV Guide,* 25 April 1992: 19–20.

Kitman, Marvin. "'Roseanne': Blue-Collar Zingers Right on Target." *New York Post,* 18 October 1988: 12+.

Kogan, Rick. "'Fat Episode' Expands Delta's Appeal." *Chicago Tribune,* 11 December 1989, sec. 2: 2.

Kunkel, D., Cope, K. M., Farinola, W. J. Maynard, Biely E., Rollin, E., and Donnerstein, E. *Sex on TV: A Biennial Report to the Kaiser Family Foundation.* Menlo Park, CA: Kaiser Family Foundation, 1999.

Lacayo, Richard. "About Face: An Inside Look at How Women Fared under Taliban Oppression and What the Future Holds for Them Now." *Time* 3, December 2001: 34–49.

Landay, Lori. *Madcaps, Screwballs, & Con Women: The Female Trickster in American Culture.* Philadelphia: University of Pennsylvania Press, 1998.

Lauzen, Martha M., and David M. Dozier. "Making a Difference in Prime Time: Women on Screen and behind the Scenes in the 1995–1996 Television Season." *Journal of Broadcasting & Electronic Media* 43 (1999): 1–15.

Leibman, Nina. *Living Room Lectures: The Fifties Family in Film and Television.* Austin: University of Texas Press, 1995.

Lengermann, Patricia M., and Ruth A. Wallace. *Gender in America: Social Control and Social Change.* Englewood Cliffs, NJ: Prentice-Hall, 1985.

Lusane, Clarence. "Assessing the Disconnect between Black & White Television Audiences: The Race, Class, and Gender Politics of *Married...with Children.*" *Journal of Popular Film and Television* 27.1 (1999): 12–20.

MacDonald, J. Fred. *Blacks and White TV: African Americans in Television Since 1948.* 2nd ed. Chicago: Nelson-Hall, 1992.

Macdonald, Myra. *Representing Women: Myths of Femininity in the Popular Media.* London: Edward Arnold, 1995.

Marc, David. *Comic Visions: Television Comedy & American Culture.* 2nd ed. Oxford: Blackwell, 1997.

Marc, David, and Robert J. Thompson. *Prime Time, Prime Movers.* Boston: Little, Brown, 1992.

McCrohan, Donna. *Archie & Edith, Mike & Gloria.* New York: Workman, 1987.

McEachern, Charmaine. "Comic Interventions: Passion and the Men's Movement in the Situation Comedy, *Home Improvement.*" *Journal of Gender Studies* 8 (1999): 5–18.

Meehan, Diana. *Ladies of the Evening: Women Characters of Prime-Time Television.* Metuchen, NJ: Scarecrow, 1983.

Miller, Mark Crispin. "Cosby Knows Best." *Village Voice,* 2 December 1986: 53–54.

Mitchelmore, Pam. *Living Single: An Episode Guide.* epguides.com/Living Single/guide.shtml.

Mitz, Rick. *The Great TV Sitcom Book.* New York: Richard Marek, 1980.

Montgomery, Kathryn C. *Target: Prime Time—Advocacy Groups and the Struggle over Entertainment Television.* New York: Oxford University Press, 1989.

Moore, Marvin L. "The Family as Portrayed on Prime-Time Television, 1947–1990: Structure and Characteristics." *Sex Roles* 26 (1992): 41–61.

Murphy, Mary. "Roseanne Bites Back!" *TV Guide,* 23 February 1991: 2–7.

NAACP Image Awards. http://www.naacpimageawards.org.

National Organization for Women. "Intense Efforts to End Wage Gap Underway." August 22, 2001. http://63.111.42.146/news/article.asp?articleid=7653).

Newcomb, Horace, ed. *Television: The Critical View.* 5th ed. New York: Oxford University Press, 1994.

Newcomb, Horace. *TV: The Most Popular Art.* Garden City, NY: Anchor, 1974.

Newcomb, Horace, and Robert Alley. *The Producer's Medium: Conversations with Creators of American TV* . New York: Oxford University Press, 1983.

O'Connor, John J. "Roseanne Smirks through the Trials of Life." *New York Times,* 18 October 1988: C22

O'Connor, John J. "2 Views of Relations between the Sexes: Cynical and Wary." *New York Times,* 28 March 1988: C20.

Olson, Beth, and William Douglas. "The Family on Television: Evaluation of Gender Roles in Situation Comedy." *Sex Roles* 36 (1997): 409–27.

Oppenheimer, Jess, with Gregg Oppenheimer. *Laughs, Luck...and Lucy: How I Came to Write the Most Popular Sitcom of All Time.* Syracuse, NY: Syracuse University Press, 1996.

Oskamp, Stuart, ed. *Television as a Social Issue.* Newberry Park: CA: Sage, 1988.

Owen, Rob. *Gen X TV: The Brady Bunch to Melrose Place.* Syracuse, NY: Syracuse University Press, 1997.

Pilato, Herbie J. *The Bewitched Book.* New York: Dell, 1992.

Press, Andrea. *Women Watching Television: Gender, Class, and Generation in the American Television Experience.* Philadelphia: University of Pennsylvania Press, 1991.

Press, Andrea, and Terry Strathman. "Work, Family, and Social Class in Television Images of Women: Prime-Time Television and the Construction of Postfeminism." *Women and Language* 16.2 (1993): 7–15.

Putterman, Barry. *On Television and Comedy: Essays on Style, Theme, Performer and Writer.* Jefferson, NC: McFarland, 1995.

Real, Michael R. "Bill Cosby and Recoding Ethnicity." *Television Criticism: Approaches and Applications.* Ed. Leah R. Vande Berg and Lawrence A. Wenner. New York: Longman, 1991. 58–84.

Reep, Diana C., and Faye H. Dambrot. "TV Parents: Fathers (and Now Mothers) Know Best." *Journal of Popular Culture* 28 (1994): 13–24.

Reese, Stephen D., Oscar H. Gandy, and August E. Grant, eds. *Framing Public Life: Perspectives on Media and Our Understanding of the Social World.* Mahwah, NJ: Erlbaum, 2001.

Rowe, Kathleen. *The Unruly Woman: Gender and the Genres of Laughter.* Austin: University of Texas Press, 1995.

Ruth, Daniel. "A New Hit? Fat Chance." *Chicago Sun-Times,* 18 October 1988: 45.

Sampson, William. "Typical Black Family? C'mon!" *Chicago Sun-Times,* 23 August 1986: 17.

Scharrer, Erica. "From Wise to Foolish: The Portrayal of the Sitcom Father, 1950s–1990s." *Journal of Broadcasting & Electronic Media* 45 (2001): 23–40.

Shugart, Helene A. "Isn't It Ironic? The Intersection of Third-Wave Feminism and Generation X." *Women's Studies in Communication* 24 (2001): 131–68.

Shugart, Helene A., Catherine Egley Waggoner, and D. Lynn O'Brien Hallstein. "Mediating Third-Wave Feminism: Appropriation as Postmodern Media Practice." *Critical Studies in Media Communication* 18 (2001): 194–210.

Siegel, Paul, ed. *Outsiders Looking In: A Communication Perspective on the Hill/Thomas Hearings.* Cresskill, NJ: Hampton, 1996.

Signorielli, Nancy. "Children, Television, and Conceptions about Chores: Attitudes and Behaviors." *Sex Roles* 27 (1992): 157–70.

Signorielli, Nancy. "Television and Conceptions about Sex Roles: Maintaining Conventionality and the Status Quo." *Sex Roles* 21 (1989): 337–56.

Signorielli, Nancy, and Aaron Bacue. "Recognition and Respect: A Content Analysis of Prime-Time Television Characters across Three Decades." *Sex Roles* 40 (1999): 527–44.

Signorielli, Nancy, and Michael Morgan, eds. *Cultivation Analysis: New Directions in Media Effects Research.* Newbury Park, CA: Sage, 1990.

Simmons, Rachel. *Odd Girl Out: The Hidden Culture of Aggression in Girls.* New York: Harcourt, 2002.

Skill, Thomas, and James D. Robinson. "Four Decades of Families on Television: A Demographic Profile, 1950–1989." *Journal of Broadcasting and Electronic Media* 38 (1994): 449- 64.

Smith, Ronald L. *The Cosby Book.* New York: S.P.I. 1993.

Smith, Sally Bedell. "Cosby Puts His Stamp on a TV Hit." *New York Times,* 18 November 1984, sec. 2: 1+.

Somerville, Janice. "Prof keeps 'Cosby Show' on Track." *Star-Ledger,* 23 September 1990: TV-22–23.

Sorensen, Jeff. *The Taxi Book.* New York: St. Martin's Press, 1987.

Spangler, Lynn C. "Buddies and Pals: A History of Male Friendships on Prime-Time Television." *Men, Masculinity, and the Media.* Ed. Steve Craig. Newbury Park, CA: Sage, 1992, 93–110.

Spangler, Lynn C. "A Historical Overview of Female Friendships on Prime-Time Television." *Journal of Popular Culture* 22.4 (1989): 13–23.

Spigel, Lynn, and Michael Curtin, eds. *The Revolution Wasn't Televised: Sixties Television and Social Conflict.* New York: Routledge, 1997.

Spigel, Lynn, and Denise Mann, eds. *Private Screenings: Television and the Female Consumer.* Minneapolis, MN: University of Minnesota Press, 1992.

Steeves, H. Leslie. "Feminist Theories and Media Studies." *Critical Studies in Mass Communication* 4 (1987): 95–135.

Steinem, Gloria. "Why I Consider *Cagney & Lacey* the Best Show on TV." *TV Guide,* 16 January 1988: 4–6.

Taylor, Ella. *Prime-Time Families: Television Culture in Postwar America.* Berkeley, CA: University of California Press, 1989.

Terry, Clifford. "Pattern Dulls 'Designing Women.'" *Chicago Tribune,* 29 September 1986, sec. 2: 5.

Tuchman, Gaye, Arlene Kaplan Daniels, and James Benet, eds. *Hearth and Home: Images of Women in the Mass Media.* New York: Oxford University Press, 1978.

Tueth, Michael V., S.J. "Fun City: TV's Urban Situation Comedies of the 1990s." *Journal of Popular Film and Television* 28 (2000): 98–107.

Turner, Richard. "The Grave Condition of TV Comedy." *TV Guide,* 21 July 1984: 4–8.

Vande Berg, Leah R., Lawrence A. Wenner, and Bruce E. Gronbeck. *Critical Approaches to Television.* Boston: Houghton Mifflin, 1998.

Wagg, Stephen, ed. *Because I Tell a Joke or Two: Comedy, Politics and Social Difference.* London: Routledge, 1998.

Waldron, Vince. *The Official Dick Van Dyke Show Book.* New York: Hyperion, 1994.

Ward, L. Monique. "Talking about Sex: Common Themes about Sexuality in the Prime-Time Television Programs Children and Adolescents View Most." *Journal of Youth and Adolescence* 24 (1995): 595–615.

Ward, L. Monique, and Rocio Rivadenya. "Contributions of Entertainment Television to Adolescents' Sexual Attitudes and Expectations: The Role of Viewing Amount versus Viewer Involvement." *Journal of Sex Research* 36 (1999): 237–249.

Washington, Mary Helen. "Please, Mr. Cosby, Build on Your Success." *TV Guide,* 22 March 1986: 4+.

Watson, Mary Ann. *Defining Visions: Television and the American Experience Since 1945.* Fort Worth, TX: Harcourt Brace, 1998.

Weaver, James B. III, and Elizabeth A. Laird. "Mood Management During the Menstrual Cycle through Selective Exposure to Television." *Journalism and Mass Communication Quarterly* 72 (1995): 139–46.

Weissman, Ginny, and Coyne Steven Sanders. *The Dick Van Dyke Show: The Anatomy of a Classic.* New York: St. Martin's Press, 1983.

Wild, David. *Friends: The Official Companion.* New York: Doubleday, 1995.

Wimmer Roger D., and Joseph R. Dominick. *Mass Media Research: An Introduction.* Belmont, CA: Wadsworth, 2000.

Winfrey, Lee. "Black-&-White Response to 'Cosby Show' Critics." *New York Daily News,* 27 August 1985: 77.

Zillmann, Dolf, Jennings Bryant, and Aletha C. Huston, eds. *Media, Children, and the Family: Social Scientific, Psychodynamic, and Clinical Perspectives.* Hillsdale, NJ: Erlbaum, 1994.

Zillmann, Dolf, and Peter Vorderer, eds. *Media Entertainment: The Psychology of Its Appeal.* Mahwah, NJ: Erlbaum, 2000.

Zoglin, Richard. "Sitcom Politics." *Time,* 21 September 1991: 44–47.

Zook, Kristal Brent, *Color by Fox.* New York: Oxford University Press, 1999.

INDEX